STUDIES

IN THE

CHRISTIAN EVIDENCES.

BY

ALEXANDER MAIR, D. D.,
MORNINGSIDE, EDINBURGH.

SECOND EDITION, REVISED AND ENLARGED.

AMERICAN TRACT SOCIETY,
150 NASSAU STREET, NEW YORK.

PREFACE.

THIS book is not written primarily for professional students, whether theological or scientific, though it is hoped that even readers of this class may find it not altogether uninteresting or unworthy of their notice. It is written expressly for that section of our intelligent Church members and adherents whose minds have been brought into contact with the religious doubts and difficulties of the age, and have in some measure felt them; and not less for those who, as Christian teachers and counsellors, are called on from time to time to deal with such doubts and difficulties as they arise in the minds of others.

The special design of the book has to a great degree determined its character. It is not meant to be a 'System of Christian Evidences;' for, as a rule, such treatises, from their very nature, are far too minute and full for the readers in view. Its purpose is rather to take up some of those points which are not only fundamental, but at the same time well fitted to meet the wants of the day, and which are easily grasped by an intelligent mind. I need scarcely say that the object specially aimed at accounts for the greater fulness of statement and use of colour and illustration than might in other circumstances have seemed necessary. It further explains why the different studies, even at the risk of a little repetition, have been made as self-contained as possible, in order that they may admit of being read independently of each other.

The particular position taken up in the book is to be carefully noted. It starts from Theism, or the belief in a personal God, as its accepted basis. Its design is to aid in removing obstacles out of the way, and in conducting the earnest reader from the position of Theism into the central truths of the Christian religion, and a reasonable faith therein. It will be understood that it lies quite beyond its sphere to attempt any full and systematic statement of the different doctrines of Christianity.

In a department which has been so long and so fully investigated by able thinkers, but little that is new can be expected. I have, of course, gone over the whole field in my own way; at the same time, it has been part of my deliberate purpose to make a free use of available material, and so to work it up as to meet present needs and forms of thought. Accordingly much that I have attempted to say has been well said by others previously; but wherever there is conscious indebtedness calling for notice, it is acknowledged. Wherever a quotation is of any length, or of special importance for the argument, the reference is carefully given. Wherever it has been deemed desirable to illustrate a point at length by quotations, this has been done in the Appendix.

In issuing a SECOND EDITION I have availed myself of the opportunity presented of submitting the whole work to a careful revision. While the curtailments have been few and unimportant, I have added a new study—the sixth—entitled, 'Some Recent Reverses of Negative Criticism,' and have also inserted several fresh paragraphs in the body of the work as well as in the Appendix.

MORNINGSIDE, EDINBURGH,
September 1889.

CONTENTS.

—o—

I.

Christianity and Physical Science.

PAGE

Present Unbelief not greater than that of last Century—Springs from the 'Spirit of the Age'—And the Prevalence of Scientific Methods—Assumes the form of Agnosticism or Materialistic Atheism—Some Men Atheists and Materialists by Conviction—Atheism sometimes springs from Moral Causes—Foremost Scientific Men not generally Materialists—The mere Scientific Specialist no Authority in Theology or Criticism—Rejection of the Supernatural in the New Testament sometimes a Question determined beforehand—Physical Science cannot reach Religious Truth—Its Instruments cannot discover it—Its Field is different — Border-lands — Bible Narrative of Creation—Genesis i. the Religious Charter of Science — Order of Creation a Question of Science—Genesis i. not yet proved wrong—Development Hypothesis—Evolution only a *Mode* of Working, and not a *Cause*—Slowness of Process makes no essential Difference—Evolution not yet proved scientifically—Christians should accept Real Discoveries of Science with Gratitude—Christianity readily adjusts itself to Real Discoveries—Our Attitude towards Science. 1

II.

Of Intellectual Difficulties in Religion.

PAGE

There are Intellectual Difficulties in Religion—Such to be expected—Belief depends on Evidence and not on Comprehension—Difficulties arise from the Objects contemplated in Religion—God—Who is Spirit—And Infinite—Man and the Mystery in him—Difficulties also arise from the Finiteness of Man's Mind—Treatment of such Difficulties—We must recognise the Limits of Human Thought—New Testament not to be rejected because of Difficulties—The Mysterious not necessarily Uncertain—We must receive the Doctrines on the Evidence—Other Systems have their Greater Difficulties—The Moral Use of such Difficulties, ... 34

III.

Of Revelation and Inspiration, and the Difficulties connected therewith.

Man by Nature a Religious Being—Natural to Expect a Religion to meet his Wants—Religious Instincts not met in mere Nature—Light of Nature not enough to guide—A 'Book-Revelation' not impossible—A Theory of Inspiration not necessary or logically possible at this Stage—Not the First Doctrine to be presented to the Anxious—Three Positions possible—Literal Inspiration—Religious Inspiration—That the Writers were Trustworthy Witnesses — Even this last is sufficient for Reasonable Certainty and Salvation—Care to be taken in presenting a Rigid Theory of Inspiration at the Outset—Importance of remembering the Special Purpose for which the Bible was given—Objection considered, that even Inspiration has not given Certainty—Real Unity of the Church, . . 52

IV.

Early Historical Testimony to the Authenticity of the New Testament.

PAGE

Subject stated—Christianity a Revelation in the Past, and hence room for Historical Evidence—New Testament generally accepted on the United Testimony of the Divided Church—Reasonableness of this—Authenticity of the New Testament a Question outside of Physical Science—Ancient Manuscripts cited as Witnesses—Church of the Second Half of the Second Century, A.D. 150 to 200—Fathers and Versions—Church of France, Irenæus Representative Witness—Church of Italy, Muratorian Canon, Ancient Latin Version, Hippolytus—Northern Africa, Tertullian—Egypt, Clement of Alexandria—Syria, Peshito—Asia Minor—Evidence summed up—Continuity of the Church—Fate of the Later Works of Aristotle—Period from A.D. 100 to A.D. 150—Witnesses cited—The General Decision of the Church remains, and not all the Evidence—The Heretics and their Testimony—New Testament could not have been forged in the Second Century—General Conclusion, ... 73

V.

The Testimony of the Unquestioned Epistles of Paul.

Romans, First and Second Corinthians, Galatians, and Revelation accepted by Negative Critics—The First Four Epistles of Paul—Testimony of Baur—Renan—Author of *Supernatural Religion*—These Four Epistles a sure Foundation—Character of Paul, the Witness—Thoroughly tested—He had the best Means of knowing the Facts—A Martyr for *Facts* and not *Opinions*—His Testimony includes the Supernatural—Chief

PAGE

Facts of our Lord's Life—Doctrine as to His Person—Chief Doctrines of Christianity—Christian Ethics—The Church—Evidence strengthened by the Churches with which Paul stood in Close Relation—Supported by the Revelation of John—Tübingen School giving up its Position—Practical Conclusion, 108

VI.

SOME RECENT REVERSES OF NEGATIVE CRITICISM.

Subject stated—Only about One-Fourth of the New Testament accepted by Baur and immediate followers as genuine—Recent Discoveries, etc., fall in with the Church's Belief in regard to the New Testament—The Epistle of Barnabas—The Refutation of all Heresies, by Hippolytus—Testimony of the Clementine Homilies to John—Tatian's Diatessaron—The Gospel of Marcion—General Survey of the Retreat of Negative Criticism—Specially in regard to the Four Gospels—Three-Fourths of the New Testament accepted as genuine—The Battle of Criticism had to be fought—Victory in view, . 137

VII.

THE CHRISTIAN MIRACLES.

What is a Miracle?—Not a Violation of the Laws of Nature—Importance of Miraculous Element in Christianity—Christianity the only great Religion that ever came claiming to be authenticated by Miracles—A Revelation to be expected—Miracles the most Direct Proof of a Revelation—Object of Christ's Miracles—Miracles not impossible—Physical Science cannot prove them to be impossible—Intelligent Voluntary Action has in it the essential elements of a Miracle—We cannot explain the Mode—Miracles not Incredible—Hume's

PAGE

Argument from 'Experience' discussed—Does any one really believe in the Christian Miracles?—Kind of Evidence to be expected — Renan's Conditions of a satisfactory Miracle—Christ's Miracles interwoven with the Narrative and Teaching—They fit into the Personality of Christ—'Signs'—What they imply, ... 157

VIII.

DIRECT PERSONAL TESTIMONY TO MIRACLES IN THE NEW TESTAMENT.

Question stated—Assuming the Authenticity of the Chief Books, the Testimony is abundant—Inquiry restricted to the Four Unquestioned Epistles of Paul — Drift of Paul's Testimony obvious—Special Revelations—His Vision of Christ—Gift of Tongues—Gifts of Healings—Explicit Testimony to Miracles in general—2 Cor. xii. 12 discussed—Miracles performed by other Apostles and in other Churches — Paul's Testimony practically that of the Church—Summing up, . . . 199

IX.

THE RESURRECTION OF CHRIST, AND WHAT IT IMPLIES.

Saying of Talleyrand—Importance of the fact of Christ's Resurrection—Kind of proof to be expected—Resurrection harmonizes with the Person and Character of Christ—Foretold by Christ—Testimony of the Roman Soldiers—Of the Apostles—Of the Acts—Of Peter—Of John—Of Paul in his Four Unquestioned Epistles—1 Cor. xv. 3–8 considered—Paul's Vision of Christ—Change produced in the Apostles—Early Success of the Church—The Lord's Day—Various Hypotheses adopted for explaining away the Resurrection—What it implies, . . . 223

X.

THE ARGUMENT FOR CHRISTIANITY FROM THE UNIQUE PERSONALITY OF CHRIST.

PAGE

Influence of Christ on the History of the World—Christ the Source of Power—His Peculiar Relation to Christianity—A Difficult Problem to Unbelievers—The Christ of the Synoptics and the Christ of John—Christ unique in His Sinlessness—Transcendent Power of His Personality shown by its Influence on the Apostles—His Teaching—His Kingdom—Universality of His Purpose—Himself the Cornerstone—Method adopted to establish His Kingdom—His Plan mature from the beginning—The Various Elements harmonize in Christ—He cannot be an Evolution of Natural Forces—Cannot be a mere Fiction—His Moral Character implies that His Claim must be well founded—His Divinity—Conclusion, ... 248

XI.

SOME IMPORTANT CONVERGING LINES, AND THE ARGUMENT THEREFROM.

Argument stated—Peculiarities in the Christian Line of History—Monotheism of the Jews—The Sacred Books—Preservation of the Jewish People—This prophesied—Christ came among this People—This also prophesied—And expected by the Jews—The Fulness of the Time—Planting of the Church—Spread of the Church—This also prophesied—Corruption of the Church prophesied—Prophecy of the Destruction of Jerusalem—The Lord's Supper and what it teaches—Mathematical Theory of Probabilities applied—Mode of Argument adopted by Antagonists—Conclusion, ... 279

XII.

Christianity proving itself by the Principle of the 'Survival of the Fittest.'

by way of correction. Still, we have the best reason for being assured that there is by no means a more deep and wide-spread unbelief existing in the country at the present day than has existed in some previous ages; for example, the greater portion of the preceding century. Of course the unbelief of the present is apt to seem to us much more intense and widely diffused than that of the past, just because in the one case the cloud is right overhead, and we feel its baleful shadow, whereas in the other we see it only in the distance, like a dark streak on the horizon. But if we compare the testimony of competent witnesses, who lived in the central eclipse of eighteenth century unbelief, with the state of things in the present age, we shall find but little reason to believe that 'the former days were better than these.' Addison declares it to be an unquestionable fact in his time, that there was 'less appearance of religion in England than in any neighbouring state or kingdom,' whether Protestant or Roman Catholic.'[1] Judge Blackstone, a thoroughly competent and trustworthy witness, has left it on record, that 'having a curiosity to know how matters stood in regard to religion, he went to every London church of note, but could not have discovered from what he heard whether the preacher was a follower of Confucius, or of Mahomet, or of Christ.'[2] This is a

[1] See Lecky, *History of England in the Eighteenth Century*, vol. ii. p. 545.
[2] See *Contemporary Review*, March 1880, p. 515.

statement sufficiently suggestive; and we may safely affirm that no man could say anything approaching to it in regard to the churches of London or Edinburgh at the present day.[1]

In the case of many in connection with the Church whose minds are in a somewhat uncertain state, this uncertainty has arisen, not so much from definite and positive arguments against Christianity, as from a particular tone of mind and way of looking at religious things. If they examine their own consciousness, probably they will not find positive, formulated reasons present to it, on which they are resting for support of their scepticism. The cause is of a more subtle kind, whether we call it the 'spirit of the age,' or by some other name. The literature in which such men indulge is of a sceptical tendency, perhaps flavoured with insinuations and sneers against religion and all very pronounced religious life and work. The influence of this reading is not unlikely backed up and intensified by the special atmosphere of the society which they keep. And living and moving and having their being in such an air, they find the result to be only too certain. Not more surely does the hand take the colour of the dye in which it is daily working; not more surely does the body become deteriorated in health by the infectious or unwholesome atmosphere which it breathes, than the

[1] See Appendix, Note I.

mind, by the very laws of its nature, becomes lowered, chilled, enfeebled in its tone of faith by such influences. It may be the case that men who are confirmed in the faith, and can discount such unhealthy literature at its true worth, may pass through such reading unscathed; but for those whose minds are yet in the plastic state, the state of formation, it is almost impossible to escape without receiving more or less of subtle injury.

Another source whence this widespread feeling of uncertainty arises may be found in the modes of proof, and the tests of certainty, which are in the highest favour in our day. The present age, as compared with any of the past, is pre-eminently the age of physical science. The scientific methods, with their instruments of research, have attained to solid and splendid results, and hence the tendency is to look on such methods as the only trustworthy and legitimate kind of proof. Not more surely were the Middle Ages the era of Scholasticism, and the favourite mode of proof that of the scholastic logic, than the present age is the era of science and scientific proof. Accordingly, men seek, and expect to have, scientific methods of proof for everything in religion; and what cannot be so proved, they are only too ready to relegate to the limbo of mere myth and fable. They forget that so-called scientific proof cannot possibly be had for everything; cannot possibly be had for things which lie beyond the special and legitimate domain of physical science. They forget that, from the very nature of things, scientific proof is restricted just as specially to physical truth, as mathematical proof is to mathematics, or historical proof to historical events, or proof by consciousness to our states of mind, or proof by moral intuition to principles or actions as right or wrong.

When we pass outside the Church, we find not a few of the philosophers and scientific men of our day taking up the position of Agnosticism. This forms a kind of half-way house between Christianity and positive disbelief, and means that man cannot attain to any certain knowledge of God and the supernatural world. Whether there is a God or not, and if there be, what He is; whether there is a supernatural world or not, and if there be, what it is, the consistent Agnostic declares he does not, cannot know. It is, however, very difficult to carry out consistently a thoroughgoing Agnosticism; and even Herbert Spencer, whom Agnostics speak of as 'our great philosopher,' finds it by no means easy to do so. It is true he calls the Mystery which takes the place of God in his system the Unknowable, but when he enters into details it appears that after all he does know a good deal about it. He knows it as actually existent,—as Energy, as Infinite and Eternal, the Ultimate and Unconditioned Reality, the Ultimate Cause. 'Belief in its existence has, among our beliefs, the highest validity of any,' and 'duty requires us neither to affirm nor deny personality in regard to it.' The 'choice is not between personality and something lower than personality,' but 'between personality and something higher;' for the 'Ultimate Power is no more representable in terms of human consciousness, than human consciousness is in terms of a plant's functions.' Furthermore, it is in a sense true, that 'by this Infinite and Eternal Energy all things are created and sustained,' and it 'stands towards our general conception of things in substantially the same relation as does the Creative Power asserted by theology.' In short, the Unknowable is the Ultimate Reality, higher than mere human personality, infinite, eternal, and unchangeable in being, power, and activity, the First Cause, the Creator and Preserver of all things. Evidently the philosopher of Agnosticism knows a great deal about the Unknowable, and it is even difficult to see why his fullest utterances might not cover a very genuine Theism.[1]

The prevailing unbelief of the age, however, goes further than a consistent Agnosticism, and manifests itself largely as Atheism or Materialism. It may assume various phases and different names, but ultimately it comes very much to the same thing. It culminates in the express denial of a personal God,—a God possessed of self-consciousness, intelligence, moral

[1] See especially the *Nineteenth Century* for July 1884, article on 'Retrogressive Religion.' *First Principles*, pp. 108 ff.

nature, and free-will. As such, we may call it Atheism. But Atheism is only a negative word, and gives merely the negative view of the typical modern unbelief. It also aspires to a positive name, and the possession of a positive theory of the universe. That name and theory is Materialism, according to which the ultimate source and explanation of all things is to be found in matter and force. Even the Pantheism which is held as a theory by some philosophers, is practically reducible to the same thing. Though it may assume various phases, in every case it distinctly implies the denial of a personal God, just as really as Materialism. It may speak of God, but it does not mean by the name a really personal Being. It means at the most only a great blind nature-power, impulse, or 'stream of tendency,' pressing itself onward and outward in the universe, somewhat like the unintelligent life of a tree. For all practical purposes—and it is in this aspect especially that we have to deal with it at present—it is the same thing as atheistic Materialism. It believes in no God but nature and the universe, with its totality of matter and force. The universe is its own creator, preserver, and governor. But as Materialism is the theory more easily and vividly grasped, just because it appeals more directly to the bodily senses, it is, and is likely to be, at least for some time to come, the most wide-spread form of unbelief.

There are some who doubt whether there is any such thing as a genuine Atheist or Materialist in the world. They think that such a character is a moral and intellectual impossibility. But this is a grave mistake. We have no right as Christians to insinuate or believe that all Atheists or Materialists are mere hollow pretenders, professing for some small reason or other to be such, when in reality they are not. We have no reason to doubt that there are many Materialists as genuine and strong in their particular convictions as honest Christians are in theirs. It may indeed seem to us incredible, as we look on the human person, soul and body, with all its wonderful and complicated arrangements, order, and adaptation of means to end, that any one can consider it seriously and thoughtfully, and suppose that it could have come into being without a working intelligence behind it. It may seem to us not less incredible that any fair mind can contemplate the mathematical order existing everywhere in the universe without inferring the presence of an intelligent God therein, just as it would seem to us incredible that a mathematician, cast upon the shore of an unknown island, could discover the figure of one of Euclid's propositions on the sand without at once inferring the recent presence of civilised man. All this, we repeat, may seem to us well-nigh incredible. Nevertheless, it would be utterly wrong to rush to the conclusion that men who deny the existence of a personal God, and attribute everything to mere matter, do not truly believe what they profess to believe. There *are* genuine Materialists and Atheists, men who are such by intellectual conviction, by virtue of reasons which seem sufficient to their logical understanding. No doubt they may be misled by some mental twist, idiosyncrasy, or bias, or by taking a very one-sided view of the evidence ; but the fact is not the less a fact. The human mind can reason itself into convictions, which are not only paradoxical, but even directly contrary to its instinctive and primary beliefs. For example, we may safely say, that belief in the existence of an external world is one of our instinctive and primary beliefs ; and yet there have been men of the highest philosophic power and character, who have doubted, or even denied, the existence of the external world. In like manner, we should not be astonished to find men who absolutely deny the existence of God, who passionately declare that there is and can be no such being as God, though His existence may seem to us to be an instinctive and primary belief, necessarily awakened in us by the intelligent contemplation of the universe.

But while Christian charity leads us to make the above statement, truth at the same time requires us to make a counter-statement. There can be just as little doubt that Atheism often springs from moral causes ;

from the heart more than from the head; from the moral character more than from the force of reason. A man, we shall suppose, has sunk into selfishness and indulgence in sin, perhaps even in sensual vice. He has a deep, real, all but irresistible liking for his favourite pleasure or besetting sin. It is the desire of his heart, the thought of his mind, the picture of his imagination, the dream of his sleep, the occupation and enjoyment of many of his waking hours. But at the same time conscience is not utterly dead within him, and it occasionally disturbs him with terrible mutterings and forebodings. It tells him of his unworthy life, of his sin and guilt, and threatens him with a righteous condemnation and punishment. It whispers in his ear that if there be a God at all, he must be liable to His just displeasure, and he knows it in his heart. This dark thought haunts him like a dismal spectre by night and day, making him uneasy and miserable, sometimes even in the midst of his sin, more frequently and more deeply so after it is over. In order to attain to peace of mind, he must give up either his sin or his lingering belief in a holy and righteous God. He cannot think, however, to give up his sin; he is so enthralled by the love of it, so completely bound with its iron fetters. Like many men, he has got just enough of belief in God to make him miserable in a life of sin, but not enough to convert him effectually from it. In these circumstances, he naturally desires that there should be no God, no judgment, no hell, in order that he may be able to sin with impunity, without fear, and without disturbance. The wish by and by ends in being father to the thought; and what he ardently wishes, and finds it his supposed interest to believe, he soon persuades himself to believe. Under his fatal bias, he is ready to listen eagerly to every argument that may tell against the existence of God, and which thus falls in with his wishes; he shuts his mind to all considerations that prove His existence; and he finally ends by persuading himself that there is no God. His sin and selfishness lead him to Atheism. Just as men are sometimes brought into Christianity by the sense of guilt, and the fear of judgment and of hell, so there are others who are by the same motives led into Atheism. The saying of Fichte is in very many cases extremely near the truth: 'Our system of thought is frequently only the history of our heart.'

It is not an uncommon boast among some of the more decided opponents of positive Christianity, that all the foremost scientific men of the present day are unbelievers, Materialists, or at least Agnostics. But the adherents of our Churches have no reason whatever to be overwhelmed with dismay, and frightened out of their faith by any such boast. Though, unfortunately, many genuine scientific men belong to the unbelieving ranks, yet it is by no means the case that this is true of the class as a whole. In proof of this, we cannot do better than quote from a writer, whose name will be accepted at once as that of a first-class scientific man and a thoroughly competent witness. Professor Tait of Edinburgh, in reply to an article by Mr. Froude, in which the allegation just referred to was maintained, speaks as follows: 'When we ask of any *competent* anthority who were the "advanced," the "best," and the "ablest" scientific thinkers of the immediate past (in Britain), we cannot but receive for answer such names as Brewster, Faraday, Forbes, Graham, Rowan Hamilton, Herschel, and Talbot. This must be the case, unless we use the word science in a perverted sense. Which of these great men gave up the idea that nature evidences a designing mind? But perhaps Mr. Froude refers to the advanced thinkers, still happily alive among us. The names of the foremost among them are not far to seek. But, unfortunately for his assertion, it is quite certain that Andrews, Joule, Clerk-Maxwell, Balfour Stewart, Stokes, William Thomson, and such like, have, each and all of them, when the opportunity presented itself, spoken in a sense altogether different from that implied in Mr. Froude's article. Surely there are no truly scientific thinkers in Britain further advanced than these!'[1] 'There is,' says Dr. Maudsley, 'hardly one, if indeed there be even one, eminent scientific inquirer who has

[1] *International Review*, Nov. 1878, pp. 725 f.

denied the existence of God.'[1] Professor Tyndall himself records his declaration that 'it is not in hours of clearness and vigour that this doctrine [Material Atheism] commends itself to his mind; that in presence of stronger and healthier thought it ever dissolves and disappears, as offering no solution of the mystery in which we dwell.'[2] This and similar utterancs on the part of earnest scientific men, who are commonly regarded as Materialists, may well lead us to the exercise of cautious charity, and remind us of the saying of Jacobi concerning himself: 'With the heart a Christian, though with the intellect a heathen.'

But even admitting that the majority of first-class scientific men were Materialists, for us to doubt the truths of Christianity on that account would be quite unreasonable. We speak at present of those who are merely physicists, and have devoted no special study or examination to the historical and critical evidences of Christianity. The well-deserved eminence which such men have attained in the field of physical science does not make their testimony in the least degree more worthy of weight than that of other men, in the department of historical and critical evidence; and this for the obvious reason that they are entirely out of their special field. Because a man is an eminent chemist and nothing

[1] *Body and Mind*, p. 335.
[2] *Fragments of Science*, vol. ii. p. 206.

more, that does not make his word of any authority in mathematics. Because a man is a splendid mathematician, that does not make him an authority in chemistry. So, on the same principle, because a man is an eminent physicist, that fact alone does not tend in itself to make him an authority in historical or Biblical criticism, any more than the fact that a man is eminent in the department of historical or Biblical criticism necessarily makes him an authority in physical science. In such cases, while the eminent specialists are trustworthy authorities in their respective departments, they entirely cease to be so whenever they pass into another department which is altogether strange. In this new field their special eminence counts for little or nothing; their testimony is simply that of an outsider, and not for a moment to be compared with that of even a very ordinary specialist in this department. In other words, just as the testimony of a very ordinary geologist is of far higher value in geology than that of the most distinguished theologian who is nothing but a theologian; so the testimony of a very ordinary theologian is of far higher authority in the theological field than that of the most eminent geologist who is nothing but a geologist. We must accordingly distinctly guard against the common but grievous fallacy of supposing that because eminent scientific specialists are high authorities in their respective fields, therefore they must also be of equally high authority in the totally different and foreign fields of theology and Biblical criticism.[1]

But it may be said that this Scepticism, or the rejection of the great facts and truths of Christianity, is not confined to mere physicists, who have never specially examined into questions of historical criticism. It is to be found strong and pronounced in men who have given a large amount of attention to such questions. We have it in such men as Baur and Strauss, Renan and the author of *Supernatural Religion.* And this is true. But then, in these and similar cases, the explanation is to a large extent plain and simple. These men were philosophers before they were critics. They had determined the question of supernatural or no supernatural in the sphere of philosophy before they approached the field of Biblical criticism; and in each of the cases mentioned, they had determined the question in the negative. Baur declares it to be a 'purely philosophical question.' He announces the standpoint of his criticism to be the 'purely historical' one, which, according to him, 'from the nature of the case,' excludes the absolutely miraculous.[2] Strauss lays it down as a fundamental canon that 'an event cannot be historical which is inconsistent with the known and otherwise universal laws of

[1] See Appendix, Note II.

[2] *Kritische Untersuchungen*, p. 225; cf. also pp. 121, 530; *Kirchen geschichte*, vol. i. pp. x. 1. 24; *Die Tübinger Schule*, p. 14.

phenomena.'[1] Renan states categorically that 'the gospels are shown to be partly legendary, *because* they are full of miracles and the supernatural.' He says, 'According to my philosophy, there is no place for individual will in the government of the universe;' and again, 'It is an absolute rule of criticism to grant no place in historical narratives to miraculous circumstances.'[2] The author of *Supernatural Religion* affirms that the miraculous is 'antecedently incredible,' and 'emphatically excluded by the whole constitution of the order of nature,' and the like.[3] In other words, their *starting-point* is, that there is and can be no supernatural. It is a pre-determined question, and hence, when they come to New Testament criticism, they must of necessity explain away, in the best manner they can, everything that savours of the miraculous. That is to say, instead of first looking at the evidence for the grand facts of Christianity, they practically foreclose the question by declaring that there is no supernatural, and therefore the gospel narratives must be mythical and fictitious, just because they contain a large element of the miraculous. The supernatural is the very subject under proof, and they reject the evidence for it, just because it contains

[1] *Leben Jesu*, vol. i. p. 103 (1837); compare *New Life of Jesus*, p. xii. (Authorized Translation).

[2] *Vie de Jésus*, p. xv., 12th edition; *Recollections*, p. 325; *Les Apôtres*, p. xlvii.

[3] *Supernatural Religion*, vol. ii. pp. 480 f., 3rd edition.

the element of the supernatural; as if the supernatural could ever be proved by anything short of the supernatural! In view of this, it is not a thing to be very much wondered at that such men should be disbelievers in the grand truths of Christianity. The necessity of their philosophy required it, and therefore the phenomenon need not occasion great perplexity.

So far as physical science, strictly so called, is concerned, it cannot possibly either directly prove or disprove any of the great verities and doctrines of the Christian faith. This will clearly appear, when we consider what are the special instruments which it employs in the discovery of truth, and what is the special field of its investigation. If we ask what are the special instruments which it uses, the answer must be, the physical senses. Its method may be generally described as the method of investigation by the trained, accurate, intelligent, and patient use of the physical senses. Even when it uses the most refined instrumental appliances as tests by which to discover the existence of the most delicate and subtle forces, it still depends on the thoughtful use of the bodily senses for its results. But if the instruments of discovery used by physical science are the senses, it necessarily follows that the field of investigation must correspond to its instruments. In other words, it must be the physical universe of matter and force, which alone can be perceived by the physical senses. This is indeed implied, and even expressed, in the name, physical science.

But if the instruments of physical science be the senses, and its special field the material universe, it follows that it can neither directly prove nor disprove the grand spiritual truths of Christianity. Its instruments, the physical senses, are, from their very nature, utterly incapable of perceiving these truths. They may perceive the things which are seen and temporal; but they cannot perceive the things which are spiritual, unseen, and eternal. The senses singly, or taken all together, can no more directly perceive such things, than the eye can perceive a sound, or the ear perceive a colour; and that for the same reason, namely, the utter want of capacity. No scientific test, however delicate, can discover the presence of God, as it discovers a current of magnetic or electric force. No physical eye, however scientifically trained, can discover the facts of the atonement, or justification by faith, or the judgment, or the immortality of the blessed in heaven. 'We observe,' says Professor Tyndall, 'what our senses, armed with the aids furnished by science, enable us to observe,—nothing more.' When the unbelieving astronomer, Laplace, declared that he had scanned the whole heaven with the telescope, but had found no God, this is exactly what we might have expected. If he had announced to the world, that he had discovered, in the depths of space, some ocean of subtle substance which he affirmed to be God, we might safely have affirmed in reply, that it was a delusion; for God is a pure Spirit, 'whom no man hath seen, nor can see.'

While mere science cannot discover the truths of religion, because its instruments are not of the kind necessary for their discovery, it cannot discover them for the further reason, which, indeed, is immediately implied in the above, that they are beyond its proper domain. This domain, as we have seen, is the physical universe of matter and force. But the fundamental truths of religion belong to the region of the unseen, the spiritual, the supernatural, which is a totally different sphere, lying quite beyond the horizon of physical science. Hence we see the force of Mr. Huxley's statement, that 'Science is neither Christian nor unchristian, but extra-Christian,' that is, occupying a sphere, in a certain sense, outside of Christianity.

From all this, it surely follows that science, strictly so called, can no more give direct testimony, either the one way or the other, in regard to the spiritual and supernatural verities of our religion, than the eye can give direct testimony in regard to sound, or taste, or the inhabitants of an unseen star in the infinite depths of space and the historical events which are being transacted there. 'Eye hath not seen, nor ear heard, neither have entered into the heart of man, the things which God hath prepared for them that love Him; but God hath revealed them unto us by His Spirit.'[1]

There must, of course, be border territories where science and revelation meet, and where the materials and interests of both are mixed up together. In regard to such border-lands, as in the case of border-lands elsewhere, there may be room and necessity for no small disputation, before we can carry out the true Christian principle of rendering unto science the things that belong to science, and to revelation the things that belong to revelation.

We have a notable instance of this border territory in the Bible narrative of the creation. We find men everywhere asking the question, some insultingly, others sorrowfully and anxiously, Does not science really come into direct and hopeless collision with revelation as to the account of creation given in the first chapter of Genesis?

Now we may safely reply that even here it does not and cannot. The first chapter of Genesis, like all the rest of the Bible, was not meant to be a revelation of science, but of religious truth. It was not written primarily to make known to us the order of physical creation, but the grand religious truth that the earth and its contents were created, and that God was the Creator. Its design is to sweep away all idolatry and mere

[1] See Appendix, Note III.

nature-worship, and to lay a solid foundation for the worship of God alone, by showing us that the universe, and all objects therein, are not independent existences, far less deities, but mere creatures of God's hand, and therefore not proper objects of worship. Its object very specially is to show that it is one and the same God who is the Creator of man and all things, the God of providence and history, and the God of redemption, and that therefore through all there is but the one only, the living and the true God. It is most certainly this all-important and distinctly religious purpose that is the supreme object of the first chapter of Genesis, and not the revelation of the scientific facts concerning the order of creation.

We may safely go farther, and say that the first chapter of Genesis, by laying it down as a fundamental truth that the universe is the creation of God, gives a religious foundation to physical science. It declares distinctly that nature is the revelation and work of God as really and truly, so far as it goes, as the Bible itself can possibly be.

> ''Tis elder Scripture writ by God's own hand;
> Scripture authentic, uncorrupt by man.'[1]

Accordingly it must clearly be our duty to study this first and simpler revelation of God as well as the second and higher. Over against 'Search the

[1] Young's *Night Thoughts*, Night Ninth, ll. 646 f.

Scriptures,' the first chapter of Genesis practically writes and inculcates 'Study nature, for it is God's revelation.' But this study of nature, of matter and force and their laws, of life and its organisms, is just physical science. Hence this chapter is really the religious charter of science, which gives it an authoritative place in the religious sphere alongside of the study of the Bible, and invests it with a religious sanction and significance. The religious standing thus given to science, it is our sacred duty fully to recognise, it is our sin thoughtlessly to ignore or despise. As surely as any man believes the truth taught in the first chapter of Genesis, that all nature is the creation of God, so surely is he under the most religious obligation to believe every truth of nature fully ascertained by science. To refuse this is a sin against this chapter, a sin against the God of creation, an act of deep religious unbelief.[1]

Leaving aside for the moment the question whether the first chapter of Genesis is an exact record of physical facts or only a pictorial exhibition of a great religious truth, in any case, it falls to science to give us, if it can, certain information in regard to the order and details of creation, and thus contribute decisive aid to the final solution of the question. When science has made known to us the truth of the matter, it will be our

[1] Compare Geikie, *Hours with the Bible; Creation to Patriarchs*, p. 39.

religious duty to accept its teaching, for this field lies within its proper domain. The essential Bible truth of the chapter, that God is the Creator of all things, can never be touched by science, for it is totally beyond its range ; but it is within its range to ascertain the order and details of creation, and when it has reached sure results in regard thereto, we are bound absolutely to accept them as the very truth of God. What we have to be certain about is, that the results shall be really scientific truth, and not a mere hypothesis. With this view distinctly before us, it is obviously our wise and proper course as Christians to possess our souls in patience, and quietly wait until science has arrived at absolute certainty. 'He that believeth shall not make haste.' If science should ever be able to prove that the actual order of creation was different from that given in Genesis, there will be no occasion for dismay. It will only be in harmony with the unquestionable fact, that the Bible is primarily a revelation of special religious truth, and not of physical science.[1]

At the same time, we by no means hold that science has as yet demonstrated that the order in the first chapter of Genesis must be considered as altogether belonging to the realistic, pictorial, or parabolic form or clothing of the truth to be taught. It seems very clear that the account in Genesis is unique among the

[1] See Appendix, Note IV.

cosmogonies. It is free from the fables and monstrosities to be found in the cosmogonies of Greece and India, and even Babylonia. And how is this to be explained? It is clear that the date of the creation, as indicated here, is of indefinite antiquity, and that the order is one of progression from the lowest to the highest types of organisms, as is the case in nature. And how are we to account for this? There appears to be from the very 'beginning' a general agreement in the order; for, though the geologic ages overlap each other, so that they are not bounded by any sharp lines, yet they seem to agree essentially with the order of Genesis. How, again, does this happen to be the case? Genesis represents man as the final and crowning step of creation, which also seems to be a truth of science; and, lastly, it would appear both from Genesis and science that, since the advent of man, God has had an age of Sabbath rest from creating new species. And how, we may ask, does Genesis turn out to be correct in these points also? Surely we may well say that it is more than wonderful that an author, writing in the midst of wild and fabulous cosmogonies and scientific night, should have hit by mere chance on so many elements of truth and soberness in regard to such a difficult question. Surely the whole suggests a higher hand than that of Moses.[1]

In close connection with this question as to creation,

[1] Compare Newman Smyth, *Old Faiths in New Light*, chap. iv.

and, indeed, forming a most important element in it, is that of evolution, or the so-called development hypothesis. This is the explanation of life and living organisms chiefly relied on by materialistic Atheists in our time, for the banishment of an intelligent Creator from the universe. Accordingly, because of the company which the hypothesis is so often found to keep, and with which it is such a favourite, many have come to look upon it with intense suspicion, and ask the question, Is it not utterly and essentially atheistic? Does it not banish the Creator for ever from the universe? But this hypothesis does not necessarily do any such thing. Even though it were scientifically proved that evolution from lower forms to higher was the method of creation, it would not change the relation of God to creation in any substantial degree. So very obviously is this the case, that the most distinguished advocates of evolution have clearly seen and admitted its consistency with the doctrine of a personal God. This is true of Wallace, and Darwin himself, and the author of the *Vestiges of the Natural History of Creation.* J. S. Mill very explicitly states that 'the theory, if admitted, would be in no way whatever inconsistent with creation.'[1] Professor Calderwood, from the distinctly Christian standpoint, is no less emphatic. He says: 'It is obvious that, even if this

[1] *Three Essays on Religion*, p. 174.

theory were accepted in the form in which it is at present propounded, not only would the rational basis for belief in the divine existence and government not be affected by it, but the demand on a Sovereign Intelligence would be intensified.'[1] It would be easy to multiply authorities; but it is unnecessary, for it can hardly be questioned that the evolution theory leaves the relation of God to creation essentially where it was before.[2]

For what is evolution or the development hypothesis, viewed from the theistic or Christian point of view? It is not a real and independent cause or power in itself, and therefore it can originate nothing, and can account for the existence of nothing. It is only a mode of operation, the method supposed to be employed by the true Cause or Creator in carrying out His work of creation.[3] It means that God, instead of creating new forms all at once out of inanimate matter, made use of lower forms, working in and on them so as gradually to push them up into higher forms. His power, His intelligence, His will wrought in the lower forms, ever giving them higher potency, pressing them upward, and directing their upward course, and moulding from within and without new organisms to suit the new stage.

Now it is surely plain that there must be very much

[1] *Science and Religion*, p. 21. [2] See Appendix, Note V.
[3] See this well thought out in Fairbairn's *City of God*, pp. 58 ff.

the same intelligence, power, and will expended on the part of God in the case supposed, as in that of immediate creation. In both cases there is needed just as much as will produce the result, and nothing more. The only essential difference is, that in the one case the divine operation is extended over a vast period of time, whereas in the other it is concentrated. But it matters not how long a man takes to climb a hill,—an hour, a day, or a year. It is a certain law of physics that he must expend exactly as much force in the one case as in the other, neither more nor less. It matters not whether the builder finish the house in a month or in ten years. He has to expend very much the same intelligence, power, and work on it in the one case as in the other. The fact that he raises it slowly stone by stone in no way radically changes the problem. By spreading the intelligence and power over the years, we do not get rid of them. We only make their movements slower, and therefore less observable. But, in either case, very much the same amount must be expended, the amount necessary to produce the result. And so it is with God in nature according to the Christian theory of evolution. The fact that He works slowly does not do away with His work. It is as necessary in the slow process as in the immediate one; and to think that because the process proceeds so slowly, therefore it proceeds without God, may be as shallow a fallacy as to suppose that, because the house is built slowly, therefore it is built without a builder, and even builds itself.

It is quite certain that there is no moral necessity as yet laid on us to accept evolution pure and simple as a scientific truth, even the highest scientific men themselves being judges. In the whole history of man we have no unquestionable case of spontaneous generation of life, or the origin of a distinctly new species. We have no experimental proof of either the one or the other, in spite of human ingenuity and observation. The experiments of Pasteur and Tyndall may, for the present, be confidently regarded as having annihilated those of Bastian, which were fondly supposed to have demonstrated spontaneous generation. Moreover, when we go back to the geologic ages, we find that the vast gulf between the brain-mass of man and that of the highest ape was practically the same as at the present day. The average brain of man, as he now exists, is more than three times that of the highest ape; and it was the same in the earliest period of which we have any knowledge. There is, therefore, no trustworthy proof of mere development gradually bridging over the gulf. Once more, our mathematical physicists seem to have demonstrated that the world has not existed in the present state nearly long enough to allow time for the slow processes of an imperceptible evolution.[1] But in

[1] See Appendix, Note VI.

any case we ought not to give way to alarm, and should allow science to work out the problem calmly for itself. If evolution should ever be demonstrated to be the method adopted by God in creation, Christians will only have reason to thank science for the discovery of the truth ; and we may rest assured that science, in the very process of proving evolution, will also educe proofs, that this is after all the method which affords the highest manifestation of creative wisdom.

Christians, as we have already seen, are bound by their allegiance to Him who is the Truth, to seek the truth, and, when they have found it, to be loyal to it whatever may betide. Their inmost spirit should ever be that expressed in the passionate cry of Augustine, 'O Truth, Truth! thou knowest how the inward marrow of my soul longeth after thee.' We ought therefore to be prepared most thankfully to accept the truth by whatsoever channel it may come. Accordingly, instead of hating and reviling science, we should remember that we have much reason, as Christians, to thank it in the past for correcting erroneous views which had mingled with current exegesis and theology, and we should be modest enough to expect that the same thing may possibly happen again in the future. There was a time when men devoutly believed that the sun rose in the east, moved through the heavens, and set in the west, and even thought this view demonstrated by the Bible.

But science has corrected this mistake, by showing that the earth moves round its own axis; and surely as Christians it becomes us to thank science for revealing to us the actual truth in the case. There was a time when the earth, and not the sun, was regarded as the fixed centre of the solar system; but science has demonstrated the truth of the Copernican view, and swept out of existence for ever the Ptolemaic system with 'centric and eccentric scribbled o'er, cycle and epicycle.' There was a time when the earth was regarded as only six thousand years old or so; but science has proved that millions of years have elapsed since the creation. There was a time when it was held that the earth had gone through its main creative stages in the space of six days of twenty-four hours each; but science has shown that each stage occupied myriads of years. Science has corrected these and similar mistakes which mingled with traditional exegesis and theology. They lay within the proper domain of science, and it has now given a final and trustworthy deliverance in regard to them. And clearly it is our duty, as Christians, to be grateful for the truth thus discovered, to accept it cordially, and frankly to acknowledge our high obligations to science for correcting the errors and revealing the real facts.

When we look at the past, we may well learn another very important lesson which may be of use in the future. That is, that Christianity has never had any great difficulty in appropriating to itself and its service the corrections of science, and adjusting its relations to new and real discoveries; and this for the simple reason that they were the truth. Many Christians were greatly terrified at the overthrow of the old Ptolemaic system of astronomy, which made the earth the centre of the universe. But, not to dwell on the fact that Copernicus, who thought out the true scientific view, was himself an ecclesiastic and a professed believer, we may safely say that no Christian of sense has any difficulty nowadays in accepting the Copernican system as true. There was no small dismay, and not a little of the rash cry of heresy, when geologists began to maintain the antiquity of the earth, with most of its various species of plants and animals. But now, no Christian of a healthful mind has any great difficulty in accepting the fact of the earth's antiquity, and thanking science for the truth. And so will it be with the real discoveries of science in the future where they turn out to collide with the views of traditional theology. Whatever flutter they may cause at first, Christianity will soon be able to adjust itself to them, and Christians will have reason to be thankful to science for revealing the very truth, and giving us a fuller and clearer manifestation of the creative wisdom of God.

In view of all that has been said, it will appear clear

to the thoughtful mind that there is no need for the feverish, blind, and unreasonable dread which possesses and excites not a few Christians in regard to physical science. She is not, and from the nature of the case cannot be, the foe of true religion, any more than geology can be the foe of mathematics, or astronomy the foe of mental philosophy or political economy; and this just from the fact that her kingdom lies in a totally different sphere. Her special kingdom, as we have seen, is the physical universe, and there she reigns legitimately supreme. There she is at home and speaks with authority, and we must accept her clearly and fully ascertained results as the truth. We are bound to do so, as Christians, by our loyalty to truth and the God of truth. But when science forsakes her own special domain, and passes into 'the regions beyond,' then she is out of her own kingdom, and ceases to speak with authority. When she enters the metaphysical sphere, the spiritual or supernatural sphere, she ceases to be physical science, and becomes metaphysical or theological speculation under the false name of physical science. Working in her own field, she may amass many physical facts and principles which imply and point to great spiritual truths, and which may help the cautious and penetrating theological thinker to correct imperfect views of the truth received by tradition; but she cannot of herself directly reach such truths so as either to prove or disprove them. She cannot be an authoritative witness in regard to them either one way or another, any more than a man who is blind can be a witness in regard to the colour of a person's dress who has just passed him at a distance. It is therefore utterly erroneous to suppose that true science can ever injure true religion, and it is unreasonable to entertain a blind fear or hatred against her because of such a supposition. To do so does not imply faith in Christianity, but a want of faith in it; a want of faith in truth and the God of truth. In short, the blind dread of science is sheer distrust of God, and a very real form of unbelief.

II.

Of Intellectual Difficulties in Religion.

While the way of salvation is so very plain that even a child can apprehend it, it is not to be denied that there are many intellectual difficulties in connection with Christianity. It ought even to be frankly admitted that these difficulties are great both in number and in magnitude. But, unfortunately, there is a class of people who, from some mental idiosyncrasy, or peculiarity of training, keep looking at these mysteries only, or at least supremely, peering into the deep and unfathomable well, until they become bewildered by the darkness. They are drawn as by a morbid spell to fix their troubled mind upon the difficulties alone, until perhaps they end by regarding Christianity as an absurd, irrational, and incredible system, not even 'a cunningly devised fable,' and are fain to seek refuge from their perplexity in Scepticism or sheer Atheism. Just as the moth keeps fluttering around the flame until it is consumed by it, so their minds keep hovering around these difficulties until they prove their undoing. The object of the present study is to deal with these difficulties in a practical way, and show what is the proper light in which to regard them, and what is the wise and healthful mode of treating them.

To many honest thinkers it is at first sight a matter of the greatest wonder that there should be any difficulties at all in a religion like Christianity, which professes to be a *revelation* from God to man; and they are ready to say, How much easier it would be to be a Christian, if only all mysterious doctrines were swept out of Christianity!

But instead of its being a reason for wonder that there are difficult doctrines in the Christian system, such doctrines are just what we might naturally expect. If any man were to declare that he had discovered or invented a religion which kept clear of all such doctrines, we might safely say that this very fact would show it to be a false and shallow religion; for a religion that has to do with such mysteries as sin, and God, and atonement, must of necessity contain difficult doctrines. If any religion avoids such doctrines, it can only do so by avoiding to grapple with those grand and awful problems which lie at the root of all genuine religion, and thus entirely failing to accomplish its end. These difficulties, accordingly, instead of being an occasion for wonder, are just what we might naturally expect, and instead of being an argument against Christianity, rather turn out, so far, to be an argument in its favour.

We may sometimes meet with people who are ready to declare that they are not under obligation to believe, and will not believe, what they cannot fully comprehend. But this is a principle which the slightest reflection will show to be utterly unsound and untenable. We must believe what we apprehend or see to be true, whether we can comprehend it or not; for our belief depends on sufficient evidence, and not on perfect comprehension of the object or event. It is a question, we repeat, of sufficient evidence, and not of complete logical analysis or comprehension. Let us contemplate, for example, the fact of our own personal existence. We must believe it on the evidence of our consciousness, though we cannot comprehend in the least the mystery of our existence. We know the *fact* that we do exist, but the *how* we cannot understand. Indeed, we need only to reflect for a moment to be convinced of the truth that creation is teeming with mysteries which we must accept on the evidence of our senses, but which we cannot in the least comprehend. In the eloquent language of J. S. Mill, 'Human existence is girt round with mystery; the narrow region of our experience is a small island in the midst of a boundless sea, which at once awes our feelings and stimulates our imagination by its vastness and obscurity. To add to the mystery, the domain of our earthly existence is not only an island in infinite space, but also in infinite time. The past and the future are alike shrouded from us; we neither know the origin of anything which is, nor its final destination.'[1] In short, all nature is full of mysteries, from the common dust beneath our feet up to the rolling world, and the still more mysterious soul of man. And surely if Nature, the first and lower revelation of God, is full of mysteries, the principle of continuity would lead us to expect that Christianity, the second and more advanced revelation, should contain similar and even greater and more numerous mysteries, as leading us into deeper depths. In any case, to quote the words of Leibnitz, 'the man who in divine things will believe nothing except what he can fully measure with his understanding, must narrow down the idea of God.'

It is natural, first of all, to inquire whence these difficulties arise. And we answer, that they partly arise from the objects contemplated in religion. One of these objects is God. He is indeed the prime object presented to us in religion, and in Him it lives and moves and has its being. But God is a being of such exalted nature, that we ought to be prepared to meet with mystery in any religion that professes to give us a revelation of Him. Mystery is indeed inseparably connected with the idea of God, and a God in whom there is no element of mystery, but who is perfectly comprehensible to us,

[1] *Three Essays on Religion*, p. 102.

would be no God at all, but a being inferior to ourselves. And accordingly the Bible invariably represents God as a being involved in mystery, and makes no pretensions to clear it away. We find the patriarchs at the dawn of revelation speaking of Him as a mystery: 'Canst thou by searching find out God? Canst thou find out the Almighty unto perfection?' Ages pass away, and the light of revelation becomes fuller; but still the Psalmist has to say, 'Clouds and darkness are round about Him.' And even when we come to the New Testament age, and the days of Him who is 'the image of the invisible God,' the mystery is not cleared up; for is not Christ Himself declared to be the great 'mystery of godliness'? Indeed, the main difference in this respect between the Old Testament and the New is, that in the former God is generally represented as a mystery because of the darkness, and in the latter because of the excessive light of glory in which He dwells.

There are many elements in the character of God which necessarily make Him mysterious to us. We can select only one or two as instances. And evidently one source of the mystery is the fact, that He is a pure and formless Spirit. 'God is a Spirit.' When we refer to this as a source of mystery, we do not mean to say that spirit is to us really more mysterious, or less clearly and fully comprehended, than matter. On the contrary, there is the best reason to hold that this is not the case;

and if any one doubts it, he can settle the matter very easily for himself. He has but to take a quiet half-hour, and think out all the properties of matter which he knows, and put them down in one column, and then all the properties of spirit, such as consciousness, thought, memory, conscience, feeling, imagination, will, and the like, and put them down in another column by themselves, and he will find, perhaps to his astonishment, that the second column is just as extensive and intelligible as the first. In other words, we have, to say the least, just as clear and as extensive knowledge concerning spirit as we have concerning matter. Even Mr. Huxley, with his usual honesty, admits it to be an indisputable truth that our knowledge of the soul is more intimate and certain than our knowledge of the body,[1] and *a fortiori* of matter in general. Still there can be little doubt that, as a rule, men are so much accustomed to use their physical senses, and to think by means of forms or symbols, that it is a difficult thing for them to think clearly of a pure and formless Spirit like God.

Another element in the nature of God which involves Him in mystery is His infinity. We are apt to overlook the meaning of infinity, and because the word is familiar to eye and ear, and slips easily over our tongue, to suppose that we fully understand it. But it really means

[1] *Essays selected from Lay Sermons*, etc., p. 139.

without all limits, and therefore beyond the possibility of our comprehension. Perhaps by an effort of recollection, we may be able to recall the time when the idea of the infinite first dawned upon the soul. We stood on a shoreless sea, or looked up into the deep blue sky, and as we endeavoured in thought to fathom the dim space around or above, the idea of the infinite was borne in upon our mind. We can, perhaps, remember the strange thrill and amazement of the soul at the birth of the new thought, and how we felt overwhelmed with the great and awful weight of mystery. Every one who has had such a vivid perception of the infinite will be prepared to expect that an infinite God must of necessity be a mystery. How much more must this be the case when we remember that in Him there is not only infinity, but infinity, as it were, piled upon infinity—infinite duration, infinite power, infinite knowledge, omnipresence in infinite space, infinite holiness, infinite love, and many more infinites besides; for is He not the absolutely infinite One? Indeed, we soon become bewildered in our attempt to realize Him, and begin to understand the saying of the old Greek poet, who declared that the longer he thought about God, the greater the mystery appeared.

Another object contemplated in religion is man. But we may be ready to say, Surely we must be at home here at least, and all this department of the field must be free from difficulty. Yet how far is this from being the case —for 'what a mystery is man to man!' Although psychologists have been engaged in the study of the human soul for ages, the mystery is very imperfectly cleared up. It is just like what the maps of Africa are, which were constructed thirty or forty years ago. There is a little fringe around the shore, which is more or less accurately mapped out, while the vast interior is marked 'unexplored territory.' And so is it even yet with the human soul. There is much of unexplored territory within it, great deeps which have been little broken up. 'We are fearfully and wonderfully made.' Our coming into life is a mystery, our departure out of it a mystery, and all the course between is a perfect web of mystery. In the language of Goethe, the great German poet and thinker, 'Man is a mysterious being; [of himself] he knows not whence he comes, nor whither he goes; he knows little of the world, and least of all of himself.' And surely when we remember that Christianity has to do with man, who is a mystery, and with God, who is the mystery of mysteries, we should not be surprised to find that it contains intellectual difficulties. Rather we should expect to discover in it 'things hard to be understood,' and which we must be content, in the present life, to know only in part.

But these intellectual difficulties arise not merely from the nature of the objects contemplated, but also from the finiteness of the human mind which contemplates them. There is no mystery about God to Himself, just because 'His understanding is infinite.' And much more must He fully comprehend us, who are the finite work of His own hands. But it is far otherwise with man. His mind is very limited, and the question at once arises, How can such a finite mind ever comprehend an infinite Being in all His infinity? And the answer must be that the thing is impossible. Some positive and important knowledge concerning the infinite God such a mind may possess, but to comprehend Him fully is impossible. Finite space cannot contain infinite space; the part cannot contain the whole: man cannot take up the ocean in the hollow of his hand, or clasp the ponderous globe in his arms; and so his finite mind cannot comprehend the infinite Jehovah, or the little plummet of his reason sound the unfathomable ocean of Deity. And hence we are forced to the conclusion, that it is impossible in the very nature of things for God to give a revelation of Himself to man which shall be clear of all difficulty. Before this can be the case, man must become God.

And how ought we to conduct ourselves in view of these difficulties? We ought plainly, for one thing, to recognise the limits of human thought. The mind may be brought to rest in regard to a truth in two ways. It rests when it fully comprehends it; but it will also sink into rest when it clearly sees that the difficulty is beyond the limits of human thought, and therefore utterly insoluble. It is indeed very much the same with the investigator of truth as it is with the mountain-climber. When the climber comes to the mountain which is the object of his attack, if he finds it accessible at all, he will not rest satisfied until he has mastered it, stands upon its summit, and enjoys the noble prospect. But when he comes to it and finds it obviously unscalable, then he ceases to waste his strength upon it, sits down satisfied in its awful shadow, and admires in wondering reverence its sublime peaks and precipices. And so with the mind and any truth or problem which is the object of its contemplation. If the truth seems soluble, it will not rest content until it has mastered it, taken its stand upon its summit, and surveyed the new landscapes beyond. But it will also rest content and cease to weary itself in vain, when it has discovered that the truth is absolutely insoluble, and beyond the limits of human thought. It will then be ready to sit down in its sublime shadow, and in its mysterious presence give way to feelings of reverence and adoration.

It does not lie within our scope at present to prove the authority or trustworthiness of the New Testament: but it does lie within it to guard against an error, into which not a few are ready to fall in reference to the

New Testament. Because they find many difficulties there, and things which are flatly contrary to their prejudices and likings, they proceed at once to throw it aside as a forgery or fiction. But this is a most unreasonable procedure, such as no practical man would follow in secular things. Perhaps we cannot see this more clearly than by an illustration. It not unfrequently happens, when a wealthy man's testament is opened and read after his death, that some of his relatives are displeased and disappointed. They have been left out altogether, or they have got very small sums; while others whom they dislike or think without any claims at all, have got far too much. But because they are disappointed with the will, and its contents do not exactly fall in with their views, this is no reason why it should at once be set aside. If the will is properly drawn out, legally attested, and unquestionably genuine, this settles the matter. The parties concerned must be content with its terms, however much they may be disappointed and displeased with them. And so, after finding out on its own appropriate evidence the authenticity and trustworthiness of the New Testament, we are not at liberty to reject it because of its difficult and disagreeable doctrines. To do so may be rationalism, but it is not reasonableness.

It may be well to utter a word of warning here against supposing that because certain doctrines are mysterious they are necessarily uncertain. There are some who incline to believe that the mysterious is always more or less doubtful, that mysterious and doubtful are very much the same thing. But this is a great mistake, for a matter is not necessarily more doubtful in the least because it is mysterious. If one of our travellers were to tell the natives of Central Africa, that in Britain long trains, many scores of tons in weight, might be seen rushing through the country at the rate of forty miles an hour, and no living creature attached to draw them ; or if he were to tell them that a man can sit in London and converse with a friend in New York, the words passing instantaneously along the bottom of the Atlantic Ocean,—they would certainly regard these statements as mysterious, and perhaps as absolute untruths: but we know that our railway system and the Atlantic telegraph are undeniable facts. We see, then, that a doctrine is not necessarily uncertain because it is mysterious. A mystery may be quite as certain as the very simplest fact. As we have already seen, certainty is all a matter of sufficient evidence, and not of mere intellectual comprehension.

What then we have to do with these difficult doctrines is to believe them on their own appropriate and sufficient evidence, and leave the solution of the mystery in the hands of God. If we accept the Bible as God's authoritative word, and find a difficult doctrine clearly contained in it, and educed from it all by reasonable interpreters, we must accept it as true; and it is quite unscientific and irrational to explain it away, or begin to pare it down to the measure of our mind and wish. What God requires us in the first place to do, is to find out, receive, and be loyal to the truth, and not to solve mysteries. To take an illustration: we cannot comprehend the mystery of the Trinity, but we find it clearly taught in the New Testament, and therefore we are bound to accept it whether we can comprehend it or not. We cannot reconcile fully the two opposite polar doctrines of God's decrees and man's freedom. But we find the former taught in the Bible and in history, and the latter in the Bible and our consciousness, and therefore, on their respective evidences, we are bound to accept them both. We may not be able to follow out the intricate interaction of the two truths; but we are not called on to do so, for we are saved by believing the truth, and not by solving mysteries. Nay, we are expressly told that a man may 'understand all mysteries and all knowledge,' and yet be nothing. In short, we must hold fast the truth attained, and leave the mysteries in the hands of God, to be cleared up in His own good time and way. This is at once the genuine spirit of true science and true philosophy, as well as of true theology and common sense.

In view of the whole state of the case, we may well

utter a word of respectful caution to many of our younger Church adherents against being moved by mere intellectual difficulties at once to renounce Christianity. It is well in such cases that thoughtful people should remember that here, if anywhere, they may have reason to bear the difficulties they have, rather than 'fly to others that they know not of.' If they think that the difficulties of Christianity are greater than those of the competing systems, it is merely because they are not yet acquainted with the latter. They know the difficulties of Christianity because they have often heard them insinuated, or dinned into their ears by its loud opponents; but if they were only half as well acquainted with the difficulties of the anti-Christian systems, they would find that they are still greater and still more numerous. Atheistic Materialism, Pantheism, Positivism, Secularism, Scepticism, Agnosticism, and the like, all present intellectual difficulties greater than those of Christianity, and moral difficulties vastly greater. They leave untouched all the grand and pressing enigmas of life, and make all its sad shadows, its sorrows and sufferings, its bereavements and trials doubly dark. They have not a single ray of hope and light to cast on the darkness of death, but rather deepen the blackness into 'a horror of great darkness.' Rousseau, in a striking passage, pictures out the different species of Atheists as met in conclave to explain the secret of the universe, and Clarke, at the close of their different proposals, enunciating the idea of God. Such an idea, he says, only needed to have been propounded last of all to command universal acceptance and admiration as the grand solution. Then he adds, in words which we may freely translate and apply to Christianity, 'The elements in Christianity which are incomprehensible to the human mind are less in number than the positive absurdities of other systems. The insoluble objections are common to them all, because the mind of man is too limited to solve them. Accordingly, they prove nothing against Christianity more than against other systems. Ought not, then, that system which alone explains everything to be preferred when it has no more of difficulty in it than the others, especially when it vastly excels them all in the direct proofs of its truth?'[1]

The difficult doctrines of our religion are not without their advantages, and it may be well to mention two or three of them.

It is obvious, for example, that they have a great educative or training power. As every one knows, there are two modes of education possible and practised. The one is commonly called cramming, according to which the scholar has all his difficulties solved for him,

[1] *Émile*, Livre IV. p. 316 (Firmin-Didot).

and only passively receives the results or facts. The man who is educated on this system may have a large store of knowledge; but his intellect will be undeveloped, and he will be feeble in practical sagacity and independence of thought and action. The other mode is that of training, in which the teacher wisely brings the scholar into contact with difficulties, and encourages him to solve them for himself. The result is, that in wrestling with these difficulties the mind wrestles itself into full and manly vigour, the intellect is well developed, and practical sagacity and independent thought and action become natural to the man. Now, in like manner, these difficult doctrines are most useful as a means of high and manly training in the religious sphere. We can conceive of God having revealed to us only a few plain and simple facts as the whole doctrinal system of our religion; and such a system might have been the means of saving us; but it could not have reared a race of vigorous and intellectual Christians. This species of Christians can be fully reared only in the midst of brave and manly wrestling with difficulties, which above most things tends to make us strong. It is the great doctrines alone that fill and expand the mind, that bring us up to perfect manhood, 'to the measure of the stature of the fulness of Christ.'

But the difficult elements in Christianity are also

useful as a means of training men in some of the most important Christian virtues. They tend, for one thing, to train the mind in faith. They present a field in which we must learn to trust God even when we cannot fully comprehend Him, in which we must be content to walk by faith, and not by sight. They also afford a very efficient means of training the soul in humility and modesty. They remind us that we are but of yesterday, and know nothing; that we are very finite creatures, utterly unable to fathom the depths and scale the heights of God and His universe. They furthermore train the soul in the exercise of habitual reverence. This highest and sublimest of all human emotions can live and grow only under the shadow of the mysterious, the infinite, and the unscalable. The presence of 'the little hills' may awaken pleasure, but it is the presence of the sublimest Alps, the Matterhorns, the Monts Blancs, the Schreckhorns, whose snowy summits reach far up into the lonely blue, which alone can awaken reverence. And, on the same principle, it is not the plain and simple truths of our religion, but rather its infinite heights and depths of mystery, which awaken and nourish the sublimest reverence and awe.

But obviously also these difficult doctrines tend to awaken and keep up intellectual interest, and make provision for intellectual enjoyment for ever. The mind has an instinctive desire for new knowledge. When it has exhausted any subject, then to be happy, after a due rest, it must pass on to something new. If it were already possessed of all knowledge, obviously in looking forward to the future, the springs of interest and of hope would to a large extent be dried up, and it would have nothing in prospect but a comparatively monotonous and uninteresting eternity. But in these mysteries we see that this cannot be the case, for it has an inexhaustible field before it for its investigation. It will be drawn on from one discovery to another, advancing from the summit of one grand mystery, now solved, to another, like a giant stepping from mountain peak to mountain peak, nearer and nearer to the infinite Jehovah, the intensity of interest ever deepening with the deepening eternity.

III.

Of Revelation and Inspiration, and the Difficulties connected therewith.

THERE can be little doubt that man is by nature formed to be a religious being. The religious capacity or instinct is a primary and essential part of his original constitution, and it is the crowning element which emphatically distinguishes him from the lower animals. Our own consciousness clearly testifies to the fact that we possess religious capacities and emotions; nor can this be denied even by those who have ceased to profess adherence to any special form of religion. But the fact is still further proved by the universality of religion throughout the human race. Every tribe yet discovered, whose manners and customs have been carefully investigated, possesses religion in some form or other; and if there be any tribes which do not, they can only be such as have sunk to the very lowest state of degradation. To say that religion is the invention of designing priests is no explanation of the phenomenon. In the first place, it is not true that this is the origin of religion; for, as Herbert Spencer says, 'A candid examination of the evidence quite negatives the doctrine maintained by some, that creeds are priestly inventions.'[1] And, in the second place, even if the assertion just referred to were true, it would be far from proving that man is not possessed of a religious capacity by nature. Rather it would prove the very opposite; for, it might be asked, why was there a demand for religions to be invented, and why were they so universally accepted after they were invented, if there be no religious capacity and instinct inherent in man?[2]

But if man has religious instincts, capacities, and cravings, it is natural to expect that there must be a religion to meet and satisfy them. We find that the principle of adaptation is carried out in the universe, and that every instinctive craving and capacity implies and has its own corresponding object. The eye implies light, the ear implies sound, hunger implies the existence of food, natural affection objects of natural affection, and the desire for knowledge a universe where this desire can be satisfied. On the same principle, we may reasonably expect that the religious instinct or capacity implies a religion to meet and satisfy it.

But it may be said that our religious instinct must, like the other instincts, be met, if met at all, in the

[1] *First Principles*, p. 14.
[2] Cf. Calderwood, *Philosophy of the Infinite*, p. 421 (3rd edition).

sphere of mere nature. We have no right, it may be argued, to look for a supernatural revelation of religion to meet our religious craving, any more than a miraculous supply of food to meet our hunger, or of scientific truth to meet our craving for knowledge. But this is by no means the case; for while it is true that our religious instincts, like the others that belong to our constitution, are real instincts, it is also true that they distinctly differ from them in being spiritual and supernatural. Accordingly, while the objects which meet our physical instincts all belong to the physical universe, and are directly within our reach, those that meet our religious instincts belong to the spiritual and supernatural sphere, which cannot be directly reached by us, and can be known with practical certainty only by revelation. In view of this consideration, we may reasonably suppose that our religious nature warrants us to cherish at least the expectation of a divine revelation. That such an expectation is reasonable is surely attested by the fact, that the human race has ever been on the outlook for supernatural revelations, and ready cordially to receive those presented to it, even though they should be forgeries or merely supposed revelations. And when we contemplate the fearful mistakes which men have made in religion through want of an authoritative revelation, as may be seen everywhere in heathendom, and still more when we contemplate the high and momentous interests at stake, it must be confessed that such a revelation is needful in a supreme degree, and most devoutly to be wished.

It is quite vain to reply that the light of nature is enough to guide the earnest inquirer with practical certainty in regard to the matter, and that we have but to look into the depths of our consciousness, to question our religious nature, and consult the oracle of reason. The anxious seeker, alas! finds no satisfaction, no practical assurance here. He looks around, and he sees that those who profess to be guided by reason have arrived at the most different results. The directions which they take, and the conclusions which they reach, are about as numerous and divergent as the lines which we can draw outwards from one and the same centre. Which of these divergent lines is the earnest seeker to follow? Which of them is the true, colourless light of reason? Is it the stark Atheism of Feuerbach or Bradlaugh? Is it the coarse Materialism of Haeckel? Is it the Pantheism of Spinoza, Schelling, or Hegel? Is it the Positivism of Comte, and the worship of collective humanity? Is it the Agnosticism of Herbert Spencer, or the Scepticism of Hume? Is it the Deism of Professor Newman? Or is it the more ethereal and lofty Theism of James Martineau? Is the seeker to believe that man has a soul, or is he not? Is he to believe that man perishes at death, or that he is certainly immortal?

Or is the most that is permissible the bare possible hope of immortality, which was the utmost that John Stuart Mill could admit? Is he to believe that heaven and hell are both realities, or is he not? Amid such inextricable confusion and diversity, and especially on such essential questions, it is evident that a reasonably certain revelation is a vital need. In proportion as we believe in a God of fatherly love and mercy, in the same proportion shall we be inclined to believe that He will come to our aid by a special revelation if He can. To some it may even appear utterly improbable, next to incredible, that such a God would leave man, His poor, lonely, ignorant child, 'an infant crying in the night,' without extending to him His hand, or giving him the torch of revelation to light up his path. The inadequacy of human reason, the character of God, and the vital importance of the matter at stake, all alike point distinctly in the direction of a special revelation. This revelation, we believe, has been given us in the Bible, and more particularly, so far as we of the present dispensation are concerned, in the New Testament.

It has been objected that an external or 'book' revelation of religious truth is an impossibility. We are writing at present only for those who are at least Theists, and therefore believe in the existence of a personal God. To such there can clearly, one would say, be no impossibility in the matter. There can be no impossibility of making such a revelation on the part of God. We ourselves can communicate new truth to men around us, and surely the infinite God can do the same, only in an infinitely higher degree. We can communicate truth to other human minds with tolerable efficiency, even though we are compelled to do so indirectly through means of arbitrary speech, spoken, written, or printed; and surely God, to whom all hearts and minds are directly open, can at least do the same. How He may do so we may not be able exactly to analyse or explain, but one would think that what is possible for man in his imperfect artificial way, must be still more possible for God in His own direct and perfect way. And, on the other hand, when once the revelation has been communicated to the recipients, and expressed by them in an intelligent and permanent form, there is nothing on the part of man to prevent him from deriving unspeakable profit from it. The student receives the vast bulk of his mathematics and history from books, so that these books become essentially to him a written revelation of mathematical and historical truth. On the same principle, why should not the New Testament be to the Christian a revelation of new truth in the sphere of religion? Man, it appears, can give to man a revelation of new truth; and to say that God cannot do the same, is to say, as one has pointedly expressed it, that 'what is possible with man is impossible with God.'[1]

It may be said at once by some, This lands us directly in the theory of inspiration, which is just the grand initial difficulty and stumbling-block. But it must be distinctly understood that at present we have nothing whatever to do with any special theory of inspiration, orthodox or otherwise. We are, as it were, only approaching the New Testament and the grand truths which form the substance of Christianity, and it is clear that we cannot as yet logically have any definite theory of inspiration. Such a theory is, indeed, not one of the first doctrines that a man logically receives, but, as a rule, one of the very last. At any rate, we must have a reasonable historical belief in the New Testament, before we can logically have any full and definite theory of inspiration; for surely it is plain that we must first of all have a general confidence established in the New Testament, if our theory on the subject before us is to rest on its teaching as a foundation. We cannot expect that we should have some special supernatural proof granted to us at the outset, in the form of miracle, or personal revelation, or inspiration, that the New Testament is divinely inspired. We will not venture as Protestants to say, that a man must accept the doctrine of inspiration merely on the dictation and authority of

[1] Compare *Eclipse of Faith*, p. 63 (5th edition).

the Church. If we are to have a scriptural faith in the inspiration of the New Testament, and a truly scriptural theory of it, we can get these only from the New Testament itself; and it is obvious that we cannot logically do so until we have a reasonable belief in its general truthfulness. But when we have once attained to such a belief, we are logically prepared to accept its testimony in regard to inspiration as well as other matters.

It is a very great mistake on the part of religious teachers to begin Christian instruction in the case of doubting, but thoughtful and anxious seekers after truth, by insisting at the very outset on the reception of some hard and fast theory of inspiration. It is to be feared that there are religious teachers who do so, who place their theory on this subject in the foreground, and almost require acceptance of it at once as indispensable to the study of Christianity, if not to salvation. But in doing so, we may safely say they act illogically, and peril the chances of Christianity, in the case of the doubting, on a doctrine which is not really fundamental or in the first rank. In adopting this course, they are guilty of the same mistake as a general would be, who would stake the fate of his country on the taking of some outpost or fortress of the second or third order, while there were many of the first class, both vastly more powerful and defensible, remaining behind. It is quite certain, in any case, that the apostles in their teaching adopted a totally different plan. They did not come to their inquirers with a definite theory of inspiration, to which they demanded assent at the very outset, and before they proceeded to take another step. On the contrary, their practice was to begin with a plain, bold statement of the fundamental and soul-saving truths and facts of the gospel. Their first supreme object was to get men saved, and then they left them to learn or work out afterwards their theory of inspiration.

Perhaps, however, the question may be put here by some, 'Is it meant that a theory of inspiration is not necessary to be believed in order to salvation? Can a man be saved without holding any definite theory of inspiration?' To these questions we must unhesitatingly answer in the affirmative. Thousands have been saved who never heard of the doctrine under consideration, and thousands are being saved in our churches who have, to say the least, no very definite theory on the subject. Thousands have been saved who never even saw the New Testament, not to speak of having formed any theory in regard to its inspiration. We must ever bear in mind, and boldly declare, that men are saved by personal faith in the Lord Jesus Christ as exhibited in the gospel, and not by any theory of inspiration. If a man has such faith, then he is assuredly in the way of salvation, whether he has any definite view or not in reference to the doctrine in question. Indeed, it is only when a man has attained to personal faith in Christ, that he is prepared for approaching this doctrine; only then does he attain to the proper standpoint from which to study it; and only then does he see it with the proper light falling upon it, so as to enable him to arrive at a right conclusion.

There are three very distinct positions which may be taken up with regard to the doctrine of inspiration, admitting, of course, of various more or less definite grades between. There is, first of all, what may be called the high traditional position. According to this theory, the Holy Spirit so completely and effectually directed and controlled the language and mind of the sacred writers, that the result was a book not only absolutely infallible in its revelation of religious truth, but also literally infallible in all its smallest details, whether scientific, chronological, historical, geographical, moral, or doctrinal.

Another position, which seems also tolerably definite, is what we may call the theory of Religious Inspiration. According to this view, the object which God has in the New Testament is to teach religion, and therefore the inspiration extends only to the religious element. The phenomenon exhibited may be represented somewhat thus: God selected men, and put them by His providence into the very best position for knowing the outward historic facts, and being both eye-witnesses and ear-witnesses. Then He moved their minds by an irresistible impulse to write; He bore in, breathed in upon their minds the religious truth which they were to write, and so directed their minds in writing that they gave an infallible and trustworthy statement of religious truth. At the same time, because His object was not to reveal scientific, geographical, or even historical truth (except so far as it was essential to Christianity), they were left very much to their own information on such matters. Accordingly, their statements in regard to them are the common views of the age in which they lived, the views of thoroughly truthful men, but which may be sifted and even corrected by reasonable criticism. This theory seems also to give a comparatively definite and logical position, and, so far as the residuum of religious or theological truth is concerned, it gives us very much the same results as the preceding.

There is yet a third and still lower ground which may be taken. We mean the position that the writers are merely authoritative witnesses of what they saw and heard and received, without any supernatural presence of the Spirit to guide them in writing. In short, they are merely thoroughly qualified witnesses of the highest moral character, whose testimony is to be received very much like that of other perfectly trustworthy witnesses.

There can be no fair doubt that even this low ground logically admits of reasonable certainty in regard to all the great facts and truths of the gospel. It admits of the same certainty as we possess in reference to other well-accredited events of past history, certainty reaching such a high degree that there can be no valid or reasonable ground for doubt. For example, if an intelligent jury be engaged on the trial of a man accused of murder, and five or six competent witnesses bear clear and concurrent testimony to his guilt, they will unanimously agree to bring in a verdict of guilty. They will do so without misgiving, even though they know the witnesses are not infallibly inspired, but are liable to make mistakes. They will do so even though there may be some points in regard to which one or more of the witnesses may appear to be in mistake, and not a few points in regard to which there may be a measure of apparent mystery and confusion which cannot be satisfactorily cleared up. Even in these circumstances, the whole jury may attain to such a high measure of certainty, that they have no doubt remaining in their minds in regard to the essential facts, to such certainty indeed, that they do not hesitate to bring in a verdict of guilty, even though it is to cost a fellow-creature his life. From all this we may clearly see that, even if the New Testament were not inspired, but only the composition of thoroughly qualified and trustworthy witnesses, immovable certainty might be produced on the mind, such certainty as we possess in regard to the lives of Cæsar, or Napoleon the Great, or the best-accredited events of past history.

These three are quite distinct and logically conceivable positions in regard to inspiration. We do not for a moment say that they are all equally scriptural or correct; but we say emphatically that they are all views which may be held by a man who has saving faith in the Lord Jesus Christ. A man must not therefore think of saying, because he cannot attain to the first view, and can rise no higher than the third, that therefore his case is hopeless, and he need not trouble himself any more in regard to Christianity. On the contrary, when a man has got the length of even the third or lowest view, he has got enough to lead him into a reasonable faith in all the great events and soul-saving truths of the gospel, in other words, enough to lead him into personal salvation. Whenever we get a man up to the point of accepting the New Testament as the testimony of thoroughly competent and trustworthy witnesses, the first grand step is gained, and we can begin to press home upon him with effect the matter of his personal salvation.

It is by no means an uncommon thing for some of the more extreme teachers of the high orthodox school, to declare and maintain that there is no logical halting-place for a man between verbal inspiration of the most rigid type on the one hand, and absolute scepticism on the other. It is not at all an uncommon thing to find such speakers and writers at times constructing very pointed and strongly-expressed dilemmas to show that the inquirer is shut up by a stern necessity either to the one extreme or the other. But such a course of procedure we may safely believe to be not only quite unwarrantable, but even quite erroneous.[1]

The average man of fair and honest mind, who looks at realities rather than formal syllogisms, sees at once, by the higher logic of common sense and practical instinct, that such a style of arguing is false. He knows that there is a sound and trustworthy pathway between absolute verbal inspiration on the one hand and absolute scepticism on the other. He knows that between these two there is the middle way of reasonable moral certainty, that practical certainty by which we are guided in regard to the general affairs belonging to human life. We have no inspiration to direct us in reference to the truths of past history, such as, for example, the leading events in the life of Alexander the Great, or Cæsar, or the first Napoleon; but it does not therefore follow that we are left in absolute scepticism in regard to these historic personages. In a trial for murder, the witnesses produced are not infallibly inspired, but the jury are not

[1] Cf. Briggs, *Biblical Study*, pp. 240 ff.

on that account necessarily left in a state of helpless doubt in regard to the guilt of the prisoner. We have no infallible certainty in the ordinary matters which make up three-fourths of our daily life, and yet we are not left in hopeless uncertainty with reference to them. On the contrary, the historian is practically certain in regard to the lives of Alexander, Cæsar, and Napoleon; the jury bring in a confident verdict of guilty against the prisoner at the bar; and we feel reasonably certain in regard to the common affairs of our everyday life. In such matters as these, we clearly have a middle way between absolute certainty on the one hand and absolute scepticism on the other. Indeed, it is only for a comparatively small proportion of practical truth that we have such certainty as amounts to anything like the absolute infallibility of verbal inspiration. And surely it is reasonably conceivable that a man may have high certainty with regard to the historical facts and doctrines of Christianity without believing in verbal inspiration. Accordingly, though a man may not see his way to adopt this doctrine in its highest type, it by no means follows that he must be shut up to absolute scepticism. He may still hold by the middle way of moral evidence, which produces that practical certainty with which we have to content ourselves in matters of history and of human life and conduct.

But the mode of reasoning just referred to, besides

being unwarrantable and erroneous, is dangerous, and productive only of evil. We shall see this at once, if we consider how it is likely to act in the case of the thoughtful inquirer who has not attained to belief in verbal inspiration, and has serious difficulties in regard to the doctrine. Such a person comes across the dilemma referred to above, acutely and strongly put, and what is likely to be the consequence? It may be that by his practical common sense he sees at once that the argument, though very clever, is not sound, and immediately he loses all confidence in the trustworthiness of the author. Or it may be that he is possessed of a timid mind, and, being filled with a just horror of absolute scepticism, he shuts his eyes firmly, and commits himself at once and for ever to verbal inspiration, not as the result of sound conviction, but of mere blind dread. In so doing, he unquestionably suffers moral injury. Or, once more, it may be that the thinker is of a strong and impatient mind. When such a man in his state of doubt meets the dilemma, he may say, I cannot possibly accept this doctrine of verbal inspiration, and as this dilemma shows that there can be no middle way in the matter, I must just be content to cast myself into the arms of absolute scepticism. In this case the clever argument is productive of enormous spiritual evil.

It is quite certain that we are not shut up by any

stern necessity of an *a priori* kind to one or other of the two extremes, to verbal inspiration or absolute scepticism. We may reasonably hold to the middle way of practical common-sense certainty. As Christians, we may, without doubt, have unspeakable ground to thank God that He has given us in the Bible a higher certainty than this, and that we have by His grace attained to it. But it does not therefore follow that we are warranted to denounce the inquirer who is in doubt in regard to inspiration, and to declare dogmatically that there is no possible halting-place between the verbal type of it on the one hand and absolute scepticism on the other. Rather we should urge him, on the ground of that which he sees to be true, to enter without delay within the sacred circle of Christianity, where alone he can be in the true position, and have the true light for arriving at a satisfactory conclusion in regard to the scriptural doctrine of inspiration.

To make our present subject complete, it is necessary to draw attention to the importance of clearly keeping in view the special purpose which the Bible was meant to serve. It was given to man to be an authoritative revelation of religious truth; to 'make us wise unto salvation;' to be 'profitable for doctrine, for reproof, for correction, for instruction in righteousness, that the man of God may be perfect, throughly furnished unto all good works.' It was not meant to be a revelation of physical science, of geology or astronomy, of chemistry or medicine; and if any man betakes himself to the sacred books for an authoritative revelation in these departments, it is quite certain that his procedure is unwarranted, and can only lead to evil. The Bible holds straight on its way, and shows its practical common sense by sticking steadily to its grand object, and giving itself no concern about the different branches of physical science. When in the course of its narrative it does require to touch on such external matters, it simply does so in the current language and forms of the age, without meaning to affirm either that they are right or that they are wrong. Nor does an apparent mistake in the fields referred to, and arising in the manner now indicated, necessarily invalidate or even impair the trustworthiness of the Bible in its own sphere, any more than such a mistake destroys the authority of the scholar in the department of his special language, or the authority of legal counsel in the department of law. Indeed, such so-called mistakes are properly no mistakes at all, for the writer or speaker, in the cases under consideration, really means to affirm nothing either as to the truth or falsehood of his incidental statements, and only uses them on his way to express the supreme leading idea which he has before his mind. But although positive mistakes were made by the Bible in the field of physical science, even that would not necessarily invalidate its authority in its own express department of religion, any more than a positive mistake in geology or astronomy would invalidate the authority of the scholar or of legal counsel in their respective spheres. And the reason of this is obvious; for in such cases the mistakes lie in an external and totally different department from that in regard to which the specialist professes to give authoritative information, and therefore they ought not to affect his full trustworthiness in his own proper sphere.[1]

It may be said that even revelation and inspiration conjoined have not succeeded in giving man reasonable certainty in regard to religion. Does not the very multitude of the Christian sects show that the matter is quite as doubtful as ever? Are not the Churches just as hopelessly divided as the philosophers or system-makers? We answer that this is by no means the case. Although the different sections of the Church are separated from one another outwardly, the division is more superficial and apparent than deep and radical. While the philosophers, as we have seen, are hopelessly divided in regard to the most fundamental questions, such as the existence of God, the soul, immortality, and the like, on all fundamental questions the Churches are at one. They are rather separate streets, squares, and quarters of the same great city of God, than separate

[1] See Appendix, Note VII.

and hostile cities. In any case, the underlying basis of unity in their common faith, spirit, and life is ten times greater, and of a hundredfold more importance, than the superficial accidents which separate them. In looking down from the summit of Ben Lomond on the lovely lake over which it presides, the traveller sees its southern end all dotted over with islands, separated from each other by reaches of flashing water. But at the basis these islands are all united, and consist of the same mother rock; and the waters of separation only require to be removed in order to make this plainly visible. And so we may safely affirm that the various branches of the Holy Catholic Church are all essentially one, and at one in regard to the fundamental truths of Christianity; and we only require to look beneath the surface in order to discover that this is the case.

We cannot see this radical agreement and unity in regard to the essentials of Christianity better than by looking into any of our Church hymn-books. We see there the unity of the faith and of the Spirit demonstrated in a very interesting and instructive way by the variety of Churches from which the hymns have been drawn. In looking into the hymnals of the three great Presbyterian Churches of Scotland, and into *Hymns Ancient and Modern*, we find therein many of the same distinctively Christian hymns, and these taken from very different Churches. From the Greek Church we have, 'Art thou weary, art thou languid, Art thou sore distrest?' from the Roman Church, 'Jerusalem the Golden;' from the German Church, 'Now thank we all our God;' from the Episcopal Church, 'Rock of Ages, cleft for me;' from the Wesleyan Church, 'Jesus, Lover of my soul;' from the Congregational Church, 'When I survey the wondrous Cross;' from the Moravian Church, 'Hail to the Lord's Anointed;' as well as from the Presbyterian Church, 'I heard the voice of Jesus say.' Surely all this is very instructive, and demonstrates the essential agreement and unity of the Church and the Church's faith, notwithstanding the outward division and the so-called 'war of sects.' It matters only in a secondary degree in what street, or square, or quarter of the holy city a man may live, provided only he be really a citizen and live within its walls.

IV.

Early Historical Testimony to the Authenticity of the New Testament.

THE object of the following study is to give a brief and clear statement of the early historical testimony to the authenticity of the New Testament. In other words, it is an attempt in some degree to answer the question, 'What historical evidence do we possess for accepting the leading books of the New Testament as genuine and authentic productions of the Apostolic Age?' The subject, therefore, is one neither of experimental nor internal, but almost solely of external, evidence. The field before us is of vast extent, and can be discussed within our present limits only in a very general way. Accordingly, we must in the sequel content ourselves with marking out boldly the leading outlines of the argument, without descending into details.

Christianity is not a purely natural religion which may be thought out in all its minutiæ by mere human reason, working on the materials which lie before it in nature, physical and mental. On the contrary, it is a religion which comes down upon nature from a higher sphere, in order to correct fallen and disordered nature. That is to say, it is a supernatural revelation, a revelation which comes out of the heavenly sphere, and therefore its contents can be known only from books or oral tradition. Very especially it is a religion which has its foundation in certain great supernatural facts, such as the incarnation, life, work, death, resurrection, and ascension of Jesus Christ. But these facts, though supernatural, just because they are past facts, can be known to us only by historical evidence in the form of books or oral tradition. In so far as we are concerned in this nineteenth century, we may drop oral tradition out of sight, and confine our attention to the evidence of books. But since the alleged historical facts and revealed truths of Christianity are contained in the New Testament, the question at once narrows itself to this: 'What historical evidence have we for accepting the books of the New Testament as the genuine and authentic production of the Apostolic Age?'

It is probable that the vast majority of Christians accept the New Testament as authentic and trustworthy, on the general testimony of the Church in the age in which they live. They look around and find a great society existing in the world, known as the Christian Church. It is spread over many countries, and it exists in many different sections—Protestant, Roman Catholic, Greek, Armenian, Syrian, Coptic, and the like. But however much these sections may differ from each other, and however bitter their mutual antagonism may sometimes be, there is one thing in which they all agree. They all accept the New Testament as the genuine production of Apostles and apostolic men, and fall back upon it as their grand foundation and authoritative charter. And this united testimony is not weakened in any way by the fact of divisions existing in the Church, but rather greatly strengthened, because it is shown thereby to be the testimony of jealous rivals.

On the general ground of the united testimony of the divided Church, Christians, as a rule, at first accept the books of the New Testament as genuine and authentic. Nor is there anything unreasonable in this procedure. On the contrary, it is highly reasonable. It is very much the same ground as that on which men generally accept the facts of past history, and books that have come down to us from distant ages. If we ask the average man why he accepts such historical facts as the battle of Marathon, or of Bannockburn, or the leading events in the life of Alexander the Great, or of Luther, he will likely reply that it is on the ground that they are accepted by the general run of historians. If we ask on what ground he accepts Hamlet as the production of Shakespeare, the Pilgrim's

Progress as the work of John Bunyan, or Paradise Lost as that of Milton, he will very likely reply that it is because they are accepted as such by the general literary world. This is quite a reasonable answer, and it is the only one which the vast majority of men, even of educated men, can give. In very much the same way Christians, as a rule, accept the books of the New Testament at first on the general ground of the concurrent testimony of the Church, and this ground, so far as it goes, is one which is quite reasonable.

When we inquire what is the nature of this evidence, and what intelligent account can be given of it, the answer must be that it is mainly a case of historical evidence. That is, it is very much the same kind of evidence as that on the ground of which we accept any other book or historical fact coming down from the past. It is not, therefore, a question with which mere physical science, distinctively so called, has anything to do; for it lies entirely beyond its proper domain. According to the principles laid down in a previous study, physical science has just as little to do with the realm of historical criticism, as historical criticism has to do with the realm of physical science. Physical science, such as geology, for example, has nothing whatever to say in regard to such historical facts as the battles of Marathon and Bannockburn. Physical science, such as astronomy, for example, can determine nothing whatever as to whether Hamlet is really the work of Shakespeare, or Paradise Lost the work of Milton. It can determine nothing whatsoever in regard to such questions, for they lie entirely beyond its horizon, in the totally different sphere of historical criticism. In like manner, physical science has nothing whatsoever to say either for or against the authenticity of the books of the New Testament. It is an investigation which belongs to the totally different department of historical criticism and evidence.

It would be a very easy matter to begin at the present day and trace our New Testament back from century to century, until we arrive at the ancient Church. But the work would be wearisome, and it is quite unnecessary. We are able to take a single leap over fourteen or fifteen centuries by the aid of three very ancient manuscripts of the New Testament, which, by a gracious Providence, have come down to our day. At this stage of our investigation, we cannot do better than cite these venerable and most valuable witnesses to give their testimony.

Before calling these witnesses into court, it will be proper to make a few remarks by way of introduction. Of course, before the art of printing was invented, the New Testament, like other books, could be multiplied only by being written or printed with the pen. This employment of printing books with the pen formed one of the chief occupations of the monks during the darkness of the Middle Ages, and many specimens of their handiwork, beautifully executed and illuminated, have floated safely down to our day. Books so written are called manuscripts. Now there are many manuscript copies of the New Testament, which have come down to us from very early ages. It is a well-known fact that many works belonging to the classic literature of ancient Greece have been preserved to our time, almost enough to form a small library. But Tischendorf, a learned German, lately dead, who had perhaps more knowledge of ancient manuscripts of the New Testament than any man of our generation, declares that 'Providence has ordained for the New Testament more sources of the greatest antiquity than are possessed by all the old Greek literature put together.' He here refers, of course, to versions, and references in the early writers of the Church, as well as manuscripts. The fact so emphatically stated is one of the very highest importance, and ought to be deeply impressed upon the mind as a means of strengthening our faith. It shows that Biblical scholars have abundance of material out of which to construct a trustworthy Greek New Testament.

The first of the three ancient manuscripts which we cite as a witness is that which is called the *Alexandrian*. It receives its name from the fact that, in the seventeenth century, it was brought from Alexandria, in

Egypt, in which city it had very probably been written. It is now preserved in the British Museum in London. It is written, or printed with the pen, in neat capital letters. It is agreed among scholars that it is about 1400 years old, so that it takes us back by a single leap to the year 450 or so. It is not quite complete, being somewhat mutilated by age and wear; but it contains portions of all the books of the New Testament, and shows us most explicitly that the Church possessed the same New Testament about the year 450 as we now possess.

The second ancient manuscript whose testimony we adduce is the *Vatican* manuscript. It is so called because it is preserved in the Pope's library in the Vatican at Rome. Like the Alexandrian, it is written in capital letters, though they are not formed quite so beautifully. It is, however, somewhat older, its age being over 1500 years, so that it carries us back at once to about the year 350 or so. It is unfortunately incomplete, wanting Revelation and some of the smaller Epistles; but it bears unmistakable testimony to the fact that the New Testament of that early age was substantially the same as we now possess.

The third manuscript which we cite as a witness is, if possible, one which is more interesting than either of the two preceding. It is that which is known among scholars as the *Sinaitic* manuscript. It is so called because it was discovered in the year 1859 at Mount

Sinai, in the old monastery of St. Catherine there. Tischendorf, the German scholar already referred to, was on a mission to the East in search of manuscripts, when he had the honour allotted to him by Providence of discovering this inestimable treasure in that ancient convent. The circumstances connected with its discovery are quite romantic; but of course we cannot enter into them at present. He succeeded in securing it, and it is now safely deposited in the Imperial Library at St. Petersburg. It is the most beautifully printed of all the three. It is about 1500 years old, having been written probably about A.D. 350. It contains the New Testament complete; and thus it affords us the most explicit testimony that the New Testament of that early age was the very same as we now possess.

We have cited these three venerable witnesses from the three capitals of Christendom,—the first from London, the capital of Protestantism; the second from Rome, the capital of Roman Catholicism; and the third from St. Petersburg, the capital of the Greek Church; and we see that their testimony is most explicit. It is not only explicit, but it perfectly agrees; and it demonstrates that the early Church possessed and used the same New Testament with ourselves about the year 350, or 250 years after the death of John and the close of the Apostolic Age.

We are now ready to take another step back, and

here we come to the main part of our argument. Let the reader try to transfer himself in thought to the second half of the second century of our era. That is, we are now to contemplate the period extending from A.D. 150 to A.D. 200. The Apostle John, it is believed, died about the year 100, so that we have now before our mind the period extending from fifty to one hundred years after the death of John and the end of what may be called the Apostolic Age. We have therefore before us a period when men, not a few, were still alive who had seen and conversed with John, and when multitudes were still living who had seen and conversed with those who had seen and conversed with him. Such is the age to which we are now introduced.

But before proceeding to call our witnesses, let us look for a little at the Church in this early period. It had spread over the length and breadth of the Roman Empire, and even into India and Ethiopia, and other regions beyond its boundaries. Probably it had not as yet the majority of the population in any large city or province, and very likely its entire adherents may have fallen short of two millions. Nevertheless, it had gained a footing in almost every city from Britain in the north to Ethiopia in the south, from Persia in the east to Spain in the west.

It must also be remembered that the books of the New Testament were habitually read on the Lord's day in the assemblies of the faithful throughout the Church. This is a fact which is not denied and not deniable. The sacred books were thus kept constantly before the eyes and minds of the ancient Christians, so that they could easily detect whether any old and acknowledged book was rejected or lost, and whether any new and unauthorized book was introduced. In other words, this universal system of reading the New Testament in the public meetings of the Church enabled all Christians to act as guardians of the New Testament and faithful witnesses to its integrity. We can easily see how impossible it would be in the present day to introduce any new book into the services of the Church, or drop any important one altogether, without all Christians noticing it, and raising a loud and universal protest. In those early ages, when the New Testament Scriptures, although not in the hands of the people, were read much more extensively in the public services than they are now, we may safely conclude, in like manner, that no new book could be introduced or old one expelled, without awakening the attention of the entire body of Christians. What, then, is the testimony of the Church of the second half of the second century to the leading books of the New Testament?

We can, of course, directly ascertain what was the New Testament of this early age only from the representative authors who lived at the time. Happily a considerable number of books have come down to us, the works of Fathers and other men eminent in the Church during that period. There were also some translations of the New Testament already made from the Greek into other languages before the year 200. We now proceed to cite as witnesses some of these Fathers and Versions, and examine them as to the books which were then accepted in the Church as genuine and authentic. We cite them from different countries, and even from different continents, in order to show all the more conclusively and impressively, that the entire Church, throughout its length and breadth, accepted substantially the same New Testament as ourselves.[1]

The first witnesses which we cite are from the Continent of Europe, and the first of these is the Church of ancient France. We call as the representative and mouthpiece of that Church Irenæus, the bishop of the well-known city of Lyons. He was a native of Asia Minor, and had sat at the feet of Polycarp, who had sat at the feet of the Apostle John, and he probably sealed his testimony with his blood by dying as a martyr in A.D. 202. He was a somewhat extensive author, and his works which have been preserved to our day are enough to form a very considerable volume. That he is a witness of the highest character and value

[1] See Appendix, Note VIII.

is beyond all possibility of contradiction. And his testimony is full and explicit. He mentions all the four Gospels; and so clear and decided is the confidence of the Church, in his day, in regard to the matter, that he declares there are and can be only four. But as nothing gives the modern mind such a firm assurance as a few statistics, even though they should be immediately forgotten, we venture to give the following statistics of his quotations. They will be found to be at least approximately correct, and we believe rather under than over the mark.[1] He mentions Matthew, and he quotes from him, either directly or by way of reference, about 180 times; Mark, and quotes from him about 15 times; Luke, and quotes from him about 125 times; John, and quotes from him over 80 times. It is therefore beyond all doubt that Irenæus and the Church of France in this early age accepted our four Gospels, and them alone. But our witness mentions also the Acts of the Apostles, and quotes from it about 50 times; Romans, and quotes

[1] It is proper to state the method adopted in arriving at the results given in the following statistics. I employed the indexes of Scripture references given in the works of the respective Fathers in Clark's *Ante-Nicene Christian Library*. I took the trouble to turn up more than a hundred references in each of the authors from whom statistics are given, ascertained in this way the relative trustworthiness of the references, and calculated the general results accordingly. With the exception of the references in Hippolytus, from which a considerable deduction has to be made, the others may be confidently accepted very much as they stand in the indexes. At all events, a deduction of five or ten per cent. will be ample.

from it above 60 times; 1 Corinthians, and quotes from it upwards of 70 times; 2 Corinthians, and quotes from it 17 times. He mentions also Galatians, Ephesians, Philippians, Colossians, and Revelation, and quotes from all of them frequently. He also mentions and quotes from many of the smaller Epistles. Such is the testimony of Irenæus, Bishop of Lyons, and witness of the Church of France. It is most explicit, and proves incontestably that already this distant Church in the latter half of the second century, from fifty to a hundred years after the close of the Apostolic Age, possessed the same New Testament as we now possess.

We now pass over the Alps into Italy, and inquire what was the New Testament of the Italian Church in this early age. We cite three witnesses as representatives of this Church. The first is an ancient list of the New Testament books called the Muratorian Canon, because it was discovered and published by Muratori at Milan in the year 1740. This interesting old canon or list of sacred books belongs to about the year 170, and therefore falls within our period. It is a very imperfect production; but it bears explicit testimony to all the books of our New Testament, except Hebrews, James, 1 and 2 Peter, and 3 John. The second witness which we cite in regard to the Italian Church is the ancient Latin Version of the New Testament. Already, at this early period, a translation had been made into Latin for the use of the Christians who spoke that language. Perhaps it had been made originally in North Africa, but an edition of it was already current in Italy. We know the books which it contained from some very ancient manuscripts and the references in the ancient Latin Fathers. It contained substantially the same books as are mentioned in the Muratorian Canon. The third witness is Hippolytus, whose chief work was discovered within the memory of the present generation. He was a leading presbyter, and probably a schismatic bishop at Rome. He died as an old man and a martyr about A.D. 237; so that much of his manhood fell within our period. Of his numerous works, enough has been preserved to form a considerable volume. And there can be no doubt as to his testimony; for it is full and explicit. He quotes from Matthew, directly or indirectly, more than 50 times; from Mark, about 6 times; from Luke, about 25 times; from John, about 50 times; from Acts, 7 times; from Romans, about 10 times; from 1 Corinthians, about the same; and in a similar proportion from most of the other Epistles, until we come to Revelation, from which he quotes about 18 times. When we take the testimony of Hippolytus along with that of the Muratorian Canon and the ancient Latin Version, we can have no hesitation, on the evidence of such witnesses, in concluding that the Italian Church in the second half of the second century already possessed substantially the same New Testament as we now possess.

We next pass from Europe over to Africa. Right over against Italy, in and around Carthage, in the region of the modern Algeria and Tunis, a flourishing Church had existed from the dawn of Christianity. It was the Church which afterwards numbered among its bishops such men as Cyprian and Augustine. At the period under review, it could already boast of one of the most distinguished Christian writers of the age. We mean Tertullian, the first in time of the great Latin Christian authors. He was born probably about A.D. 160, and died probably about 220; so that his testimony is valid for our special period. We cite him as the representative witness of the North African Church. And his testimony is most explicit and abundant. His extant works are somewhat extensive; and in them he refers to, or quotes from, all the books of the New Testament, except Philemon, 2 Peter, 2 and 3 John. He quotes from, or refers to, Matthew, about 400 times; Mark, about 80 times; Luke, about 500 times; John, about 240 times; Acts, about 110 times; Romans, about 160 times; 1 Corinthians, about 350 times; 2 Corinthians, about 120 times; and so on proportionately through all but the very smallest Epistles, until we come to Revelation, from which he quotes about 80 times. Such evidence as that just given requires no comment. Tertullian and the North African Church clearly testify that they used our present New Testament in the second half of the second century.

We pass eastward along the northern coast of Africa, until we come to Alexandria, in Egypt. In this ancient city, Christianity was planted in the Apostolic Age, and toward the end of the second century, it already possessed a flourishing theological school, which produced a number of famous Fathers and Christian authors. We have more particularly to do at present with the well-known Clement of Alexandria, who falls within our special period. Like Tertullian, he left somewhat extensive writings behind him, many of which have survived to our day in the original Greek. They contain quotations from, or references to, almost every book in the New Testament, the exceptions again being such small Epistles as Philemon, 2 Peter, and 3 John. He quotes from Matthew, or makes reference to his Gospel, about 180 times; he quotes from Mark above 20 times; from Luke, about 110 times; from John, above 60 times; from Acts, about 20 times; from Romans, about 110 times; from 1 Corinthians, about 150 times; from 2 Corinthians, more than 30 times; and in a similar proportion from all the remaining Epistles, with the exceptions already mentioned, until we come to Revelation, which he quotes about 12 times. The outcome of all this testimony is very plain. The

Church of Alexandria, the most learned, critical, and scientific Church of the age, acknowledged, beyond all contradiction, the same New Testament in the second half of the second century as we now possess in the nineteenth.

We now enter the Continent of Asia, in which most of our sacred books had their origin. We begin by citing the ancient Syrian Church as a representative witness. In Syria, the country lying to the north of Palestine, bounded on the west by the Mediterranean, and stretching away eastward to the Euphrates and beyond it, Christianity was already planted in the Apostolic Age. But as the Syrian language was totally different from Greek, being in fact a language cognate to the Hebrew, a translation of the New Testament soon became a necessity. Accordingly we find that a translation was made into Syriac at a very early date, probably in the first, certainly in the second half of the second century. This very ancient version, slightly modified, not only exists to the present day, but is the 'authorized version' used by all the different sections of the Syrian Church—sections which go back to the fourth century. It is known by the name of the Peshito. It contains all the books of our present New Testament, except 2 and 3 John, 2 Peter, Jude, and Revelation. This testimony might be further corroborated by that of Syrian authors belonging to this period, of whom some remains have been preserved to our day. But the Peshito itself is a sufficient witness, and testifies most explicitly to the fact that the Syrian Church already possessed substantially the same New Testament as ourselves, probably in the first, and certainly in the second half of the second century.

From Syria we may pass northward to Asia Minor, and cite the Church of this region as a witness. Irenæus, whom we have already examined as the representative witness of the Church in France, was a native of this region, and passed his early youth, he tells us, under the instruction of Polycarp, Bishop of Smyrna, who was the disciple of the Apostle John. He speaks of no divergence in regard to the leading sacred books as existing between the Church of Asia Minor and that of France. He rather teaches the very opposite ; so that this testimony may be fairly regarded as implying that substantially the same books were accepted by the Church of Asia Minor as were accepted by the Church of France, and as are accepted by ourselves. But, in addition to his testimony, we shall immediately see that long before the second half of the second century, the leading New Testament books can be proved to have been in current use in the Church in question. In other words, we conclude from circumstantial evidence of the very strongest kind that in the second half of the second century the Church in Asia

Minor used substantially the same sacred books as the Church in the nineteenth century.

Let us now endeavour to sum up this evidence, and ascertain the conclusion to which it points. We must remember that the evidence adduced is not that of individual, private, isolated men. It is the evidence of the Churches to which the writers belonged, of which they were office-bearers, and which they represent. Accordingly, the first conclusion evidently is, that already in the second half of the second century—from 150 to 200—and within fifty years or so of the Apostolic Age, the Church, over all its length and breadth, from Syria in the east to Italy in the west, from France in the north to Egypt in the south, beyond all contradiction possessed substantially the same New Testament as we at present possess.

The testimony just adduced is extremely strong, though at first it may be somewhat difficult fully to realize its strength. It is that of a continuous, organized society, whose life flows on without a break. The Church began with the Apostles. It spread out from Jerusalem; it continued to live and grow without the least interruption, like a healthy human being. It might change its members to some extent, from year to year, by death at the one end and conversions at the other, just as the human body changes its constituent particles of matter. But amidst all this it retained its continuity and identity, just as the human body retains its continuity and identity, though it is said to change its substance entirely every seven years. We might in a way regard the Church as a gigantic mystic person—'the body of Christ'—living on continuously through the ages, changing its constituent particles slowly, but constantly keeping up an unbroken continuity of life. Its testimony accordingly is, in a manner, like that of an intelligent being who keeps on living through the ages, but whose eye becomes not dim nor his force abated through the lapse of years. We might even say that it is like that of several independent mystic persons; for the Churches of Rome, Alexandria, Syria, and Asia Minor assuredly had an independent continuity of existence from the Apostolic Age, so that their testimony is also largely independent. Keeping this organic, living continuity of the Church vividly before our mind, we may most certainly accept the testimony of the Church in the second half of the second century, as valid not merely for the age in which it was given, but for eighty years before—that is, for the Apostolic Age. In other words, the testimony of the Church in the period specified, is valid in the highest degree for the age of the Apostles, and bears that the leading books of the New Testament are the genuine and authentic production of that age.

We may be pardoned for dwelling a little longer on

this point, partly because of its importance, and partly because of the extreme difficulty which we have, in this age of the printing-press, in realizing the power of a corporate body to hand down facts correctly by tradition. Perhaps we may feel the force of the argument still more vividly if we look at the matter thus. Let us start with the year 150. We have already seen that the Church most certainly accepted the leading books of our New Testament at that date. But the majority of Church members living in A.D. 150 were living in A.D. 145, and even 140; of those living in A.D. 140, the majority were living in 130; and of those living in A.D. 130, the majority again were living in 120; and so by a few steps we reach the Apostolic Age. The older members of the Church are constantly overlapping and living alongside of the new ones, thus keeping up an unbroken life and tradition, so that the testimony of the Church to our sacred books in A.D. 150 really reaches back to the first century. We can thus pass on from year to year, because of the vital organic continuity of the Church, until we reach back to the Apostolic Age, feeling firmly safe at each step; and conclude, with the highest certainty attainable in historic evidence, that the New Testament books are the genuine production of the age of the Apostles. Nowhere is there any break in the life of the Church, as if all its members had died out at any date, and, after an utter gap, the Church had been somehow started anew. In that case the argument would not have held with such force. But the continuity is most assuredly uninterrupted — the vast majority of the members of any given year overlapping the members of several previous, and also of several succeeding years; nay, forming a constituent part of the membership of several preceding and succeeding years, so as to transmit the sacred books with an unbroken tradition.

This living continuity, the vast majority of presbyters and members of one year overlapping on the one side those who die, and on the other those who are admitted in the same year, makes it next to impossible that any book once accepted should have been lost or rejected, and that any new and forged book should have been surreptitiously introduced. We only require to contemplate how utterly impossible such an incident would be in the present day, to see how impossible it must have been even then. And what makes the argument stronger still is the fact that even the most determined scrutiny by the most hostile critics has not succeeded in pointing out the date, place, and circumstances after the Apostolic Age, in which any book of the New Testament was forged and palmed off upon the Church as genuine, and finally inserted in the list of sacred books.

Perhaps it may help the reader to see more clearly

and feel more vividly the force of the argument, if we adduce as an illustration the fate of the later works of Aristotle. He was, as every one knows, the greatest philosophical thinker, with perhaps only one exception, of all antiquity. His later works some time after his death entirely disappeared from the view of the world. They had been carried away from Athens to Asia Minor by a man of the name of Neleus. This man died, and the manuscripts remained in possession of his family. But when the kings of Pergamus began to collect their famous library, and were everywhere gathering up books for this purpose, the family of Neleus, afraid to lose their precious treasure, hid the manuscripts in a cellar. There they lay for a period of one hundred and fifty years, during which they seem to have been utterly forgotten by the world, or at least given up for lost. But when they were again found and brought to light, learned men had no difficulty, from a great variety of grounds, in coming to the assured conclusion that they were the genuine works of Aristotle. And this though they had been utterly hidden out of sight for a hundred and fifty years! If learned men could attain to such certainty in regard to the works of Aristotle, which had entirely disappeared for a hundred and fifty years, much more may we trust the testimony of the Church in the second half of the second century in regard to the genuineness of the books of the New Testament, when we consider that this testimony extends back only over eighty years or so, and that the sacred books were not buried out of sight, like those of Aristotle, but publicly read in the meetings of the faithful on the Lord's day throughout all the Church, north, south, east, and west.

But we are not left to bridge over the gap between A.D. 150 and the age of the Apostles simply by an elaborate argument. We have also direct evidence of the utmost value. Happily a few small books and fragments have come down to us even from that early period, the period between the Apostles and A.D. 150. In these literary remains we find explicit testimony to our New Testament books as already existing and forming the spiritual food and the palladium of the Church. Of the works of Justin Martyr, who was born in Palestine about A.D. 100, wrote at Rome about 140 and later, and suffered martyrdom there about 166, enough has come down to us to form a fair-sized volume. His works are not addressed to Christians, and are not of such a nature as to admit of extensive quotation from most of the New Testament. But in his remains he refers explicitly to the Gospels, though he does not mention the evangelists by name, and quotes from them all, although, like the ordinary preacher, often from mere memory. Indeed, his references to the life of our Lord are so numerous and abundant, that a very full narrative might be constructed out of them.[1] He mentions also Revelation, and if he does not quote from the Epistles, it is because they do not lie in his way. This testimony of Justin is valid possibly for Palestine and certainly for Rome, and for the first half of the second century.

Another writer whom we can adduce as witness from this period is Papias, the Bishop of Hierapolis in Asia Minor, a Church mentioned in the last chapter of Colossians. He lived and flourished in the early part of the second century, say about 120, and was the contemporary, if not the disciple, of the Apostle John. He certainly overlapped the Apostolic Age. Only a very few fragments of his works have come down to us, the whole of which might be printed on a single page. But from these fragments and the few notices preserved in ancient writers, we know that he used Matthew, Mark, and probably John, 1 John, 1 Peter, and Revelation. This testimony is largely supplemented by that of Polycarp, martyr-bishop of Smyrna, also in Western Asia. He was both a contemporary and disciple of the Apostle John, so that his life also overlaps the age of the apostles. A small epistle of his has come down to us, written probably about the year 115. It is not quite so large as

[1] See Sanday, *The Gospels in the Second Century*, pp. 91 ff.; Westcott *The Canon of the New Testament*, pp. 101 ff. (4th edition).

Colossians, and yet it contains upwards of forty quotations from, or references to, our New Testament, taken in all from ten or twelve books. The testimony of Papias and Polycarp is valid for the Church in Asia Minor at the beginning of the second century.

We mention only another contemporary of John, Clement of Rome. His life lay largely within the Apostolic Age. He wrote an Epistle to the Corinthians, which happily we still possess entire. It dates from about the year 95, so that it is probably as old as some of the books of the New Testament. In this Epistle we find many sayings of our Lord which are found in our present Gospels, though Clement does not refer explicitly to the Gospels as his source of quotation. But he distinctly implies, either by quotation or allusion, the existence of Romans, 1 Corinthians, Ephesians, Hebrews, James, and 1 Peter. Such is the testimony of Clement, and it is obviously valid for Rome and the close of the first century.

The testimony just adduced might even be considerably increased, if we were to descend into minute details. But the above will be sufficient to bridge over the chasm between the second half of the second century, in which the testimony is full and irresistible, and the Apostolic Age or close of the first century. The witnesses just adduced, especially when viewed in the light of our previous argument, distinctly show that about the year 100 the same sacred books as we possess at present were known and received in the Church. But this was a time at which the Apostle John was just dead, and, in any case, when multitudes were living who overlapped the Apostolic Age, who had themselves been the disciples and friends of the apostles, and who had even seen and used the original manuscripts. We therefore conclude that the leading New Testament books must have been the genuine and authentic productions of apostles and men of the Apostolic Age.

Before leaving this department of the subject, it may be well to remark that it would be a grand mistake to suppose that we now have all, or even one-tenth part, of the evidence on which the early Churches accepted the books of the New Testament as the genuine productions of their authors. The vast bulk of the evidence which they had before them, and on which they came to their decision, has been lost for ever. Only the decision remains, with some stray and, for the most part, accidental facts of the evidence. But that is just what might have been expected, and it should in no way shake our faith. When we look back on important judicial trials or events of past history, we sometimes find that we possess only the decision of the judges or of the age in regard to them, but not the facts on which it was founded. Yet we have little difficulty in accepting as trustworthy the decision of competent contemporaries when that decision is consentient. And so it is here. The mass of evidence has disappeared, but the decision remains. We know that the Churches in Rome, Egypt, Syria, and Asia Minor, Churches which had a continuous existence from the days of the apostles, and had all the facts before them, substantially agreed. The case has been tried, as it were, by different independent juries, in widely distant parts of the world; they unite in returning practically the same verdict; and surely we may accept the agreement, or rather unanimity, of the verdict as a reasonable substitute for the lost details of the evidence.

We now pass on to notice briefly the testimony of the ancient heretics to the sacred books of Christianity. In doing so, we shall cite our witnesses only from the first half of the second century. We know that heretics had already appeared upon the scene in the days of the apostles, and they were only far too numerous still. One positive benefit, however, which they achieved for the Church in all succeeding ages was to leave behind them their decided testimony to the Christian Scriptures. In their case we have to do with the testimony of men who, for the most part, lived outside the Church, who were more or less hostile to orthodox Christianity, and therefore were sure to criticise its sacred books with no favourable eye. In the view of many, perhaps of all, this fact should make their testimony more valuable, as being that of men free from all friendly bias, as being in some degree the testimony of enemies.

Now it is a singular and important fact that their testimony is very explicit. They fall back, as a rule, for their support on the same sacred books as the Church itself. So far as we can judge from their scanty remains, they seem even to quote more largely from them than the orthodox, and certainly some of them speak more profusely about them as 'Scripture,' using the very same method of quotation as they do in regard to the Old Testament. And this mode of procedure is most significant; for it implies that the Christian Scriptures were accepted by the Church of the age as the authoritative books, on which every system of doctrine must of necessity be founded.

We adduce the testimony of only two heretical teachers from this early period, from A.D. 100 to 150. The first witness whom we cite is Marcion. This man was a native of Pontus, in the north of Asia Minor, and a son of the Bishop of Sinope, a maritime city in that region. He was born about the year 100, and afterwards removed to Rome, where he was already known as a full-blown leader of heresy about 140. And what is his testimony in regard to our New Testament? We know, on the best of evidence, from different sources, that he positively accepted an abbreviated Luke and the first ten Epistles of Paul. But one of the great accusations brought against him was just the fact that he mutilated or rejected sacred books which the Church regarded as authoritative. In addition to the books which he positively accepted, he bears distinct testimony, by a tolerably explicit rejection of them, to the other three Gospels and Revelation. In other words, about the year 140, Marcion, the heretic, bears explicit testimony to three-fourths of our present New Testament; and this testimony may be regarded as valid even for remote Pontus, and certainly for Rome and the more central regions of the catholic Church.

We cite as witness only another and still more ancient heretic. His name is Basilides, and his chief sphere of life seems to have lain in Egypt. He flourished about A.D. 120, and, without doubt, overlapped the Apostolic Age by a number of years. A few very small fragments of his writings have come down to us in the form of quotations by the Fathers who wrote to refute his opinions. He laboured to support his views by the authority of the New Testament, and he often quotes from it, and generally as Scripture. We have explicit proof from the fragments and references which we still possess, that he accepted at least Matthew, Luke, and John, Romans, 1 and 2 Corinthians, Ephesians, Colossians, and 1 Peter; that is, decidedly more than one-half of our present New Testament. Of course it is not to be inferred for a moment that, because no allusions are made to the other books in the scanty remains which survive, they did not exist or were not acknowledged by Basilides. In other words, we see that this ancient heretic bears most important testimony to our sacred books, and it is the testimony of a man who not only was outside the pale of the Church, but whose life reached back into the Apostolic Age.

The conclusion from all this is very forcible. It means that the Christian Scriptures were so firmly established, so widely accepted, and so well authenticated by evidence which could not at that time be controverted, that even heretics felt compelled to accept them and make the attempt to found their systems upon them. We may be well assured that if they had known them to be forgeries, they would have followed a different course, and shown them up as such. But not even Marcion, who rejected some of the books, pretended to do so, so far as we know, because they were forgeries, but only because in his view they were too Judaistic and one-sided. We may therefore extend to the New Testament generally the saying of Irenæus in his great work, *Against Heresies:* 'So great is the certainty in regard to the Gospels, that even the heretics themselves bear testimony to them, and every one of them starting from these Gospels endeavours to found his teaching thereupon.'

But after all, it may still be said, Is it not quite possible that the books of our New Testament may have been forged about the beginning of the second century? To this we answer, quite apart from the preceding evidence, that the thing is all but impossible. We know very well what the authors of that period could do, and there was not one of them capable in the least degree of forging books like those of the New Testament. We have but to read the New Testament carefully, and then go on to read the Christian literature of this age, in order to see and feel at once what an unspeakable chasm exists between the two. In passing from the Christian Scriptures to these productions, we are coming down from heaven to earth.[1] Something like this is felt by all thoughtful readers, and frankly acknowledged even by such hostile writers as F. W. Newman. We know of no man, at the opening of the second century, who could forge a single book of the New Testament. But the New Testament must have been written by at least seven or eight different authors. This must appear evident, even to the most uncritical reader, from the difference of style in the books. If, therefore, our sacred books were forgeries of this early

[1] Compare Rogers, *Superhuman Origin of the Bible*, p. 354; Schaff, *Ante-Nicene Christianity*, vol. ii. p. 634.

age, there must have been several forgers at the work. But if there was not one man capable of carrying out such a forgery, much more certain is it that there were not seven or eight. If it, nevertheless, be said that the names of those able forgers have been forgotten, while the names of far feebler men have been preserved, we may safely answer that this is well-nigh incredible. We can scarcely conceive that the Church should have utterly forgotten the names of its seven or eight ablest authors, and preserved the names of men who, while they were heroic Christians, were nevertheless possessed of only average abilities, and very moderate literary power. This consideration of itself makes the hypothesis of wholesale forgery all but incredible, and even impossible. How difficult it is to explain and account for things, when people will not accept the simple, reasonable truth!

To sum up: when we remember the unbroken continuity of the life and testimony of the Church, and the agreement of that testimony so early as the second half of the second century, in remote countries of Europe, Africa, and Asia; when we bear in mind that the New Testament was the very foundation and life of the Church, that precious palladium for which it lived, and for which it willingly shed its best martyr-blood; when we consider that the sacred books were constantly read in the assemblies of the faithful, so that they were familiar to the eyes and ears of all, and also that no lynx-eyed enemy has been able to point out the occasion posterior to the Apostolic Age when any one of the books was surreptitiously introduced; when we remember that, by means of the scanty fragments which survive, we can trace them back into the Apostolic Age, and that even the heretics who lived on the very border of that age, unite in bearing the most explicit testimony to their existence and authority; and when we further reflect that Church History knows of no man in the first half of the second century capable of forging a single important book of the New Testament, not to say the whole of it; we may surely see that the proof is about as strong as we can reasonably expect. No doubt we no longer possess all the details of the evidence on which the early Church accepted the sacred books; but if we do not possess these details, we have the decision of the jury; we might say, not of one jury, but of many, and some of them unfavourably prejudiced. Men skilled in legal and historical evidence do not hesitate to accept as most trustworthy testimony the old charter of an ancient family or city which has been hid out of sight in the muniment chest for a century or two; with how much more confidence may we accept the united witness of Christians and heretics in the second century to the authenticity of the New Testament, which is the charter of the Church, the true family and holy city of God, when we remember that only a few years had then passed away since this sacred charter was actually written out, and that, by the constant exhibition and reading of it on the Lord's Day, it was kept continually before the eyes and the minds of the Christian people!

V.

The Testimony of the Unquestioned Epistles of Paul.

The argument contained in the previous study may seem to many too distant, too long and difficult to master and remember, for men involved in the hurry and hard driving of a fast and feverish age. We can suppose such persons ready to ask, Is there no more brief and simple argument, which can be easily grasped and held as it were with the hand, by which we may be reasonably assured in regard to the ground of our faith? Are there not some New Testament books, for example, which are so well authenticated, and so undeniably genuine, as to command the unwavering assent of all reasonable and competent men, believers and unbelievers alike? To this question we now proceed, first of all, to reply emphatically in the affirmative, and thereafter we shall go on to deduce the legitimate and very important consequences.

We pass, in the present study, from the testimony of the ancient Church and ancient heretics to the testimony of modern unbelievers and hostile critics. It is well known to all that the New Testament, during the last hundred years, has been subjected to the fiercest criticism, of the most minute and searching description, and not unfrequently by men whose eyes were preternaturally sharpened by the extreme of bitter antagonism. With the common ruck of ignorant and ribald enemies, whose minds have been utterly blinded or maddened by hatred of Christianity, and who can in no sense be regarded as authorities by competent men on either side, we have at present no concern whatever. There are hostile critics who, for their splendid scholarship, laborious investigation, and reasonable spirit, clearly stand out as representative men, and are universally acknowledged on both sides as such. With these we shall follow the same course as in the previous argument, and cite as witnesses a few of such acknowledged representatives, selected also from representative countries.

The object immediately before us at present is, to discover what are the books which the school of extreme negative criticism leaves remaining untouched as unquestionably authentic productions of the Apostolic Age, and of the authors whose names they bear. We take no books whatever into consideration in this study, except those whieh such critics with practical unanimity admit to be undeniably authentic. These books, it is well known, are the first four Epistles of Paul—Romans, 1 Corinthians, 2 Corinthians, and Galatians—and the Revelation of John.

We fix our attention first of all, and more especially, on the four Epistles of Paul which we have just mentioned, and which the reader will do well to impress upon his mind. We have now to show that they are unhesitatingly accepted as authentic by the learned school of negative criticism with which we have at present to do. In order to do so more effectively, we proceed at once to cite as witnesses the three highest representatives of the school in Germany, France, and England respectively.

We begin with Germany, and summon Baur as the representative witness. He was for many years professor at Tübingen in Würtemberg, and hence his followers are sometimes called the Tübingen School. He died in 1861. He was perhaps the most distinguished scholar and the ablest critic that the negative school has as yet produced, and he may be regarded as its head and grand authority in the present generation. But the testimony of Baur is most abundant and explicit. He says:—'In the Homologumena [or acknowledged Epistles of Paul] there can be reckoned only the four great Epistles of the apostle, which take precedence of the rest in every respect—the Epistle to the Galatians, the two Epistles to the Corinthians, and the Epistle to the Romans. *There has never been the slightest suspicion of unauthenticity cast upon these four Epistles, and they bear so incontestably the character of Pauline originality, that there is no conceivable ground for the assertion of critical doubts in their case.*'[1] This testimony is strong and emphatic in the highest degree, and is well worthy of being read a second time. We may just mention, in passing, that Strauss, whose name is perhaps more widely known in this country than that of Baur, and who created such a sensation in 1835 by his *Life of Jesus*, frankly admits the same thing. He speaks of it as a well-known fact, in regard to these Epistles, that their 'genuineness is not contested.'[2]

We pass from Germany to France, and cite as representative witness, Renan, the author of the romantic *Life of Jesus*, which startled the Christian world about twenty-six years ago almost as much as the earlier work of Strauss had done. But in regard to his testimony to the four Epistles under consideration, the head and representative of the French School is no less emphatic and categorical than that of the German School. He speaks of these Epistles as '*indisputable and undisputed* (épîtres incontestables et incontestées);' and adds, 'We have nothing to say of these Epistles [in the way of adverse criticism]; the severest critics, such as Baur, accept

[1] *Paulus, der Apostel*, p. 276. English translation, vol. ii. pp. 110 f.
[2] *Der alte und der neue Glaube*, 8te Aufl., p. 41.

them without objection.'[1] In another place he speaks of them as 'being texts of an *absolute authenticity, of complete sincerity, and without legends*;'[2] and once more he characterizes them as being, '*by the acknowledgment of all, of indubitable authenticity.*'[3] He accepts as genuine several other Epistles of Paul, in addition to these four; but what we have to note at present is his emphatic testimony to Romans, 1 and 2 Corinthians, and Galatians, as incontestably genuine productions of the apostle.

From France we return to England. As the representative witness of the Home School of extreme unbelieving criticism, we cite the anonymous author of the work called *Supernatural Religion*. Like the representatives of Germany and France, he announces himself as 'accepting the Epistles to the Galatians, Corinthians, and Romans in the main as genuine compositions of the Apostle Paul.'[4] The expression, 'in the main,' refers probably to the last two chapters of Romans, which he agrees with Baur in rejecting. He also declares in another passage: 'As to the Apostle Paul himself, let it be said, in the strongest and most emphatic manner possible, that we do not suggest the most distant suspicion of any historical statement he makes. We implicitly accept the historical statements,

[1] *Saint Paul*, p. v. [2] *Les Apôtres*, p. xxix. [3] *Les Évangiles*, p. xi.
[4] *Supernatural Religion*, vol. iii. p. 323 (2nd edition).

as distinguished from inferences, which proceed from his pen.'[1] This testimony is scarcely less emphatic and explicit than the preceding.

We do not need to produce further witnesses, for the testimony is most positive, unhesitating, and convergent. And the sum of the matter is this. We have cited as witnesses the heads and representatives of the unbelieving schools in Germany, France, and England, and we find them uniting in the admission, that the first four Epistles of Paul are incontestably genuine and authentic. We have only to add that the critics in question agree in holding that the apostle lived at the time usually accepted by Christians. Baur holds that he died as a martyr under Nero in the year 64, and with this view the representatives of the French and English schools agree.

Here then we have a definite and unassailable foundation on which to stand, even our opponents themselves being judges. The representative critics of the hostile school agree in accepting Romans, 1 and 2 Corinthians, and Galatians, as unquestionably genuine Epistles of Paul, and have no doubt that they were written previously to A.D. 64. We now accept this result as our basis, and proceed to inquire what it distinctly implies. In the sequel, it will be our object to show that even if our New Testament were cut down to these four

[1] *Supernatural Religion*, vol. iii. p. 496.

Epistles, we should still possess a clear statement of all the fundamental historical facts and doctrines of the gospel, and these at the same time supported by the very highest evidence.

In proceeding to this department of our work, it will be our duty at the present stage to ascertain the value of the witness, who gives us his testimony in regard to Christ and Christianity in the four Epistles in question. In doing so, we have to begin by ascertaining the condition and character of Paul before his conversion; and, of course, we are restricted to the four Epistles as our sources of evidence. From these we learn that he was a Jew. He speaks of himself as a Jew by nature (Gal. ii. 15). In contrasting himself with the false teachers, he says, 'Are they Hebrews? So am I. Are they Israelites? So am I. Are they the seed of Abraham? So am I' (2 Cor. xi. 22); and in Rom. xi. 1 he further declares that he was of the tribe of Benjamin. As to his religion, he tell us that he was of the 'Jews' religion,' and was 'exceedingly zealous for the traditions of his fathers' (Gal. i. 14), which points to the fact that he was a Pharisee. He made pre-eminent advancement in his Jewish studies, was what we would call a most promising student, and had every expectation of preferment. 'I made progress,' he says, 'above many who were my equals in years in mine own nation' (Gal. i. 14). To crown all, he was a bitter persecutor of Christianity, and gloried in wasting the Church. To this fact he refers again and again. He not merely says of himself, 'I am not meet to be called an apostle, because I persecuted the Church of God' (1 Cor. xv. 9), but refers to his persecuting zeal and activity as both excessive and notorious: 'Ye have heard of my former way of life in the Jewish religion, how that beyond measure I persecuted the Church of God and wasted it' (Gal. i. 13). Here then we have a bigoted Jew, full of his own Pharisaic self-righteousness, with the highest hopes of preferment in connection with his own religion, and at the same time a well-known and furious persecutor. His position is the most directly antagonistic to Christianity which the imagination can conceive; his education and his worldly interests are all against it; he has taken up his position in the most public and decided manner possible; and consequently, if such a man should ever become a Christian, we may conclude that the reasons and causes which lead to his conversion must appear to his mind to be of the most convincing and overwhelming kind.

But the conversion of Paul to Christianity did take place, as appears from the four Epistles beyond the possibility of a doubt. Baur admits frankly that he was suddenly converted on the way to Damascus, and that 'the apostle recognised in his conversion a supernatural event, a miracle, a thing incomprehensible even to himself.'[1] Of the fact of his sudden conversion and its thorough genuineness, Baur and the other witnesses now before us do not entertain the shadow of a doubt. It is written in letters of sunlight on all the pages of the four Epistles. The burden and spirit of them all is Christ. 'God forbid that I should glory save in the cross of our Lord Jesus Christ.' 'I am crucified with Christ: nevertheless I live; yet not I, but Christ liveth in me; and the life which I now live in the flesh, I live by the faith of the Son of God, who loved me and gave Himself for me.'

But not only does the genuineness of Paul's conversion appear from the statements and general tone of his Epistles; it was also tested in the most thorough manner conceivable and possible. The witness was sifted, cross-questioned, examined, we might almost say, by torture, and yet he adhered unflinchingly to his conviction and his testimony. He was a Jew, and gave up his people for the society of the unclean and hated Nazarenes. He was a proud and self-righteous Pharisee, and gave up his old religion for the religion of the despised and crucified Jesus. He gave up friends, and property, and worldly prospects for hostility, and loss, and worldly ruin. He who before had been a mad and malignant persecutor, not only became, with all his heart and soul, a Christian, but exposed himself to all manner of per-

[1] *Paul*, vol. ii. p. 275.

secution in turn for his new religion, and bore it willingly, unflinchingly, exultingly. He submitted not only to hatred, shame, and contempt at the hands of Jews and Gentiles, but to scourging, imprisonment, and even at last to a martyr's death. Space does not permit us to refer to, far less quote, all the passages which might be adduced from the Epistles before us in illustration of his manifold trials and persecutions. One passage will be sufficient. In 2 Cor. xi. 23–27 he speaks of himself as being 'in labours more abundant, in stripes above measure, in prisons more frequent, in deaths oft;' and then he continues, 'Of the Jews five times received I forty stripes save one. Thrice was I beaten with rods, once was I stoned, thrice I suffered shipwreck, a night and a day have I been in the deep: in journeyings often, in perils of rivers, in perils of robbers, in perils from mine own countrymen, in perils from the Gentiles, in perils in the city, in perils in the wilderness, in perils in the sea, in perils among false brethren; in weariness and painfulness, in watchings often, in hunger and thirst, in fastings often, in cold and nakedness.' And if it be asked how the apostle bore these trials and persecutions, he is ready with his reply: 'I take pleasure in infirmities, in reproaches, in necessities, in persecutions, in distresses for Christ's sake' (2 Cor. xii. 10). Surely when we see such a transformation taking place, the furious and bigoted persecutor becoming himself the persecuted Christian; when we see him so tested and cross-examined by trial, and suffering, and death, we may certainly conclude that his belief in Christianity was of the deepest and intensest kind, and that he regarded it as the undeniable, irresistible truth of God.

But we go on to say that if Paul believed Christianity to be true, then it must have been substantially true, for he had every possible means of attaining to certain knowledge. Our representative critics hold that he died in the year 64, four years earlier than the date usually assigned. Accordingly he must have been contemporary with the events connected with the founding of Christianity; for in the Epistle to the Galatians, which was written in A.D. 56 or 57, we have mention made of seventeen years (three and fourteen, Gal. i. 18, ii. 1) which had elapsed since his conversion, not to speak of the unknown years between the close of these seventeen years and the date at which that Epistle was written. This plainly points to the year 35 or 36 as the time of his conversion; and when we remember that he was old enough to have become a notorious persecutor before that date, we see that he was certainly contemporary with the events recorded in the Gospels. His very position and occupation as a persecutor, closely connected with the Sanhedrim, if not actually a member of it (Acts xxvi. 10), must have given him the very best opportunity of becoming acquainted with the facts, of sifting them thoroughly, and of hearing all that could be said by the most able and learned Jews against them, or in explanation of them. He tells us also distinctly of his intercourse with Peter and John, the apostles, and with James the brother of the Lord, who were eye-witnesses of our Lord's life, and must have had the best opportunity of examining into the historic facts of that life (Gal. i. and ii., and 1 Cor. xv.). He must have come into personal contact with some of the five hundred brethren referred to in 1 Cor. xv. 6, the greater portion of whom were still alive, and to whom he confidently appeals for testimony. He actually saw the risen Lord for himself, and received his revelations directly from Him. He speaks of miracles taking place in the circle of his own experience, he is conscious of possessing the power, at least at times if not always, of working miracles, and obviously declares that he wrought such miracles himself. We adduce these facts just now only for the purpose of showing that Paul had the best conceivable means of arriving at the truth; and therefore the facts and doctrines to which he testified by his teaching and his suffering, his life and his death, must have been true.

We do not overlook the objection which may at first sight be started to the statement now made, namely, that many men have suffered and died as martyrs for beliefs which we now know to have been quite unfounded; in other words, that many men have been 'martyrs by mistake.' This is no doubt the case; but it is not the case before us, not the case of the Apostle Paul. The martyrs referred to died for mere opinions or beliefs which were founded only on inferential and indirect evidence which might be and was fallacious; but the apostle died for facts for which he had the most direct, overwhelming, and infallible evidence, and in regard to which he could not possibly be mistaken. He suffered and died, in short, not for *opinions*, but for *facts*, which he might have learned, and undoubtedly did learn, from the most direct witnesses, and to many of which he had the testimony of his own senses and his own consciousness. He could not possibly be mistaken in regard to what he saw with his own eyes, and heard with his own ears, or felt within the circle of his own natural consciousness, or actually wrought with his own hands, as in the case of his own miracles. We say he could not be mistaken in such a case, unless he was positively insane; and when we find him suffering shame, loss, scourging, imprisonment, and death itself, for the facts and doctrines to which he testified, we must surely accept his plain statements as the plain truth. Accordingly, while the ordinary martyr by his sufferings and death only proves the genuineness of his *belief*, the Apostle Paul by his sufferings and death proves not only his own invincible belief, but also the moral *certainty* of the facts for which he suffered and died. In short, he had such means of arriving at the truth that he could not possibly be deceived, and hence, when he testifies to the historic facts and doctrines of the gospel, his testimony must be allowed the greatest weight conceivable and possible.

Such, then, is the character of the witness with whose testimony we have at present to do, as it is recorded in the Epistles to the Romans, Corinthians, and Galatians. We now proceed to consider the substance of that testimony somewhat in detail. And first of all, we would draw attention to the witness which the apostle directly bears to miracles and the supernatural as palpable and undeniable realities. We do not enter into this department minutely at present, preferring to reserve it for a separate discussion. But we draw attention to the fact that in these Epistles, the apostle bears explicit testimony to the gift of tongues (1 Cor. xiv.), and to his own supernatural vision of the Lord (1 Cor. ix. 1, xv. 8). He bears testimony no less explicit, though indirect, to the resurrection of our Lord (1 Cor. xv. 4–7). He speaks of miracles as undeniably existing in the Church (1 Cor. xii. 9, 28, 30, etc.), and even when reasoning with his bitter opponents at Corinth, he appeals, in proof of his apostleship, to the miracles which he himself had actually wrought among them, and which they could not possibly deny (2 Cor. xii. 12). According to all reasonable and fair interpretation of his language, there cannot be a shadow of a doubt that Paul in the four Epistles bears the most explicit and emphatic testimony to miracles and miraculous gifts as notorious and undeniable matters of fact.

When we turn to our Lord's life, we find the fundamental historical events in it referred to most distinctly by the apostle in the Epistles before us. If any one thinks that the references of this kind are strikingly few, it is at least a sufficient answer to reply that they are more numerous in the four Epistles than in all the other books of the New Testament, the Gospels and the Acts excepted. The facts to which the apostle testifies are mainly these: Our Lord was not only a Jew (Rom. ix. 5), but of the seed of David according to the flesh (Rom. i. 3). If the statement that He was 'made of a woman' (Gal. iv. 4) does not imply the miraculous conception, it is still more certain that the other statement that He was of the seed of David does not exclude it. He lived most obviously in the first part of the first century, for He had already ascended before Paul's conversion, which took place, as we have seen, before A.D. 40; and yet not long before this, for James the Lord's brother was a contemporary of the apostle. Our Lord had certain brethen (1 Cor. ix. 5), sons of Joseph and Mary, as we understand, and one of them was called James. He gathered round Him twelve apostles (1 Cor. xv. 5), chief among whom were Cephas and John, 'who seemed to be pillars.' He lived a life which was at once sinless (2 Cor. v. 21), and yet deeply marked by poverty and suffering (2 Cor. i. 5, viii. 9). At the close of His ministry He was betrayed at night, after instituting the sacrament of the Supper (1 Cor. xi. 23 ff.), evidently at the season of the Passover (1 Cor. v. 7). He died by crucifixion (as we learn from numerous passages), and that at the hands of 'the rulers of this world' (1 Cor. ii. 8). He was buried, He rose again the third day, and appeared to Cephas and to James, twice to the twelve, and to more than five hundred brethren at once (1 Cor. xv. 3–7). The apostle refers also to the fact of our Lord's ascension: 'It is Christ that died, yea rather, that is risen again, who is even at the right hand of God, who also maketh intercession for us' (Rom. viii. 34, x. 6). Indeed, the death, resurrection, and ascension of Christ are everywhere interwoven with the texture of the Epistles. We may also safely agree with Baur with all assurance when he says, 'He who could speak so definitely and in such detail about matters of fact in the gospel history as the apostle does, could not have been unacquainted with the rest of its chief incidents.'[1]

[1] *Paul*, vol. i. p. 94.

The views of the apostle in regard to the person of Christ obviously imply both a human and a divine element. No proof is needed that the former is the case, and accordingly our attention must be directed to the latter. With our unbelieving critics, the person of our Lord is next to nothing; He is only a man, dead for eighteen centuries, and we may hold the absolute religion without any reference to the person of Jesus at all. But with the Apostle Paul the person of Jesus is everything. 'Christ Jesus was made unto us from God, wisdom, and righteousness, and sanctification, and redemption' (1 Cor. i. 30). 'Other foundation can no man lay than that which is laid, which is Jesus Christ' (1 Cor. iii. 11). He says, 'I determined not to know anything among you, save Jesus Christ, and Him crucified' (1 Cor. ii. 2), and he speaks of his gospel as the 'gospel of the glory of Christ' (2 Cor. iv. 4). He everywhere makes salvation depend on our relation to the personal Saviour: 'There is therefore now no condemnation to them who are in Christ Jesus' (Rom. viii. 1); and 'If any man be in Christ, [he is] a new creature' (2 Cor. v. 17). Such a person as this implies must be more than human, and accordingly Baur admits it to be clear that we cannot believe Paul to have regarded Christ's personality as originating only at His human birth. The apostle speaks of Christ as the Son of God, God's own Son (Rom. viii. 32), in a way which evidently implies His exalted nature. He contrasts his human nature with the 'Spirit of holiness' (Rom. i. 4), in which His Sonship had its basis. He speaks of God as sending His Son in such a way as clearly to imply His pre-existence (Gal. iv. 4), and he calls Him, as distinguished from 'the first man,' 'the second man [the Lord] from heaven' (1 Cor. xv. 47). In Rom. ix. 5, he speaks of Him as 'over all, God blessed for ever;' and again in 2 Cor. iv. 4 as the 'image of God,' in whose face the glory of God is seen (ver. 6). He is the 'Lord Jesus Christ, by whom are all things, and we by Him' (1 Cor. viii. 6). The apostle names Him in the Trinity of the apostolic benediction even before the Father (2 Cor. xiii. 14), and distinctly regards Him as an object of worship and prayer, invoking grace and peace, and other spiritual blessings from Him equally with God the Father (Gal. i. 3, etc.). He describes Christians as those 'who call upon the name of Jesus Christ our Lord' (1 Cor. i. 2); and again, he says, 'Whosoever shall call upon the name of the Lord (Heb. Jehovah) shall be saved' (Rom. x. 13, quoted from Joel ii. 32, LXX.), a verse in which he clearly refers to Christ, and practically applies to Him the name Jehovah. Christ is also reigning Mediator (1 Cor. xv. 24 ff.), and is to be the final Judge (Rom. xiv. 10; 2 Cor. v. 10). But the fact is that no reference to a few selected texts can possibly convey any idea of the importance and dignity of Christ's person in the eyes of Paul. He plainly looks upon our Lord's divinity as an axiomatic gospel truth, and we have only to read the four Epistles with the purpose of discovering his views in regard to this question, in order to have this fact borne in overwhelmingly on the mind.

When we come to the grand doctrines of Christianity, we find them all laid down in our Epistles in the clearest language. We find there the doctrine of the Fall: 'By one man sin entered into the world, and death by sin' (Rom. v. 12). We find the universal sinfulness of man clearly taught: 'for all have sinned' (Rom. iii. 23). Our Lord's death is sacrificial and substitutionary: 'Him who knew no sin, God made sin for us, that we might become the righteousness of God in Him' (2 Cor. v. 21). He died for all, so that all died in Him (2 Cor. v. 14). He is the propitiation (Rom. iii. 25), our Passover Lamb who is sacrificed for us (1 Cor. v. 7); and He 'redeemed us from the curse of the law, being made a curse for us' (Gal. iii. 13). The salvation wrought out by Christ becomes ours by faith: 'A man is not justified by the works of the law, but by the faith of Jesus Christ' (Gal. ii. 16). The doctrine of the sovereignty of God is clearly taught (Rom. ix. and xi.), and the need of the Holy Spirit to quicken the merely natural soul (1 Cor. ii. 14). The apostle inculcates the necessity of sanctification (Rom. vi.), and clearly teaches the doctrines of the resurrection, the final judgment, and everlasting life in heaven (1 Cor. xv.). It is obvious also that he regards his gospel as a finality, as the ultimate revelation, so that there is no room for change in regard to its substance: 'Even though we or an angel from heaven preach any other gospel unto you than that which we have preached unto you, let him be accursed' (Gal. i. 8).

While we find in the four Epistles a full statement of the system of Christian doctrine, we find a no less complete statement of the system of Christian ethics or morality. We do not need to enter into this at length, for it is beyond the possibility of doubt. The root of Christian morality, according to the apostle, is 'faith working by love' (Gal. v. 6). He inculcates perfect holiness of body and spirit towards God (2 Cor. vii. 1), and a complete surrender of ourselves to His service (Rom. xii. 1; 1 Cor. vi. 20). Towards our fellow-men 'love is the fulfilling of the law' (Rom. xiii. 8 ff., xiv. 10; 1 Cor. xiii.); and he teaches us to carry it out into all the relations of life, not forgetting the conscientious discharge of our duties as citizens (Rom. xiii.). In short, while the true root of Christian morality is love, the perfect pattern of it is Christ (1 Cor. xi. 1; 2 Cor. iii. 18).

We also find in these Epistles tolerably distinct teaching in regard to the Church, its sacraments, and office-bearers. The apostle recognises the existence of a

'Church of God' (Gal. i. 13), broken up into distinct churches or congregations (Gal. i. 2; 1 Cor. xvi. 19). This Church is composed of those who are believers or consecrated persons (1 Cor. i. 2, vii. 14), who are evidently admitted within its pale by baptism (Rom. vi. 3; 1 Cor. i. 13 ff.). He refers once and again to the Lord's Supper, and gives the full and well-known account of the institution which we have in 1 Cor. xi. 23–29. The Lord's Day is apparently the day of worship in the Church (1 Cor. xvi. 2), and the services consist in offerings, praise, prayer, and preaching. When we come to the office-bearers, it is true that we have no specific mention in the four Epistles of elders and deacons by name. But we find a Church constitution plainly taken for granted in our Epistles. In Rom. xii. we have distinct references of this kind. The man who is charged with the ministry is to wait on his ministry; the teacher on his teaching; and he that ruleth is to do so with diligence (vv. 7, 8). In 1 Cor. xii. 28 the apostle mentions 'teachers,' 'helps,' and 'governments,' which we may reasonably suppose to embrace the two departments of ruling and teaching that belong to the office of the presbyter, and also the diaconate. In Gal. vi. 6 he speaks of the teacher having a right to temporal support, and he inculcates submission to those who 'have set themselves to minister unto the saints' (1 Cor. xvi. 16).

It may tend in no small degree to strengthen our

argument if we consider the extent to which the Church, according to our four Epistles, had already spread. We learn explicitly from their casual statements that before the year 58, when not more than twenty-eight years had passed away since our Lord's ascension, Christianity had spread far and wide throughout the length and breadth of the Roman Empire. We read in these Epistles not only of the church at Jerusalem, but of the churches in Judæa (Gal. i. 22). We find that the Church has made itself a home in Syria, and especially at Antioch (Gal. ii.). The gospel has been preached in Cilicia (Gal. i. 21), while far north in Asia Minor, 'the churches of Galatia' are already in existence (1 Cor. xvi. 1), and the apostle addresses to them one of his four unquestioned Epistles. We also read of 'the churches of Asia,' that is, of the Roman province of that name (1 Cor. xvi. 19), and Ephesus is expressly mentioned (1 Cor. xvi. 8, 19). We read of 'the churches of Macedonia' (2 Cor. viii. 1), and the gospel has been preached even in wild and remote Illyricum (Rom. xv. 19). We read of the churches of Achaia, or Greece; and of these we have special mention made of that at Cenchreæ (Rom. xvi. 1), while to that at Corinth two of his unquestioned Epistles are addressed. By this time there is also a flourishing church in Rome, how and by whom planted we cannot tell, whose faith is famous throughout all the world, and to which he addresses his most celebrated Epistle about the year 58, and certainly not later than 59. In short, though darkness still covers the earth, yet here and there we see multitudes of little fires already kindled, whence the sacred flame is sure to spread on every side until it meets, and all the Roman Empire is enveloped in the blaze. All this shows most distinctly that the Church reaches back to the very time of Christ, and that therefore multitudes of His contemporaries, who had every means of testing the truth of the gospel facts, cordially accepted the faith, the self-same faith as we now possess. In other words, we have in these Epistles not merely the testimony of the apostle, but testimony accepted by a wide-spread Church whose members were really contemporary with most of the events.

What, then, is the conclusion which we are warranted to draw from the above, and that with the highest historical assurance? We see that the most hostile criticism, as represented by the acknowledged masters of the school in Germany, France, and England, unites in unhesitatingly accepting the first four Epistles of Paul as indisputably genuine and authentic. We have seen that the apostle is a witness who had the best possible opportunity of arriving at a full and direct knowledge of the facts, a witness who not only was a man of the very noblest and loftiest moral character, but who gave his testimony at the constant peril of his life, and finally confirmed it by dying as a martyr for the truth. We have further seen that his testimony is most explicit in regard to the fundamental facts of our Lord's life, in regard to all the important doctrines of Christianity and the duties of Christian life, and in regard to the existence of the Church and the sacraments. Surely this result is most satisfactory. Surely we may feel confident in our conviction that in these four Epistles of Paul we have our feet upon the rock, and are at the very fountainhead of the stream of Christian truth. Surely we may reasonably rest content as having attained the highest historical and personal evidence which we can possibly expect in regard to facts or truths transmitted from the distant past: for the evidence is practically the same as if the apostle were really standing before us, as if we saw him distinctly with our eyes, as if we had put him under oath, and heard him answer our questions with our own ears.

But, it may be remembered, it was stated at the outset that there is another book of the New Testament which the representatives of extreme negative criticism are agreed in accepting as genuine. This book is the Revelation of John. It will not be at all necessary to enter into the discussion in regard to it with anything like the same detail. Let it suffice to say that Baur declares that 'the *undoubted* result of convergent lines of proof' is that it is the work of the Apostle John, written about the year 68,[1] and with this conclusion Renan and the author of *Supernatural Religion* substantially agree. But when we look somewhat carefully into Revelation, we soon find that even this peculiar book, whose object is not primarily to teach Christian doctrine, contains explicitly or implicitly the great facts and truths of our most holy faith. It teaches that our Lord is possessed of a human nature, is sprung from David (xxii. 16), was crucified (xi. 8), and rose again (i. 18, ii. 8). But He is obviously more than man. He is 'the Word of God' (xix. 13), 'the beginning of the creation of God' (iii. 14), 'the Alpha and the Omega, the beginning and the end, the first and the last' (xxii. 13), and the object of the highest adoration (i. 5, 6, v. 11, 12). The doctrine of the atonement is distinctly taught. Christ is the 'Lamb that was slain' (v. 12, etc.), who 'redeemed us by His blood' (v. 9), who 'loved us and washed us from our sins in His own blood' (i. 5). The followers of the Lamb are 'called, and chosen, and faithful' (xiv. 12, xvii. 14). The present system of things is to be wound up with a resurrection and a general judgment in which Christ will be Judge, and which is to be followed in the case of the saints by a blessed immor-

[1] *Kritische Untersuchungen*, pp. 365 ff., 376; *Kirchengeschichte d. drei ersten Jahrhunderte*, p. 147.

tality (xx., xxi., xxii.). We have even the trace of Church government not merely in the four and twenty elders, but in the angels of the churches. Here, then, we have the testimony of Paul in his four unquestionably genuine Epistles corroborated by the testimony of John in his unquestionably genuine Apocalypse, and it must be borne in mind that the latter was not only the contemporary, but the immediate disciple and companion of our Lord. Surely we may reasonably assume that his evidence contributes in no small degree to strengthen the evidence of Paul, which we have already seen to be so overwhelmingly strong.

Before closing, it may be of importance to mention that in this study we have taken as our sources only the minimum of New Testament books, only the books which have been, we may say, unanimously accepted by the extreme representatives of the hostile school of criticism. It would be a great mistake, however, to suppose that these are all the books accepted by the general body of hostile critics. The truth is, as we shall see more fully in the next study, the present representatives of the negative school are gradually coming back to the recognition of more books as genuine productions of the Apostolic Age, and in regard to the so-called spurious books they agree in dating them much nearer that age than was done by Baur.[1] Hilgenfeld, the present head of Baur's immediate school, accepts not only the last two chapters of Romans, the three closing verses excepted, as the genuine production of Paul, but also 1 Thessalonians, Philippians, and Philemon. He regards the Epistle to the Hebrews as not the work of Paul, but certainly written in the Apostolic Age, and probably before A.D. 66. He accepts the present Matthew as written soon after the destruction of Jerusalem in A.D. 70, and as founded on a still older Gospel, while he assigns Mark and the Epistle of James to the reign of Domitian, A.D. 81 to 96. He also regards the portions of Acts narrated in the first person ('we') as genuine, and probably the work of Luke. In like manner, Renan accepts as genuine Pauline Epistles 1 and 2 Thessalonians, Philippians, Colossians, and Philemon in addition to the four unquestioned Epistles, not to speak of the fact that he assigns to Ephesians, Hebrews,[2] Mark and Matthew, Luke and Acts, James and 1 Peter,[3] a date far within the limits of the first century and before the death of the Apostle John.

We have a practical remark of the very highest importance to make in conclusion. The object of the

[1] 'The number of those who represent Baur's standpoint whole and entire is, at least among German theologians, very small. In Tübingen there is now no longer a Tübingen School.'—Christlieb, *Modern Doubt and Christian Belief*, p. 547 (Clark).

[2] *St. Paul*, p. lx.

[3] *St. Paul*, p. xxxiii.

preceding discussion is not merely to satisfy the logical understanding, but to lead up to intelligent faith in Christ: and unless this be achieved, very little is gained. It is quite true that such faith implies a moral element or state of soul, as well as an intellectual one, but the intellectual element is an important, even a necessary preparatory factor. Our present object is to contribute in some small degree to this intellectual preparation and element. And what we would now emphatically say is this, that in these five New Testament books, the minimum left us by the extreme representatives of hostile criticism, we have far more than enough to warrant saving faith in Jesus, to form the firm foundation of such faith, and to nurture it into the highest degree of intelligence, power, and fulness. The man who has a reasonable assurance of the genuineness and truthfulness of the books specified has no sufficient ground for remaining a moment longer apart from Christ, and does so at his peril. His bounden duty as a guilty sinner is, without a moment's delay, to cast himself at the feet of Jesus as an expression of his penitence, faith, and self-surrender. And the very instant he does so as a real act of his soul, these books assure him that he is pardoned, accepted, made a son of God, and if a son then an heir; 'an heir of God and a joint-heir with Christ.' And as he comes to know the reality of Jesus and His truth in the experience of daily life, he will soon be able to say with the Samaritans of old, 'Now we believe, not because of thy saying: for we have heard Him for ourselves, and know that this is indeed the Christ, the Saviour of the world.'

VI.

Some Recent Reverses of Negative Criticism.

It is generally and confidently acknowledged by the highest authorities of the modern schools of negative criticism that there are certain books in the New Testament which are unquestionably genuine. As we have seen in the previous study, such men as Baur and Strauss, Renan and the author of *Supernatural Religion*, agree in accepting Romans, 1 and 2 Corinthians, Galatians, and the Revelation of John as books incontestably genuine and authentic. That is, these representative leaders of modern learned unbelief agree with catholic Christians in holding fast by the unquestionable genuineness of about *one-fourth of the New Testament*, and that a fourth containing over and over again all the essential facts and doctrines of the gospel. In regard to the remaining books of the New Testament, the position originally taken up by Baur and his more immediate followers was, that *they were composed far on in the second century, and mainly between A.D.* 130 *and* 170. It is the object of this study to show that the followers of Baur, and negative critics in general, have been compelled to retreat step by step from such an extreme position.

One of the most convincing proofs of the correctness of a theory or principle is the fact that it is found exactly to fit into and harmonize with every new discovery, and to apply in every new region brought to light. For example, it is an overwhelming proof of the truth of the Newtonian law of gravitation that it has been found to hold good in the case of every new planet, satellite, and comet that has been discovered, and even in the case of distant stars whose movements have been reduced to observation. Now, the same test can be applied in some measure to the catholic or common Church view with regard to the age of the New Testament books. It is an interesting and well-known fact, that of late years not a few manuscripts of ancient Christian books have been unexpectedly discovered; and the question becomes an interesting and practical one, Whether does the catholic or the antagonistic view harmonize better with these discoveries? Do the recently discovered books fit in better with the view that the New Testament belongs to the Apostolic Age, or with the view that it belongs mainly to the second century? We venture to affirm that there can be no reasonable doubt as to the answer. The discoveries referred to not only harmonize with the catholic view, but administer to the opposite view decided reverses, which at several points have even compelled its leaders to give up their position and beat a retreat. It is our object in this study to show that this is the case by adducing a few instances in detail. It may be true that the line of proof is not one which can be called direct, but we believe it to be an interesting side argument, which may, perhaps all the more on that account, tend to confirm our faith in the catholic view.

We begin with the so-called *Epistle of Barnabas*, which was written about A.D. 120.[1] Until 1859 this book was known only in an imperfect form, the first four and a half chapters being extant in Latin but not in the original Greek. At the close of the fourth chapter it contains these words, 'As it is written, Many are called, few chosen.' The expression here quoted is found nowhere in ancient sacred literature except Matt. xxii. 14.[2] Hence the conclusion was naturally drawn that this was a quotation from Matthew, and that the quotation was made as if it was acknowledged Scripture. The unbelieving school, however, in effect, replied, 'No. This is only the Latin translation. The quotation was very likely inserted by the translator, who was some biassed Christian. If we only had the original

[1] Hilgenfeld, the present head of the so-called Tübingen school, holds that it was written in A.D. 97.—*Einleitung*, p. 38.

[2] It is also found, of course, in the T.R. in Matt. xx. 16; but there it is probably not genuine.

Greek, we should find that it is not there.' But two original Greek copies have now been discovered, one by Tischendorf at Mount Sinai in 1859, and another more lately at Constantinople by Bryennios, now Metropolitan of Nicomedia. And what is the result? The old Latin version is absolutely correct; for the quotation is found in the original Greek almost exactly as in Matthew. The conclusion from this is obvious; the Gospel of Matthew was already written and apparently acknowledged as Scripture. It is noteworthy that the author of *Supernatural Religion* still endeavours to wriggle out of the iron grasp of the necessary inference. In a way which must fill many readers with amazement, if not with something worse, he still struggles to show that it is not a quotation from Matthew at all, but from 2 (4) Esdras viii. 3: 'There be many created, but few shall be saved.' Surely comment is unnecessary. The discovery of the Greek copies of Barnabas settles the question on the side of the catholic view, as even Hilgenfeld, the present head of Baur's school, most cordially admits.

In the year 1842 there was discovered at Mount Athos a copy of a long-lost book called *The Refutation of all Heresies*, the work of Hippolytus, an author who lived at the close of the second century and the beginning of the third. This discovery has proved one of the first importance for various reasons, and very especially for the references or quotations therein given from the works or teaching of the ancient heretics. It is well known that Baur regarded the Gospel of John as written about A.D. 160–170. But what do we learn from Hippolytus? He deals at length with the heresy of Basilides, who flourished about A.D. 125, and he tells us that this heresiarch fell back on the Gospels, specially including John, for support to his views. He thus writes: 'And this, he [Basilides] says, is that which has been stated in the Gospels: "He was the true light, which lighteth every man that cometh into the world."'[1] This quotation is unquestionably from John i. 9, and it is scarcely less unquestionable that, according to the laws of Greek grammar, Hippolytus puts the quotation into the mouth of Basilides, and even seems to quote from a book of his which he has in his eye. In other words, John was not written after A.D. 160, as Baur holds, but before the time of Basilides, that is, before A.D. 125. It may be noticed also that Basilides refers in the above quotation to 'the Gospels,' and uses them as being of acknowledged authority.

The so-called *Clementine Homilies* played a most important part in the hands of Baur and his immediate followers in the contest as to the dates of the New Testament books. Down to 1853 these Homilies

[1] *Refutation of all Heresies*, Book vii. 22. For English see Clark's Translation, vol. i. p. 276; and for Greek, Charteris, *Canonicity*, p. 173.

existed only in an imperfect copy which stopped short in the middle of Homily xix. ch. 14; eleven chapters and a half of Homily xix. and the whole of Homily xx. being lost. The date of their composition is assigned to the middle of the second century, or a little later, say about A.D. 160.

We restrict our attention at present solely to the bearing of the Homilies on the Gospel of John. Baur contended that they contained no proof of the existence of the fourth Gospel at the date of their composition. It is true that even in the imperfect edition we have quotations or reminiscences from John, which seem unmistakable to the ordinary reader, and which, if they occurred in any modern author, would be unhesitatingly referred to the fourth Gospel. We read in Homily iii. ch. 52 these words: 'Wherefore He [Christ], being the true prophet, said, I am the gate of life; he who entereth through Me entereth into life,' a passage which can scarcely fail to recall John x. 9, 'I am the door; by Me if any man enter in, he shall be saved.' In the same chapter of Homily iii. we further read: 'Wherefore also He cried and said, . . . My sheep hear My voice,'—an expression which seems obviously quoted from John x. 27, 'My sheep hear My voice.' What makes it still more likely that these quotations are taken from John is the fact that they are both found in the same chapter of the Homilies, and correspond to passages in the same chapter of the fourth Gospel, a circumstance most naturally accounted for by the theory of actual quotation. Once more, the old and imperfect edition of the Homilies contains in Homily xi. ch. 26, the statement, 'For thus the prophet has sworn to us, saying, Verily I say to you, unless ye be regenerated by living water into the name of the Father, Son, and Holy Spirit, you shall not enter into the kingdom of heaven,'—a passage which naturally appears to contain a free but undoubted reference to John iii. 5, 'Except a man be born of water and of the Spirit, he cannot enter into the kingdom of God.' Such were the references to John in the older edition of the Homilies, and yet Baur and his followers, like the author of *Supernatural Religion*, could hold that they contained no proof of the existence of that Gospel, and therefore it did not exist, or had just come into existence, at the time when the Homilies were written. Consequently John could not have been written before A.D. 160, the approximate date of the Homilies.

But we now have the Clementine Homilies entire in Greek. In the year 1853, a German scholar of the name of Dressel published a complete edition from a manuscript which he had found in the Ottobonian library in the Vatican. Now it so happens that the new and concluding fragment contains testimony of the utmost importance. For one thing, it settles that the author of the Homilies knew and used Mark, which had been doubtful up to that date. But it also settles to all reasonable minds the fact of the previous existence and the use of John. In the portion discovered by Dressel we have the following passage in Homily xix. ch. 22, 'Whence our Teacher, when we inquired of Him in regard to the man who was blind from his birth, and recovered his sight, if this man sinned, or his parents, that he should be born blind, answered, Neither did he sin at all, nor his parents, but that the power of God might be made manifest through him in healing sins of ignorance.'[1] This passage is obviously a free but real quotation from John ix. 1–3: 'And as Jesus passed by, He saw a man which was blind from his birth. And His disciples asked Him, saying, Master, who did sin, this man, or his parents, that he was born blind? Jesus answered, Neither hath this man sinned, nor his parents; but that the works of God should be made manifest in him.' So obvious is the quotation, that the controversy may now be regarded as settled in the estimation of reasonable men. Hilgenfeld, the present head of the dying Tübingen school, at once acknowledged the question as finally closed.[2] 'Volkmar admitted and admits that the fact of the use of the Gospel must be

[1] For the Greek of the quotations from the Homilies, see Charteris, *Canonicity*, pp. 184 f.; or Sanday, *The Gospels in the Second Century*, pp. 287 ff. The English given above is from Clark's Translation.

[2] *Einleitung*, pp. 43 f., note.

considered as proved. The author of *Supernatural Religion* stands alone in still resisting this conviction, but the result, I suspect, will be only to show in stronger relief the one-sidedness of his critical method.'[1]

We now come to another interesting and most important point. It is well known that Tatian, the Assyrian, who flourished about A.D. 150–170, and of whom we possess one work, his Address to the Greeks, was the author of another work called the *Diatessaron.* The testimony of antiquity is so uniform and distinct, that thus far there never could be any reasonable doubt. This Diatessaron, as the name naturally implies, is declared by ancient writers to have been a Harmony of the four Gospels. The importance attached to this fact by catholic scholars and critics on the one hand, and by Baur and his school on the other, was naturally very great. If, as catholic critics generally held, it was a veritable Harmony, it was a clear proof that at the time when it was constructed, and of course long previously, four Gospels were regarded as occupying a position quite distinct, approaching to what we call canonical. Further, critics of this class naturally considered that these Gospels must have been the present four. But if so, then John must have been received in the time of Tatian as genuine, so that it could not possibly have seen the light only so late as A.D. 160, or even later,

[1] Sanday, *The Gospels in the Second Century*, p. 288.

as Baur's School maintained. It was therefore of the utmost importance for this school to undermine the argument of the catholic critics, by showing that the Diatessaron was no Harmony whatever of the four canonical Gospels. The English reader may see how this is attempted by the author of *Supernatural Religion* in his second volume (pp. 152 ff.). He makes statements like the following: 'There is no authority for saying that Tatian's Gospel was a Harmony of four Gospels at all.' 'No one seems to have seen Tatian's Harmony, for the very good reason that there was no such work.' And again, 'It is obvious that there is no evidence whatever connecting Tatian's Gospel with those in our canon.'[1]

The question, however, seems of late to have been finally settled to the utter discomfiture of the school of Baur, and the complete demonstration of the perfect correctness of the traditional view. According to the testimony of antiquity, Ephraem, the Syrian, wrote a commentary on Tatian's Diatessaron. This commentary was regarded as hopelessly lost until lately, when an Armenian translation of it was found in the library of the Mechitarist monks, in the island of S. Lazzaro at Venice. This translation was published in Latin in 1876 by Professor Mösinger of Salzburg. Now, Professor Zahn of Erlangen has recently subjected this

[1] Vol. ii. pp. 158, 160, 161.

ancient commentary to a most thoroughgoing criticism and treatment, and the conclusion to which he comes is most interesting and astonishing. It turns out actually to be Ephraem's Commentary on Tatian's Diatessaron. And even since the above discovery an Arabic translation of the Diatessaron has been found, and was published at Rome last year.[1] We therefore now know exactly what was the nature of Tatian's famous work. And what is the result? It is found to be a consecutive Gospel narrative constructed out of a blending of our four canonical Gospels on a somewhat free principle. And Tatian uses John the most extensively of all the Gospels, adopting the chronology of that Gospel as the framework of his Harmony. 'It may be observed that a difference is so far made between the evangelists that the text of St. John is almost completely adopted, perhaps with the sole exception of chapter iv. 46–54; next in completeness comes that of St. Matthew, while St. Luke and St. Mark are much more incompletely represented.'[2] The meaning of all this is obvious. The Tübingen School, in their blind and desperate attempt to maintain the late origin of all the Gospels, and especially of John, have suffered themselves again to be misled. In the words of Professor Wace: 'There is no

[1] Lightfoot, *Essays on 'Supernatural Religion,'* p. 288.

[2] Article by Professor Wace, *Expositor*, Oct. 1882, p. 301. Cf. Charteris, *Croall Lectures* for 1882, pp. 177 ff. Zahn's *Geschichte des Neutestamentlichen Kanons*, pp. 389 ff.

longer any doubt that all the four Gospels existed in full, and substantially as we now have them, in the time of Tatian, and therefore of Justin Martyr;' for, as the author of *Supernatural Religion* expressly acknowledges, 'Tatian simply made use of the same Gospel as his master, Justin Martyr.'[1]

One other point remains on which we wish to say a few words. It is the issue of the controversy in regard to *Marcion's Gospel.* This heretic was a native of Pontus, but lived and flourished at Rome in the time of Justin Martyr, that is, about A.D. 140. He used a Gospel which, according to the consent of antiquity, and especially of Irenæus, Tertullian, and Epiphanius, was a mutilated Luke. There was no substantial reason for doubting this statement. But if it was true, then it was plain that Luke must have been written a considerable time before A.D. 140. This could not be admitted by Baur and his immediate followers, whose hypothesis required them to hold the late origin of that Gospel. What was then to be done? Of course, Marcion's Gospel must be held and proved to be the earlier and the original Gospel, of which that of Luke was only a later enlargement.

In Germany, the rectification of this grievous error came in its final stage, to its honour be it said, from within Baur's own school. Volkmar and Hilgenfeld,

[1] Vol. ii. p. 159.

two distinguished members of the school, were not only led by their own study to renounce the view of Baur and return to the traditional view, but by their thorough investigation as nearly proved as such a thing could be proved, that the ancient view was right, and that Luke was the original, from which Marcion had derived his Gospel by mutilation. So effectual was the demonstration, that even Baur withdrew from his original position. The question may now be regarded as finally settled in Germany in favour of the priority and originality of the Gospel of Luke.[1] The statement of the Fathers is proved to be substantially correct, and Marcion's Gospel turns out to be a mutilation of Luke.

But the matter was not so speedily brought to a conclusion in England. The author of *Supernatural Religion,* as might have been anticipated, still held out. He could even write: 'The statement of the Fathers that Marcion's Gospel was no original work, but a mutilated version of Luke, is *unsupported by a single historical or critical argument;*' and again, 'If we except the Gospel according to the Hebrews, Marcion's Gospel is the oldest evangelical work of which we hear anything, and it *ranks far above the third Synoptic in that respect.*'[2]

[1] 'It is enough to remark that the existence of Luke before Marcion was proved by Volkmar, Köstlin, Hilgenfeld, Ritschl, and Zeller.' Holtzmann, *Die syn. Evangelien,* p. 403.

[2] *Supernatural Religion,* vol. ii. pp. 138 f. (4th edition). The italics are ours.

But Dr. Sanday in his well-known volume, *The Gospels in the Second Century*, entered once more into an elaborate investigation of the question, and succeeded in practically demonstrating the priority and originality of Luke. So convincing is his argument, that he has had the unlooked-for satisfaction of seeing even the author of *Supernatural Religion*, after the example of abler and wiser men, withdrawing from his wild position, and finally admitting that Luke and not Marcion's mutilation is the true original. He now acknowledges that Dr. Sanday's 'able examination of Marcion's Gospel has convinced us that *our earlier hypothesis is untenable*, . . . and, consequently, that our third Synoptic existed in his time, and was substantially in the hands of Marcion.' He says that Dr. Sanday's argument must 'prove irresistible to all' critics, and that 'it is not possible reasonably to maintain' his previous view.[1] After such an admission coming from such a quarter, we may safely say, with Professor Salmon of Dublin, 'The theory that Marcion's form [of the Gospel] is the original, may be said to be now completely exploded.'

In the preceding pages we have dwelt on individual points by way of illustration; it now remains for us to give an indication of the general current of the tide of opinion in the critical world. Even in the negative

[1] *Supernatural Religion*, complete edition (1879), vol. ii. pp. 138 f.

critical world, in the very school of Baur himself, the current of opinion in regard to the dates of the leading books of the New Testament, has begun distinctly to flow back. A brief general statement will be sufficient to make this luminous. Baur regarded Matthew as written after A.D. 130; Hilgenfeld, the present head of Baur's School, holds it to have been written 'immediately' after the destruction of Jerusalem, say about A.D. 70; while Renan regards it as written about A.D. 84. Baur originally regarded Luke and Mark as written about A.D. 150 or later; but both Hilgenfeld and Renan agree in placing their date more or less decidedly within the first century, and therefore within the Apostolic Age. The case with John is very instructive. Baur regarded it as written about A.D. 160 or even 170; Hilgenfeld assigns it to A.D. 130–140; while Renan, after a good deal of vacillation, holds at present to about A.D. 125. Baur held Acts to be written about the middle of the second century; Hilgenfeld regards it as written after the close of the first century, but maintains that the portions narrated in the first person were the genuine work of Luke; while Renan assigns it to the first century. Baur regarded Romans, 1 and 2 Corinthians, and Galatians, as the only genuine Pauline Epistles; but in addition to these, Hilgenfeld accepts also 1 Thessalonians, Philippians, and Philemon; while Renan, also in addition, accepts 1 and 2 Thessalonians, Philippians,

Colossians, and Philemon, and although he regards Ephesians as doubtful, yet he says that 'in any case it belongs to the Apostolic Age.' Baur relegated all the remaining books of the New Testament, except, of course, the Revelation of John, to the second century; besides those specified above, Hilgenfeld assigns to the first century Hebrews (c. A.D. 66) and James (A.D. 81–96); while Renan assigns to the same century, Ephesians, Hebrews, James, and 1 Peter. In like manner Holtzmann, in addition to the first four Epistles of Paul, accepts 1 Thessalonians, Philippians, and Colossians and Philemon in the main, as the production of that apostle; while he not only accepts Revelation as the work of John, but assigns Matthew, Mark, and even Luke and Hebrews to the first century.

It may be interesting to concentrate our attention for a moment on the four Gospels, in order to discover the amount of retreat which has taken place more especially with regard to them. For the sake of clearness, and with the view of bringing the state of matters under the eye at a single glance, we have summed up the general results in the following table, which will speak for itself. The separate columns are headed with the names of well-known representative critics; and under the names are found the dates to which these critics respectively assign the composition of the different Gospels. The name of Weiss is added for the sake of comparison, as a liberal representative of the catholic or common Church view.

	Baur.	Volkmar.	Schenkel.	Hilgenfeld.	Renan.	Keim.	Holtzmann.	Weiss.
Matthew,	130+	c. 110	70	70+	84	66	68	70+
Mark, .	150+	73	58	81+	76	100	75	69
Luke, .	c. 150	100-3	80	c. 100	94	90	80	80
John, .	160+	c. 150	120	130+	125	130	c. 125	c. 95
	605	434	328	396	379	386	348	319

The above table may be accepted as approximately correct. We have summed up the different columns, making allowance for the indefinite dates marked +, in order that the general results may strike the eye all the more forcibly. These results are very significant. The sum-total under Baur is 605, and by comparing with this the numbers under the other names respectively, the reader will notice at once the aggregate retreat in years in each case. It will be seen that the retreat is very substantial, being considerably more than 200 years on the whole, and the movement is still going on in the the same direction. In view of all this, Holtzmann makes the frank confession: 'We find in the Tübingen School a universal movement backwards, until at last Hilgenfeld makes the Gospel literature end at the date at which Baur had only made it begin.'[1] It should also be remembered that most of the authors adduced in the table hold that written documents or Gospels existed at a decidedly earlier date than the canonical Gospels, and furnished the main substance of the latter; so that, with regard to their original material, we are carried back to a time quite within the period generally assigned by the Church for the composition of the Gospels.

If we now try to sum up the above in a general way, we have the following striking result. *According to Baur and his immediate followers, we have less than one-fourth of the New Testament belonging to the first century. According to Hilgenfeld, the present head of Baur's School, we have somewhat less than three-fourths belonging to the first century, while substantially the same thing may be said in regard to Holtzmann. According to Renan, we have distinctly more than three-fourths of the New Testament falling within the first century, and therefore within the Apostolic Age.* This surely indicates a very decided and extraordinary retreat since the time of Baur's grand assault, that is, within the last fifty years.

Such are a few of the reverses sustained of late years by the critics of the extreme negative school, and such is their substantial retreat. The general result of the whole is most significant, and confirmatory of the

[1] *Die synoptischen Evangelien*, p. 403.

catholic belief in regard to the age of the leading books of the New Testament. And let it be noted that the strength of the argument is to be seen not so much in the points separately as in the general drift of the whole. Every new discovery has not only fallen in harmoniously with the view commonly held in the Church, but has distinctly tended to confirm it, while in some cases it has been dead against the extreme school of unbelief. Moreover, the distinct and general tendency of the leading authorities on the side of negative criticism, has been to move the date of the chief New Testament books back nearer and nearer to the Apostolic Age, until at last, as we have seen, instead of only *one-fourth*, they agree that about *three-fourths* of the New Testament were actually written before the death of the Apostle John.

When the age of historical criticism came, it was impossible that the books of the New Testament could escape the fire. They had of necessity to pass through the ordeal just like other ancient books, and it will be found in the long run that it was well for the Church that it was so. We have reason to believe that the battle of dates is drawing near its close, with the victory obviously inclining to the side of the catholic view, namely, that the Christian Scriptures belong to the Apostolic Age. When the battle has once been fought out, and our sacred books have been proved and acknowledged even by negative critics themselves to fall within the first century, we may reasonably hope that a day will dawn of firmer faith than ever in these books. After they have stood the fire of such criticism as no ancient books have ever undergone, and the unwilling testimony of enemies is found substantially to coincide with the testimony of friends, surely all future ages may regard them as practically unassailable. The battle had to be fought out; but the victory is now in view, and fought out once, it is fought out for ever.

VII.

The Christian Miracles.

It is our object in the present study to discuss the subject of miracles, which may be emphatically said to be one of the 'burning questions' of the age. In approaching it, it is not at all necessary for our purpose that we enter into any abstruse analysis or elaborate definition of what a miracle really is. Our object is mainly practical, and all that is required is a definition which is essentially correct and sufficient for working purposes.

We find around us everywhere in the world a realm and order of physical nature, in whose network we live. This system is made up of matter, physical force, and the so-called laws of nature. Viewed from the merely scientific side, these laws work by physical necessity, moving on in straight lines, so that their action can be expressed by mathematical formulæ or equations. But when a being possessed of intelligence and free-will interferes with the necessary course of nature, works on or in nature, so as by means of his intelligent volitions or will to make an entirely new beginning, and produce an entirely new result or event which never could have been produced by mere physical forces themselves, working according to their own laws, then we have the essential element of a miracle. It matters not whether the action be that of a man, an angel, or God: in the direct interference of an intelligent will in the iron course of nature, so as to produce a new and designed result totally above the power of mere physical forces, we have the very soul of the miraculous and supernatural. In ordinary language, however, the term miracle is generally restricted to visible results produced in nature by superhuman agents; and more particularly still, to visible results produced in nature for a definite purpose by the special and direct volition of God. As examples of what we mean may be instanced any of the miracles of Christ, such as stilling the storm, changing water into wine, healing the sick, raising the dead, and all by a direct volition brought to bear in and upon nature. It is with the word in this last sense that we have more immediately to do.

It must be obvious that miracles, as now described, cannot be ordinary events. If they were so, they would not indeed cease to be essentially miracles, but they would lose much of their evidential power, and would largely interfere with human action and moral training. In such a case, God by His constant miracles would not only cast a slight upon His laws of nature which He has established for man's guidance, but would make a scientific knowledge of those laws, and calm confidence in them, next to an impossibility. The true view is, that for ordinary life and history we have to look to the ordinary laws as the visible or perceptible factors, while the miracles with which we have now to do are only introduced in connection with the birth of Christianity to authenticate the divine Commissioner, and show that the new religion is one of supernatural origin and contents, power and purpose. Just as man sprang into being at first in a special way, which, whether the way of direct creation or modified evolution, has never been seen in a single case in all the countless millions that have lived since history began, so also was it with the origin of Christianity. Just as a singular manifestation of divine volition and power was put forth at the origin of the new race, so, in like manner, a singular manifestation of divine power and volition in the form of miracles accompanied the introduction of the new religion into the world. But as the new race after its origin was left, as a rule, externally to the ordinary laws of nature and history which were pre-ordained with a view to its life, so was it to a large extent with the new religion. Continuous visible miracles were no more required in this case than in the other, and the new religion was left to make itself at home in the current of physical forces with their laws which had been pre-ordained of God with this purpose distinctly in view. When a person empties a vessel full of highly coloured dye into the mountain stream, it produces in the act of falling into it no small disturbance and commotion, and sends out wavelets on every side; but soon it mingles with the water, and afterwards flows on quietly with its current, only giving to it its own peculiar tinge. So has it been in a manner with the entrance of Christianity into the stream of the world's history; the miraculous manifestations accompanying its introduction in due time giving way to the course of more ordinary law.

It is not a right mode of expression to speak, as Hume and many others do, of the New Testament miracles as a 'violation of the laws of nature,' or as a means of introducing disorder into the course of the world. The very opposite of this is the case. God is the God of order, and His miracles take place only in the interests of the highest order. If there had been nothing in the world but constant and unchangeable physical laws, there would of course have been nothing in the world but mechanical order, and therefore no occasion for miracles. But then the world would have been a very poor world, however large. It was the entrance upon the scene of a moral being like man, a being possessed of free-will, and therefore with the power to sin, that changed the whole. As a most certain fact, man fell into sin and sinful courses, and it is this dark fact of sin which is the great disturber of order, the grand cause of disorder in the world. And just in this deep and ruinous disorder which has been caused by sin, do we find the true root and ground of miraculous intervention. It was designed to put an end to the dire disorder and misery, and restore the divine order; and in doing so, the supernatural religion no more violates the order of nature than the physician, who, by skilful medicine and treatment, arrests the progress of the disease, or removes it altogether, and restores the suffering patient to perfect health. It was sin that introduced the real violation of the laws of nature, and it is against it alone that the charge of disorder is to be brought. Christianity, the supernatural religion, was introduced and exists in the interests of divine order.

The truth just now touched on, namely, that miracles are in accordance with the principle of the highest order, will appear the more clearly the more carefully we consider it. There is obviously an ascending gradation in nature, of which we may name as outstanding steps, matter, chemical force, vegetable life, animal life, spiritual life. The Theist naturally believes that in this scale the lower exists for the higher; matter for chemical force; chemical force for vegetable life; vegetable life for animal life; and all for spiritual life, which is the apex of the pyramid. Surely, then, if the spiritual or highest element should by any means become the prey of disorder and disease, it cannot be but that the lower stages must admit of being used in such a way as to conduce to the restoration of order and health therein. To say that their common order or laws of working must never be interfered with, even though the supreme object for which they exist should collapse in disorder and disease, surely seems contrary to reason. Rather it would seem most reasonable that these lower stages should, from the very nature of the case, admit of being so used as to contribute to the healthful order of the highest. In a great house, all the furniture, the servants, and the different arrangements exist and work for the welfare of its inhabitant and lord; and surely we may reasonably expect, that when he falls into disease or trouble, all the arrangements must admit of being changed as far as may be obviously necessary to secure his recovery. To say that such a change is impossible would be simply preposterous. It would be to esteem the means more important than the end, the house than its inhabitant, the lower order than the higher. The Theist regards the world and its laws as made for man, and not man for the world and its laws. Accordingly, if man should fall into spiritual disease and disorder, then the world and its laws may be used by God, even in the way of miracles if necessary, to contribute to the restoration of his spiritual health and order. It is the soul of the very highest order that the lower laws and powers should be used in the interest of order in the supreme or spiritual sphere. A so-called miracle, therefore, even though it may appear to cause a momentary disorder of a lower kind, may be in strict accordance with the highest order. On the other hand, the absence of miracles may, in certain cases, be a breach or failure in the principle of the highest or spiritual order.

There are some who look on the miraculous element in the New Testament as of little importance. They think they can reject it entirely, and yet hold fast by Christianity. We do not need to enter into any lengthened discussion, in order to show that this is impossible. The miraculous element is the very backbone of the Christian system, and all, or almost all, that distinguishes it from other systems is to be found in this very element. Christ is Christianity, and His incarnation, person, life, resurrection, and ascension are all things which are intensely supernatural or miraculous.[1] Accordingly, the man who leaves all the

[1] Is it necessary to say anything as to the distinction between the *supernatural* and the *miraculous?* By the *supernatural* we mean that world of mind, and especially the Divine Mind, which exists above mere nature. Every *direct* or *immediate* manifestation or act of a supernatural being is essentially a miracle, and every *direct* or *immediate* act or manifestation of God is a miracle in the narrower sense with which at present we have

supernatural out of Christianity must leave out Christ. In any case he can believe in Christ only as a mere man, who lived and died like other men, whose body saw corruption, and whose dust has long since been scattered to all the winds that blow. Not only are all the supernatural facts gone, but also all the supernatural doctrines which were accredited by the facts, such as our Lord's true divinity and atonement, justification by faith, the resurrection, judgment, and immortality. All are gone, at least to a shadow, and there is left little more than the mere morality, with perhaps a few of the doctrines of natural religion, and these without their grandest proof and authentication. The man who renounces all the supernatural in Christianity, and who still flatters himself that he is a Christian in the New Testament sense, or indeed in any really distinctive sense, is only deluding himself.

It is a common remark in certain quarters that Christianity is just like other religions in professing to have its origin accompanied with, and authenticated by legions of miracles. This statement is made and

especially to do. We say every *direct* or *immediate* act or manifestation; for all nature is an indirect or mediate manifestation, and all its operations indirect operations of the supernatural Creator and Upholder. Accordingly, we would say that the growth of the grain is not a miracle, because it is an *indirect* manifestation of a supernatural power; but that the incarnation and miracles of Christ are properly miracles, because they are *direct* manifestations of such power. In short, a direct or immediate supernatural manifestation or action is a miracle.

reiterated, we have reason to suspect, to throw discredit upon the miracles of Christianity, and get them all swept away at once, without inquiry, along with the mass of fabled prodigies which encircle these other religions. But the statement, we are convinced, is mainly a mistake. So far as can be proved by the evidence of contemporary writers, Christianity is the only great religion of the world which came claiming from the very first to be authenticated by objective miracles; and Christ is the only founder of a great historical religion, who came professing to work such miracles in attestation of His mission. Of course, no one denies that in the lapse of time the origins of these other religions referred to became the centres of whole nebulæ of fabulous marvels; but when we go back to the founders themselves, we do not find from contemporary evidence that they laid claim to the working of physical miracles. Beginning in the distant east, we have Confucianism, the religion of the majority of the Chinese; but it does not appear from contemporary evidence that Confucius, its founder, ever claimed or professed to work miracles. When we come to India, the original home of Buddhism, we find the same thing true in regard to the founder of that religion. While it is the fact that in later ages the Buddha became the centre of an exuberant jungle of monstrous prodigies, yet it seems totally certain from the best authorities that he made no claim to work miracles, and even discountenanced the idea. And last, and most conspicuous of all, we have the case of Mohammedanism. Here, also, we find the usual host of fabulous marvels growing up in course of time around its prophet, but it is a well-known fact that Mohammed did not claim to work physical miracles in attestation of his professed revelation, and persistently evaded the challenge to do so. As he expresses himself in the thirteenth chapter of the Koran, he was 'commissioned to be a preacher only, and not a worker of miracles.'[1] In short, so far as can be gathered from anything like contemporary evidence, Christianity is the only great religion which claims from the very beginning to have been ushered into the world authenticated by physical miracles, and Christ is the only founder of a great religion who came professing to work miracles in attestation of His commission. Accordingly the assertion that Christianity is just like other religions in having its origin accompanied with crowds of miracles, is false, and quite insufficient to warrant the fair inquirer in sweeping away the Christian miracles without examination into the general limbo of discredited prodigies and myths. Rather, the striking difference between Christianity and the other religions

[1] This has been a staple argument against Mohammed from the earliest days of Mohammedanism. See, for example, the interesting *Apology of Al Kindy*, composed at the Court of Al Mâmûn, Caliph of Bagdad, about A.D. 830, pp. 55 ff. (2nd edition, by Sir William Muir).

in this respect challenges special attention, and almost constitutes an argument in its favour.

There are not a few who see that the miraculous is evidently an essential element in Christianity, but find herein their greatest obstacle to its reception. Theodore Parker says, 'Miracles hang like a millstone about the neck of many a pious man, who can believe in religion, but not in the transformation of water into wine, or the resurrection of a body.'[1] 'If miracles,' said Baden Powell, 'were, in the estimation of a former age, among the chief supports of Christianity, they are at present among the main difficulties and hindrances to its acceptance.'[2] They are so, no doubt, to those who are determined not to believe in the supernatural or any special action of the supernatural, and will have no religion but that of mere nature. But, as we have seen, the supernatural element is just the very essence and soul, the glory and power of Christianity; and to desire a Christianity without this element is to desire fire without the power to burn, matter without gravitation, electricity without the power of giving a shock, a mind without free-will.

Revelation implies the supernatural, and it can scarcely be denied that a revelation is desirable and not unreasonably to be expected. In a world in which

[1] *Discourse on Matters pertaining to Religion*, p. 186 (Trübner).
[2] *Essays and Reviews*, p. 168 (12th edition).

immortal men are sunk in sin, and liable to all the miseries which accompany it here, and the woes which may possibly accompany it hereafter; in which earnest souls in all ages have yearned, and wrestled, and peered into the thick and silent darkness with the deepest anguish, crying in agony for light; in a world in which death reigns, and men, as they feel its terrible shadow beginning to darken over them, are filled with an awful anxiety to know whether there be a hereafter, a heaven or a hell, or both; in a world where men are utterly at sea as to whether or not there is salvation for the lost, and if so, how it is to be obtained, guess warring against guess, speculation against speculation, system against system, surely no one can deny that a reasonably certain revelation is a thing most devoutly to be desired. To those who believe in a personal God it must seem to be a thing not impossible. To those who have any idea of God as a being possessed in some degree of a father's goodness and love, it must appear to be a thing not utterly unlikely, but rather most likely, that He should reveal to His children that truth which they so deeply need, for which they so earnestly cry, and which it is of paramount importance for them to know, but which, as all history proves, they cannot possibly discover for themselves with any reasonable degree of certainty.

But, when we think of such a revelation, the question

at once arises, How can it be proved to be really a revelation from heaven? How can the messenger be sufficiently accredited as an authoritative commissioner from God? The distinct answer is, that it must be mainly by miracles. No doubt, the moral character of the messenger must be of the right kind; but this of itself is no sufficient authentication; for there have been multitudes of the best of men who have not been commissioned from heaven to reveal truth beyond the reach of human reason. Therefore, we say, the special credentials of the divine messenger must be miracles.

There is the best reason to believe that the human mind, when unsophisticated and unbiassed, naturally and instinctively regards miracles as the appropriate credentials of an authoritative commissioner from heaven. Men as a rule have held this view in every age, and, notwithstanding all the acute reasoning of philosophers, nothing will ever drive this conviction out of the general mind of man. For even instinctive logic and practical common sense perceive at a glance, that nothing can prove a supernatural commission but supernatural credentials. Nothing but distinct manifestations of mathematical or musical power could ever prove to us, that a person who is a complete stranger is a distinguished mathematician or musician, and so nothing but supernatural credentials, or miracles, can possibly prove a messenger to have a supernatural commission. Mere natural credentials can no more prove a professed teacher of truth to be supernaturally commissioned, than the ability to speak or write English can prove the stranger referred to above to be a great mathematician or musician. The proof must naturally correspond with the thing to be proved, and positively imply it. Clearly, therefore, from the nature of the case, nothing but a supernatural action can ever prove a supernatural commission, nothing but miracles can immediately and satisfactorily authenticate a man to be an authoritative messenger from God. Neither the excellence of the morality alone, nor the apparently high moral character of the teacher, nor both combined, can be sufficient for this purpose; for all these may be within the reach of mere human nature. To authenticate in a sufficient way a teacher of supernatural truth, that is, truth beyond the reach of mere reason, miracles are necessary; at least they are the most direct and natural proof. Hence, while Mozley says that 'a supernatural fact is the proper proof of a supernatural doctrine;' and Mansel, that 'a superhuman authority needs to be substantiated by superhuman evidence;' even J. S. Mill frankly affirms that 'a revelation cannot be proved divine unless by external evidence, that is, by the exhibition of supernatural facts.' To sum up with the expression of Butler, 'Revelation is miraculous, and miracles are the proof of it.'

That the Lord Jesus Himself meant His miracles to be credentials of His divine commission, can scarcely be denied or even doubted. In various texts He expresses most explicitly what their purpose was, and what their effect should be. 'I have greater witness than that of John,' He says; 'for the works which the Father hath given Me to accomplish, the very works that I do, bear witness of Me, that the Father hath sent Me' (John v. 36). And again He says, 'The works that I do in My Father's name, they bear witness of Me' (John x. 25). When the disciples of John the Baptist came to Him to ascertain whether He was the true Messiah or not, He replied, 'Go your way, and tell John what things ye have seen and heard; how that the blind receive their sight, the lame walk, the lepers are cleansed, the deaf hear, the dead are raised' (Luke vii. 22). To the cavilling Jews He answered, 'That ye may know that the Son of man hath power on earth to forgive sins, (then saith He to the sick of the palsy,) Arise, take up thy bed, and go unto thine house' (Matt. ix. 6, 7). Accordingly we also find that the Jews were declared to be highly culpable for rejecting the evidence afforded by His miracles: 'If I had not done among them the works which none other man did, they had not had sin' (John xv. 24); and again, 'Woe unto thee, Chorazin! woe unto thee, Bethsaida! for if the mighty works which were done in you, had been done in Tyre and Sidon, they would have repented long ago in sackcloth and ashes' (Matt. xi. 21 ff). All this is extremely plain, and means beyond doubt that our Lord meant His miracles to be credentials of His heavenly mission.

It has been occasionally objected by a certain class of thinkers from the time of Spinoza downwards, that miracles are impossible. But surely, if we reflect, we may well ask, What mortal man can venture to make such a sweeping assertion with modesty and reasonableness? Only the man who absolutely knows that there is no personal God: only the man who is an absolute atheist, materialist, or pantheist: for obviously, if there be a God at all, it must be rash and unwarrantable in any mere man to assert that a miracle is an impossibility. The position assumed in this book is that of Theism, and as Theists we believe that God has interfered in nature from time to time to make new beginnings in it, and each of these is substantially a miracle. As geology rolls back the volume of the earth's history before our eyes, we come at last to a time when man most certainly did not exist upon the earth. Here man is, but there man is not, and between these two leaves he sprang into being. But his coming into being, whether by creation or development, was a new beginning, and essentially a supernatural action on the part of God. And if God could perform a supernatural action then, we cannot suppose that He, who is from everlasting to everlasting, is unable by a direct act of His will to make a new beginning in nature, or perform a supernatural action now. All nature is God's nature; its matter, forces, and laws are God's matter, forces, and laws, and surely it must be unwarrantable to suppose that they are not His obedient servants, and that He cannot use them for supernatural purposes or to bring about supernatural events. It may be the case that we cannot tell how God's will directly works on nature so as to accomplish the miracle, any more than we can tell how our own will raises our hand to perform the human miracle of holding up the stone that is in it. But in spite of all the mystery, we know that our will does raise our hand. And the laws and forces of nature are but the hands of God, and may be infinitely more obedient to His will than the human hand to the human will. To say that God created nature and its laws, but that He cannot now use or even modify them, looks very much like an absurdity, if not a contradiction; for surely it is a far less thing to use, or even modify those laws and forces, than to create them at first. In short, we must remember that God has made nature not to be His master, but His servant.

But does not modern physical science prove that miracles must be impossible? We confidently answer that it has never proved and never can prove any such thing. As we have seen in a previous study, it cannot even reach God, for He is quite beyond its sphere; and much more must it lie beyond its sphere to affirm that God cannot perform a miracle. It can no more prove that it is impossible for God to use the laws of nature to bring about a supernatural event, than it can prove that it is impossible for man to use the laws of nature to make a stone rise in the air. What physical science shows is that the forces and laws of nature, as a rule, are constant after they are brought into existence, not that they must be constant by a metaphysical necessity in spite of the will of God. But this so-called uniformity of nature does not exclude supernatural action on the part of man, and much less does it exclude it on the part of God. If man, in spite of this uniformity, is able not merely to act on nature from without, but even to use its laws and forces as a means to his end, surely this must be true much more of God. What physical science has shown is, that the miracles of Jesus are absolutely beyond the power of nature or of man, and must therefore be miracles in the highest sense; but it has not proved, and it cannot prove in the least, that miracles are impossible.

It has been already implied that man can perform that which is essentially a miracle. And this is the certain truth. We find in nature a system in which constant laws rule, which act of necessity, and only on their own lines. But in man we find a mind and the elements of intelligence and free-will. Man, in virtue of this mind, can act upon the forces of nature from without, and knowing their fixed laws can use them to accomplish new results and introduce new beginnings into the course of nature, which mere nature itself never could introduce. Every intelligent volition which takes effect in outward action is such a new beginning, introducing something quite new into the course of nature, and therefore it contains within it the essence of a miracle. In other words, when we form an intelligent plan, and use our free-will to set action going to carry it out into realization, we do a thing which the forces of nature, working according to their constant laws, never could have done, and which is therefore essentially supernatural. We really bring a supernatural act into being, and in doing so, we may appear even to 'violate' some of the laws of nature. But after all we are only using the laws of nature as they were meant to be used, as the trusty servants and instruments of intelligent free-will. Every law of nature still continues to act in its own way, and where we appear to 'violate' these laws, it is only by counteracting them by other laws of nature or by the laws of mind.

Perhaps it may be well to make this clear by an example or two. When we hold up a stone in the hand, it is plain that we are counteracting, 'violating' let us even say, the law of gravitation. But it is plain that we are counteracting the law of gravitation only by the higher laws of mind making use of the physical power of the arm for this very purpose. Yet even in this simple act we have all the different and all the difficult elements of the miraculous, an intelligent will producing a totally new effect in nature which nature itself never could produce. Or again, let us take the case of the steam-engine. In the production of such an object we have all the essential difficulties of the miracle. We have an entirely new thing produced by an intelligent will acting in and upon nature, a thing which mere nature never could have produced itself. Yet it is all produced by mind thinking out the thought, putting forth the will, and using the forces and laws of nature, so as to make them co-operate to realize the intelligent purpose. The mind seizes and utilizes the law of gravitation, the laws of the air, of iron, of motion, of fire, of water, of steam, and the like, unites them all and plays them off against each other, and so produces the useful steam-engine.

In all such cases as the above, we have first the intelligent plan in the mind, then the volition to carry it out, the setting free of new force, or transmutation of dormant energy by the will, in order to move the arm, perform the act, or execute the work, and the skilful use of the laws of nature so as to carry out our purpose. The step here which is the central mystery where the supernatural essentially lies concealed, is the intelligent action of the will, the setting free of new power which would have otherwise remained only dormant potential energy, and the passage over of that action and power into realization as a new existence in the world of sense. It is quite true that this step is enveloped in mystery; we cannot give a logical analysis or statement of it in detail; but the fact is as certain as any fact of consciousness can be. Now, if the finite mind of man can form such new and intelligent plans, can by the action of the will originate new beginnings, can set free new power or transmute and direct potential energy, and can use the forces and laws of the physical world so as to accomplish its supernatural ends, surely the infinite mind of God may do the same, and that in an immeasurably higher degree. He who is the supreme intelligence can form the new purpose; He who is the fountain of all will can put forth the new volition; He to whose will all power and potential energy lying in the unseen are entirely subject, can, by an act of His will, at once set free that energy in actual form so as to make it spring up in the seen in a new existence; He to whom all nature is under direct and complete control, even more than the arm is under the control of our will, can, by His will, use the powers and laws of nature as His pliant instruments, whether in the way of action or counteraction, so as to accomplish the end which He wills.[1]

We cannot, of course, in the least understand, far less exactly analyse and state, how God breaks through nature, and works in and by the forces of nature and their laws, so as to produce a new beginning or event. We know almost nothing as to how our own mind works in and through means of the brain. We know absolutely nothing as to how the will sets free nerve force, or whatever it may be, to command and move the muscles. We know next to nothing about the manner in which it works in and by the muscles to raise the arm, as to how it changes in the act of volition mere potential into actual energy. We are almost totally ignorant as to how mind works in, and on, and through means of matter, although we know the fact for certain. 'The problem of the connection of the soul and body,' says Professor Tyndall, 'is as unsearchable in its modern form as it was in the pre-scientific ages.' In like manner, we can still less expect to know and analyse the mode in which the mind of God may act in nature to produce a new beginning or a new event. It may be that, in some instances at least, He uses only natural laws to produce the miracle. Or it may be, as Lotze holds, that the natural laws remain unaltered, but that God so modifies the essential condition of the existing forces

[1] See Appendix, Note IX.

and elements of matter directly bearing on the special case, that they now work out the miracle according to the universal laws of nature.[1] Or, it may be, as the authors of the *Unseen Universe* hold, that God accomplishes the miracle by the direct transference of new energy through an act of the divine will from the invisible into the visible universe, by 'the transmutation of energy from the one universe into the other.'[1] Shall we say that just as the touch of the telegraph clerk sets free the electricity in the battery, so as to make it flow along the wire and produce the signal at the other end, or just as the will sets free the potential nerve force to flow into the arm to move it; so God by His divine volition injects a new influx of power, or sets it free to flow from the invisible into the visible sphere, leading men to say, 'Here is the finger of God, a flash of the will that can'? But perhaps, after all, it is more modest and safe to say that we cannot tell how the end is accomplished in the case of God any more than in the case of man. The New Testament never presumes to explain to us how a miracle is wrought. 'Such knowledge is too wonderful for us; it is high, we cannot attain unto it.' What we know for certain is, that God has produced such new beginnings and events, as the records of creation both in Scripture and in the structure of the earth declare, and as the records of Christianity

[1] See Appendix, Note X.

both in the New Testament and the continuously existing Church no less explicitly proclaim.

But though we may not be warranted in declaring miracles impossible, nay, even though we expressly admit them to be possible, it is further objected that they cannot possibly be proved. This is the position taken up by Hume in his famous argument. No better statement of the argument can be given than his own. 'A miracle is a violation of the laws of nature; and as a firm and unalterable experience has established these laws, the proof against a miracle, from the very nature of the fact, is as entire as any argument from experience can possibly be imagined.'[1] That is, the miracles of the New Testament are proved by testimony, but 'experience' tells us 'that testimony sometimes deceives us,' whereas it tells us that the laws of nature are absolutely 'uniform.' When testimony, therefore, comes into collision with the 'uniformity of nature,' the former must go to the wall. But in the miracle this is what takes place: and therefore we must reject the evidence of testimony for the miracle, as being more than counterbalanced by the 'uniformity of nature.' In other words, miracles cannot be proved, and are utterly incredible.

Now, that Hume's argument is very acute is no doubt the case. But it is more of a logical puzzle than anything else. At any rate it is tolerably certain that the

[1] *Essay on Miracles*, Part i.

instinctive common sense of men in general regards it more in the light of a puzzle than of a solid argument. It is a puzzle of somewhat the same kind as those who maintain the freedom of the will regard the argument of Edwards against that doctrine to be. While few can logically unravel or refute it, just as few believe it; for though they cannot solve the puzzle by logic, they nevertheless directly solve it by consciousness. It is a puzzle somewhat like the argumentation employed by Hume himself, and by the idealists, against our certainty in regard to the reality of the external world. It is extremely subtle, and difficult to refute logically; nevertheless but few believe in it; for though they may not be able to refute it by logic, they do so readily by instinct and common sense. In like manner men in general feel that though Hume's argument against miracles may be very subtle, and difficult to refute logically, it is quite as easily and directly refuted by consciousness and common sense as either of the preceding. Men have an instinctive perception and conviction that the argument is fallacious. They have an instinctive and invincible conviction that there is such a thing as sufficient evidence of the senses and of testimony for the unquestionable certainty of outward objects and events. Indeed such a conviction is one of the primary facts of our nature, and in the healthy and unbiassed mind will always prove itself victorious against any logical puzzles, or subtle long-drawn arguments from the 'uniformity' of the laws of nature. Accordingly when that sufficient evidence exists, men feel constrained to accord their belief, even to miracles, as is shown by the fact that they have in all ages almost universally believed more or less in miracles. Instead of regarding them as incredible and unprovable, they have no difficulty in certain circumstances in regarding them both as credible and proved. To use Hume's own words employed elsewhere: 'We need not fear that this philosophy will ever undermine the reasonings of common life. Nature will always maintain her rights, and prevail in the end over any abstract reasoning whatsoever.'[1]

In any case, the argument or puzzle notwithstanding, we know that things which are flagrant violations of the 'uniformity of nature' may be as certain as any historical fact in the universe, and believed to be as certain. Perhaps we shall see this most vividly by means of a simple illustration. It is quite certain that it is contrary to all 'experience' in Hume's sense of the word, that man should come into existence in any other way than by ordinary generation. All 'experience' declares that this is the only way: and therefore we should believe that man must have existed from all eternity by ordinary descent. But it is perfectly certain that there was

[1] *Inquiry concerning Human Understanding*, Part i. sect. v.

a time when man did not exist upon the earth. There must therefore have been a first man. And how did he come into existence? It matters not for our present purpose whether he was evolved or created, he clearly did not come into existence by ordinary human birth. But whether he sprang into existence by evolution or immediate creation, either is alike contrary to all 'experience.' The evolution or creation of a man has never been seen in all the ages of history, and being contrary to all experience, it ought to be unprovable and incredible. Man therefore must certainly have existed from eternity; at least we ought to believe this, if we are to trust Hume's argument. But in spite of his argument, we know that man did not exist from all eternity, that he did at some past time or other come into existence in a way entirely contrary to universal human 'experience.' So in like manner, in spite of Hume's argument or puzzle, miracles, though contrary to 'universal experience,' may have taken place, and we may have reasonable assurance of the fact.

But after all, from the Christian point of view, the Christian miracles, and those of Christ in particular, are not 'contrary to experience' in Hume's sense of the expression, and therefore his argument does not apply. We are not to think of the miracles as sporadic, purposeless, accidental occurrences. Like everything else in the universe of the reasonable God, they can never take place without a sufficient reason. Accordingly to show that miracles do not take place when there is no sufficient reason for them, proves nothing whatsoever against the credibility of the Christian miracles. We must remember that they stand in living and organic connection with the incarnation of Christ, and His mission as the Divine Saviour and the Founder of the ultimate world-religion. They are the proper credentials of His heavenly commission, and a vital part of the new religion. The case of the Christian miracles is therefore entirely unique. It stands utterly alone in the history of human 'experience.' We have no 'experience' whatsoever in regard to the introduction of such a religion and the advent of such a Person into our world. We have no more 'experience' in regard to such a thing than we have in regard to the creation of the world. As there is only one case of each in the past, we cannot be said to have any experience in regard either to the one or the other. Our 'experience' cannot say what is likely or is not likely to be the mode of procedure at the creation of a world, for we have never had any experience in regard to the matter. Accordingly, to say that it was accompanied with this or that class of phenomena cannot be said to be 'contrary to experience.' In the same way our 'experience' can prove nothing about the improbability of miracles as phenomena accompanying the origin of Christianity and the advent of Christ, for we have no 'experience' whatsoever in regard to the introduction of such a religion. In other words, our 'experience,' in Hume's sense, has really nothing to say on the matter, nothing at any rate which can prove miracles in such a conjuncture incredible.

In any case, this so-called argument against miracles from 'experience' may be checkmated in another way. Let it be granted for the moment that miracles in the general sense are 'contrary to experience;' it is also 'contrary to experience,' that evidence such as we have for the Christian miracles should be false. A jury has no hesitation in giving a fatal verdict of guilty against a murderer on the evidence of two honourable and trustworthy eye-witnesses of his crime, so certain is our confidence in proper human testimony. But here we have the best testimony converging upon the Christian miracles. The witnesses are beyond all doubt men of the highest moral character, not to speak of our Lord, who plainly claimed the power of working miracles, and speaks as if He actually wrought them. No one can believe the apostles and their fellow-disciples to be wilful deceivers. All selfish interests must have disposed them to abjure and forsake Christ, if He had been an impostor; but, on the contrary, they forsook all for Him. For His sake they exposed themselves to shame and scorn, to worldly loss and ostracism, to unremitting persecution and death. They were not merely cross-examined, they were examined by suffering and torture; and yet they held fast to their testimony and sealed it with their blood. They did not hear of the miracles at second hand; they saw them with their own eyes, heard them with their own ears, felt them with their own hands, so that they could not possibly be mistaken. The witnesses were not merely two or three, but numerous; not merely twelve, or even a hundred and twenty, but hundreds. They were not only numerous, but in spite of all their persecutions no one ever came forward and divulged the secret imposture, or showed up the falsity of the juggle. Not even Judas the traitor, not even the hostile Jews attempted such a thing, for it is notorious that they admitted our Lord's miracles to be really such, however they might seek to evade the proper inference. These miracles were wrought not in darkness, but in open day; not in private, but in public; not merely among friends, but before the most determined enemies; not with any previous preparation, but as the event presented itself, so that any collusion was impossible. They were, as we have already seen, the naturally-to-be-expected concomitants and credentials accompanying the introduction of a divine religion. They were followed by the spread of the new religion in the midst of enemies, in the very places where they are said to have been wrought, and when there was no worldly inducement to believe except shame and loss, persecution and a martyr's death. They were followed by the rise of the Christian Church, which has had an unbroken continuity of existence down to the present day. This is a brief but imperfect summary of the evidence for the Christian miracles. It is evidence of such a nature that it is contrary to all 'experience' that it should be false. There never has been a single case in which such evidence has been found to be false in the whole history of man. Accordingly, if a miracle be 'contrary to experience,' it is no less contrary to all experience that such evidence, or anything approaching to it, should be utterly false.[1]

But after all, what has 'experience' to say, as a witness, against the miracles of Jesus? Directly, it can say nothing positive. At the very utmost, it can only say that it cannot bear witness in their behalf. It can say little more than this: I was not present to see, and therefore I am not a proper witness and ought to be out of the witness-box. The matter is one beyond my competency, and not having been present at the time, I can bear no valid testimony against those miracles, if I can bear none in their favour. But the testimony presented in the New Testament, and of which a summary

[1] See this well discussed by Chalmers, *Evidences of Christianity*, Book i. chap. iii. sect. iv.

has just been given, is positive testimony. In other words, we have the testimony of thc most trustworthy and thoroughly tested witnesses, all on the same side, backed up by varied and important circumstantial evidence, and that must decide the verdict. In the case of a trial for murder, it would avail the murderer but little if he should offer to produce as witnesses a hundred, or a hundred million men, who were ready to swear that they had not seen him commit the murder. The question would immediately be raised, Were they actually present, so as to be able to see what was going on at the time and place at which the murder was committed? If they were not present, their testimony would go for nothing, they would properly speaking have no testimony at all to give; and if two trustworthy witnesses swore that they positively were present and saw the murder, the prisoner would be unhesitatingly condemned. In somewhat the same manner, the millions represented by Hume's general 'experience' were not present on the unique occasion, so as to be able to see whether or not the miracles of Jesus were actually wrought. They are, therefore, not properly witnesses in the case, and are out of court; their testimony, if it does not exactly go for nothing, is at the best only indirect; while the direct and positive testimony that remains is substantially untouched, and therefore the verdict of the jury must be in favour of the reality of the Christian miracles.

But it may be objected, After all, does any intelligent man nowadays *really believe* in the Christian miracles? Does not every man totally reject the idea of miracles in practical life? When we hear that some professed miracle has taken place, as for example the miracles at Lourdes, or others of the Romish Church, does not every intelligent man, whether a Christian or not, at once reject them without examination as absurd? Do we not set them down as mere delusion and imposture, and does not this show that every man in his heart of hearts really disbelieves in miracles? It does no such thing. If we take even the unwarrantable case of the man who positively disbelieves that any miracles can, or do, or will take place in these later Christian ages, we may easily see that such a position is quite consistent with a firm belief in the gospel miracles. No one believes in instances occurring at the present day in which men are directly created by God, and thus come into the world in the same way as Adam did; but very clearly that position is in no way inconsistent with the belief of man's original creation. No one believes in cases of man being developed out of the ape in the present age, and yet that may be quite consistent, it is held, with a belief in development in the past. The creationist and the evolutionist alike believe in the unique origin of man according to their respective theories; but after the beginning was made and man inserted in the course of nature, they may both hold that he was left to the reign of ordinary natural law. So in like manner, the Christian may consistently believe that Christianity was miraculously introduced at first, and inserted into the course of the world's life, but that afterwards it was left to the mere ordinary laws of history, without the constant intervention of miracles. What was necessary both for man and Christianity in order to bring them into existence, is by no means necessarily required for their continuance. After the Founder of Christianity has duly authenticated His mission and work by miracles, it is possible that they may be safely withdrawn. When a foreign ambassador arrives in our country, he must at the beginning of his residence show his credentials, in order to authenticate himself: but when once his position has been acknowledged, and still more when he has become in a manner naturalized in the country, he no longer flaunts his credentials in the eyes of men, or 'wears them on his sleeve for daws to peck at.'

We must, of course, be careful to distinguish what is the only kind of evidence which we can naturally and reasonably expect for the New Testament miracles. We cannot expect the evidence of universal, or even general, experience from age to age. That is precluded to a large extent by the very idea of a miracle, which is just this, that it is something outside of the course of positive general experience. And just as plainly we cannot have the evidence of direct intuition, such evidence as we have for a mathematical axiom, or a first principle in morals. The miracles of the New Testament are to us events of past history, and accordingly as such they can be known as true not by general experience or by intuition, but only by historical testimony. This follows from the very nature of the case. A man may no doubt say that he will not accept historical testimony as sufficient, even along with the moral and circumstantial evidence by which it is supported; but if so, there is no help for him. He rejects the only evidence of which the case admits, and the matter is at an end so far as he is concerned. If a man will not accept mathematical evidence for a mathematical truth, or experimental evidence for a physical truth, he is doomed to remain in unbelief; and in like manner, if a man will not accept historical evidence, even when well supported all round, for a past historical fact, he must be content to remain in unbelief. He rejects at the very threshold the only kind of evidence of which the case admits, and which can be had, and thus he practically shuts himself out from the possibility of conviction.

The conditions have indeed been sometimes laid down, which alone would be sufficient to demonstrate the reality of a miracle. Renan has done this more than once.[1] According to him, in order to make the result completely satisfactory, Jesus in raising a dead man to life, for example, should have submitted to some such conditions as the following. A committee of distinguished physiologists and physicists should have been formed. They should have selected the corpse, and tested scientifically that it was really dead. They should have fixed on the hall where the experiment was to be made, and if it could only have been in Paris so much the better. They should, in short, have taken all the necessary scientific precautions; and then, in the face of day and before an excited assembly—but we leave the rest of the picture to the reader's imagination. And even the performance of the miracle once and again after this fashion would not have been sufficient. It must have been repeated in different circumstances, and on different dead bodies. Such is a sketch of the necessary conditions. But who does not instinctively feel that such a method partakes far too much of the mere theatrical, and is quite foreign to the spirit of Jesus, to the natural way in which His miracles always sprang up out of the actual life and history, and to the real gospel meaning of the miracles, as object lessons teaching positive truth? And further, we may safely say that such a method would never have satisfied even

[1] *Vie de Jésus*, p. 51, 12th edition; *Les Apôtres*, p. 44.

Renan himself. For he doubtless would have said, as he does say, that miracles are not performed nowadays; no man ever sees or ever saw a miracle in our age; and therefore they cannot have taken place then. The committee who conducted the experiments must either have been deceived themselves, or must have united with Jesus in His deception. In any case, it is much more than likely that deception took place somewhere; for are not miracles contrary to all experience?

In a previous study we have discussed the authenticity of the leading books of the New Testament, and of course we now accept them as veracious and trustworthy witnesses in behalf of the Christian miracles. But it may strengthen their testimony, especially in view of the consideration that there are some who think they can reject the miracles and yet accept our Lord's teaching, if we emphasize the fact that the New Testament miracles are often closely interwoven with the ordinary narrative, the dialogue, and the teaching. So closely are they interwoven at times, that they cannot be separated without the utmost arbitrariness and violence, without producing confusion, and making much of the teaching unintelligible. We see this very clearly in regard to the miracle of feeding the five thousand recorded in the sixth chapter of John, when viewed in connection with the discourse which follows concerning the bread of life. We see it again illustrated in the narrative of the raising of Lazarus (John xi.); for here the conversation is closely connected with the miracle, and the miracle in its turn becomes the means of stirring up further hostility on the part of the Jews. We see the same thing in the account of Paul's conversion (Acts ix.), in which the natural incidents, the miracles, the dialogue, and the resultant new life fit into each other and are inseparably interwoven. Accordingly nothing can be more capricious or arbitrary than the way in which such critics as Renan, for example, are compelled by their foregone denial of the supernatural to deal with such narratives; for while they accept substantially the natural facts, the dialogue, and the teaching, they utterly reject the miraculous element, though the evidence for it is exactly the same as for the elements which they accept. 'The miracles,' as Godet remarks, 'are not, as people often believe, a mere embroidery upon the web of the gospel history; they form part of the very web itself.' And hence, in the words of Dr. M'Cosh, 'it is impossible to separate between the ordinary acts and discourses of our Lord on the one hand, and His miracles on the other. They are woven through and through each other as the weft and woof. They could be separated only by tearing the garment to pieces.'[1] This fact is im-

[1] This is clearly perceived and fully acknowledged even by Strauss. He says: 'If the Gospels are really and truly historical, it is impossible to exclude miracles from the life of Jesus;' and he goes on characteristically

portant and instructive, and greatly strengthens the testimony of the New Testament books to the miracles.

But while miracles are so inseparably interwoven with the narrative and teaching, it may still further confirm their credibility when we reflect that they exactly fit into the nature and personality of Jesus. In other words, there is a perfect congruity or consistency between them and Him.[1] He is represented as altogether a supernatural Person; and this He Himself explicitly claims to be. In like manner, true to all this, He acts as a supernatural Person. But to act like such a Person is to do supernatural things, that is, to work miracles. In other words, it is as natural for Him to perform miracles in the higher sense, as it is for man to perform intelligent, voluntary actions, which are miracles in the lower sense. Richter somewhere remarks that 'miracles on earth are nature in heaven.' This saying has its truth; and, applied to Jesus, it means that what appear the highest miracles to us were nature to Him. We feel that there is a consistency in it that Jesus should perform miracles, as He was Himself the grand miracle. We even find it difficult to conceive that He who was incarnate God should have gone through life without miraculous manifestations, just as

to remark: 'If, on the other hand, miracles are incompatible with history, then the Gospels are not really historical records.'—*New Life of Jesus*, vol. i. p. 19.

[1] See Appendix, Note XI.

we find it difficult to think of a man going through life without the usual manifestations of humanity. It is a fundamental law that everything should act according to its own nature, and for Christ to act according to His true nature is to perform supernatural actions in the highest sense. 'Being a miracle Himself, it would be the greatest of all miracles, if He did not work miracles.'[1]

Once more, it is worthy of remark that the miracles of Jesus were not fantastic, puerile, meaningless monstrosities, like the miracles of the apocryphal Gospels and of later Mohammedanism. On the contrary, they were the natural expression of what was in Jesus, of what His grand purpose was. They were 'signs,' full of significance. They served not only as credentials to authenticate the Messenger and His teaching, but they were also the actual means of expressing and teaching the truth. They extend over all the realms of nature, the wind and the sea, the vegetable and the animal kingdoms, the bodies and the minds of men, the world of death and the world of evil spirits: and they prove thereby that Christ is truly Lord of all. They are all miracles of healing, of mercy and benevolence, and thereby they proclaim that His mission was one of mercy and healing, that He is the life and the light of men, the bread of life, the resurrection and the life. We

[1] See Appendix, Note XII.

may read the gospel in His miracles as well as in His doctrinal teaching and His parables, and we find that it is the self-same gospel. In other words, the miracles harmonize not merely with the person but also with the mission and teaching of Jesus, and this consistency becomes another powerful consideration establishing their reality.

We close the present study with a simple statement of what the miraculous element in Christianity, once reasonably established, distinctly implies. When taken along with the moral character of Jesus, it demonstrates His divine commission and the full authority of His teaching. By doing so, it proves in the only way in which they can be proved the supernatural doctrines which He proclaimed. More especially it proves the doctrines of His divinity and propitiation, salvation by grace through faith, the resurrection, the final judgment and immortality—doctrines which are clearly beyond the reach of mere reason to ascertain with practical certainty, and which could only have been made known by a supernatural revelation. The miraculous element carries with it, in short, all those high doctrines which make our religion full of the unsearchable riches of Christ and the treasures of the Godhead, and without which it would have been poor and feeble indeed, and would long since have vanished as a living power from the earth. It proves that the supernatural is a great reality, the reality of all realities, in which the soul of the spiritual man lives and breathes as in an unseen, ethereal air, interpenetrated by its subtle presence through and through. It shows us that the little circle of our life on earth is surrounded on its utmost horizon by a supernatural zone, from which there shoots up 'a glorious rose of dawn,' giving us the good hope through grace, that when our 'life's star' sets in the west, it only sets to rise beyond the ridge of the everlasting hills in that heavenly sphere where all is life and day.

VIII.

Direct Personal Testimony to Miracles in the New Testament.

Our object in the following study is to discuss the question whether we have in the New Testament any indisputably direct personal testimony to miracles. Do any of the writers, speaking undeniably in their own name, explicitly bear their immediate testimony to miracles as matters of fact? Is there, in short, any first-hand testimony? To this we answer emphatically in the affirmative; and as the matter is sometimes spoken of as if it were doubtful, we proceed to investigate it at some length.[1]

Assuming the authenticity of the chief books of the New Testament, which has been already treated of in a

[1] For example, the author of *Supernatural Religion* speaks as follows: 'Throughout the whole New Testament, . . . there is no instance whatever, that we can remember, in which a writer claims to have himself performed a miracle. Wherever there has existed even the comparatively accurate means of information, which a person who himself performed a miracle might possess, the miraculous entirely fails, and it is found only where faith or credulity usurps the place of knowledge.'—*Supernatural Religion*, vol. i. pp. 200 f. (4th edition). This statement the author endeavours to justify at length in vol. iii. pp. 325 ff.

previous study, we might say at first sight that the direct personal evidence is abundant. There is the testimony of Matthew, who was an apostle and companion of the Lord, and therefore an eye-witness of many of the numerous miracles which he reports. There is the testimony of Mark, who was 'the interpreter of Peter,' and who 'wrote accurately all that he remembered' of that apostle's narratives. There is the testimony of Luke, who, though like Mark not an eye-witness himself, nevertheless, as he tells us in the preface to his Gospel, narrates the Gospel incidents as 'they delivered them unto us, who from the beginning were eye-witnesses.' In other words, his Gospel is a narrative of what he had directly received from the eye-witnesses. There is above all the testimony of John, which is direct and personal in the highest sense, and embraces some of our Lord's most striking miracles, and more especially the raising of Lazarus from the dead. 'He saw and believed,' even 'the disciple who testifieth these things, and wrote these things,'[1] in the fourth Gospel. Accordingly in the Gospels we have full and explicit testimony to our Lord's miracles, in two direct, in two indirect no doubt, but indirect very much in the sense that their authors are the immediate reporters of the testimony of those who were eye-witnesses.

When we pass to the other books of the New Testament,

[1] Compare John xx. 8 and xxi. 24.

we find similar and direct testimony. The Acts of the Apostles was written by Luke, and as we have already seen, he relates a considerable portion of it in the first person, 'we.' That is, he narrates as one who had been present as an eye-witness. But it will be found that those portions which he narrates in his own name are just as full of miraculous events as the other portions. He relates in the personal passages the expulsion of 'the spirit of divination' from the damsel at Philippi (ch. xvi. 16–18); and also, we may safely say, the miraculous deliverance of Paul and Silas from the prison in that city (xvi. 25–40). We find in the narrative given in the first person, the restoration of Eutychus to life (xx. 6–12), Paul's deliverance from the evil results of the viper's bite in Malta, and the healing of Publius and others of their diseases in that island (xxviii.). Again, passing to the Epistle to the Hebrews, we find its author also bearing direct personal testimony to miracles as well-known facts. He testifies that the gospel 'was confirmed unto us by them that heard [the Lord], God also bearing them witness with signs and wonders and divers miracles, and gifts of the Holy Ghost' (Heb. ii. 3, 4). In view of the peculiar nature of the book, we do not adduce the evidence of the Revelation of John, though it is accepted by the most negative school of critics as the genuine production of that apostle. Enough has been said to show that we have abundant personal testimony of the direct kind to miracles in the New Testament, and that it is given in such a way as to imply that they were regarded in the Church as undeniable facts.

We come now, however, to what is more especially the object of this study, namely, to consider the unquestioned and unquestionable evidence of Paul to miracles. In doing so, we restrict ourselves, as in a previous study, to his first four Epistles, — Romans, 1 and 2 Corinthians, and Galatians. We restrict ourselves rigidly to these Epistles for the reason there referred to at length, that while the extreme school largely reject the Gospels, the Acts, and the other New Testament books except Revelation, they are united in accepting these four Epistles. Baur, the representative and late head of the negative school in Germany; Renan, the representative of the school in France; and the author of *Supernatural Religion*, the representative of the school in England, — all unite in accepting these Epistles as indisputably genuine.[1] Here then we have a firm and sure foundation on which to stand, even in the judgment of our most determined opponents. Accordingly we confine our attention at present to these incontestably genuine Epistles, and we affirm that in them Paul

[1] See Study V., 'The Testimony of the Unquestioned Epistles of Paul;' and especially pp. 110 ff.

bears his explicit and direct personal testimony to miracles.

We do not need to dwell at present on the character of the witness. We have done so already, and have seen that he is a witness of the very highest class, who proved his truthfulness by forsaking all for Christ, by suffering for His sake shame, persecution, and a martyr's death; who lived in the midst of the events, and had, both as persecutor and apostle, the very best means of sifting the whole matter to the very bottom, so as to arrive at the absolute truth.

It seems almost certain that no man of average intelligence and unbiassed mind can read the four Epistles just referred to without concluding that Paul himself believed in miracles, and that he appears to bear his testimony to their existence as a fact notorious in the Church. This is admitted even by the negative school itself. The author of *Supernatural Religion* says: 'It must not be supposed that we in the slightest degree question the fact that the Apostle Paul believed in the reality of supernatural intervention in mundane affairs, or that he asserted the actual occurrence of certain miracles.'[1] Of course these critics must try to break down this testimony in every possible way. They attempt to do so partly by affirming that Paul was an ecstatic visionary, partly by the rationalistic process of

[1] *Supernatural Religion*, vol. iii. p. 346.

explaining away words and passages, and partly by what we cannot but call the process of special pleading; in short, by the most arbitrary and capricious methods. What we now mean to do is, to collect the testimony of the witness, and place it clearly before the minds of readers in its simple and natural meaning, leaving them as the jury to come to a decision for themselves.

We merely mention at present the apostle's narrative of the testimony of 'the twelve' (twice), of Cephas and James, and of the more than 'five hundred brethren,' to the miracle of our Lord's resurrection (1 Cor. xv. 3–7). The apostle came into close contact with many of these witnesses, so that if his testimony in that passage is not quite first-hand, it is certainly second-hand testimony of the very highest type. But we pass over the passage at present, not merely because it may be said to contain second-hand testimony, but because it will come up in its proper place in the following study.

We now come to the apostle's direct personal testimony. We find him bearing testimony to the fact that he had received revelations of truth directly from Christ. He says in Gal. i. 11, 12, 'I certify you, brethren, that the gospel which was preached of me is not after man; for I neither received it of man, neither was I taught it, but by the revelation of Jesus Christ.' The plain meaning of such language is, that Paul had supernatural or miraculous revelations of the truth, though in what particular way we may not be able exactly to tell. We cannot get rid of the force of this by affirming, that this was only his way of expressing the dawning of the truth on his mind by the natural processes of thought or logic; for he can and does distinguish clearly between his own thoughts or opinions and such revelations. Hence we find him speaking of certain things as being his own 'judgment,' and distinguishing explicitly between his own teaching and commandments, and those of the Lord (see 1 Cor. vii. 6, 10, 12, 25, 40). That is, he can and does distinguish between his own views, and truth received by direct revelation from Christ; so that, when he speaks in such emphatic terms as he does in the passage quoted above, of having received the gospel 'by the revelation of Christ,' we may confidently accept his statement as a simple fact. In other words, he bears direct personal testimony, the testimony of his own consciousness, to a miraculous event.

Another most important contribution to the apostle's testimony to the miraculous is his own vision of the risen Lord. He says, in 1 Cor. ix. 1, 'Have I not seen Jesus Christ our Lord?' And again, in 1 Cor. xv. 8, after recounting five different appearances of the risen Saviour, he adds, 'Last of all, He was seen of me also, as of one born out of due time.' When we view this vision in the light of Gal. i. 15–17, we may well believe that it took place on the way to Damascus. In any case, it was clearly a view of Christ, as an external object, by the physical eye. He says, and means his readers to believe, that he saw the Lord Jesus on that occasion, as an outward reality, in the same way as He was seen by Peter, James, the eleven apostles, and the five hundred brethren between His resurrection and His ascension. This is proved by the facts that it is mentioned along with the five appearances, and that the very same word is used in reference to it as in reference to these appearances. Beyond a doubt Paul means the reader to believe that it was a view of Christ with his bodily eyes. It is true that he tells us in 2 Cor. xii. 1 ff. of an ecstatic vision which he had had; and the objection is at once raised, May not this appearance on the way to Damascus have been merely a subjective vision also,—the vision of a mere enthusiast with excited nerves,—a vision which had no corresponding external reality? But the apostle clearly means to distinguish between the two. His vision of Jesus he regards as a case of actual sight with his eyes; the other vision was a vision by the mind in a state of ecstasy or rapture, he classes it with 'visions and revelations,' and declares that he cannot tell whether he was in the body or out of the body. And surely the consideration that he distinguishes so explicitly between physical and ecstatical vision, should confirm our belief that the appearance of

Christ to him on the way to Damascus was an objective fact, that is, a real miracle.

The next step in our argument is his testimony to the existence of miracles and miraculous powers in the early Church. And first of all we make a passing reference to the 'gift of tongues.' This gift is referred to once and again in 1 Cor. xii., and at great length in chap. xiv. What was the exact nature of this phenomenon may be matter of dispute among Christians themselves; but one thing at least is plain—viz., that it was something supernatural or miraculous. The apostle bears explicit testimony to the existence of the gift as notorious in Corinth, and he declares that he himself spoke with tongues more than any of them. That is, he testifies to the gift of tongues as existing around him in the Church, and declares that he himself possessed it. Could he mistake the testimony of his own ears and his own consciousness?

We admit, however, that the dust and difficulty which have been raised around the gift of tongues, even among evangelical writers, is so great as to mar the force of the evidence to the supernatural which it involves. Accordingly we pass on to other forms of the apostle's testimony, and come next to the 'gifts of healings,' of which we find reiterated mention in 1 Cor. xii. (vers. 9, 28, 30). The obvious and natural meaning of this expression is very plain. It signifies gifts or powers of miraculous healing, which manifested themselves in miraculous healings. We cannot explain it away by saying that, as some of the other gifts mentioned in the chapter may be explained on merely natural principles, therefore this may be merely natural too, and may only mean natural skill in dealing with sickness, and a knowledge of medicine. This, it seems very apparent, is a process of the purest rationalism. There can be no reasonable doubt as to the intended and fair meaning of the words. There can be no doubt as to the way in which a Greek would interpret them, and there can be as little doubt as to the New Testament usage. We not only find that many miracles of healing were performed by our Lord, but we also find it said that 'He *gave* His apostles *power to heal* all manner of sickness and all manner of disease' (Matt. x. 1; Mark iii. 15, xvi. 18; Luke ix. 1). We also see in the Acts that His apostles are stated to have performed '*miracles of healing*' (Acts iii., etc.); and when we compare the expression 'gifts of healing' with the above expressions, we see, from their close similarity, that something miraculous is meant, and not merely natural skill in medicine. No doubt, the texts just referred to will be said by negative critics to be taken from New Testament books which were written long after the Epistles of Paul; but even on their own supposition that they were written in the first half of the second century, they are sufficiently near the age of the apostle to establish the force of the expression, especially when we consider that, as even these critics admit, the language must have been used orally long before the writing of the Gospels and the Acts. We conclude, therefore, that the apostle bears distinct testimony to the existence of miraculous gifts—and therefore miracles—of healing.

But we also find the apostle bearing testimony to the existence of miracles as a fact apparently undenied and undeniable in the Church. In 1 Cor. xii. we find him saying: 'To another (is given) the working of miracles'[1] (ver. 10); 'God hath set in the Church miracles'[2] (ver. 28); and again, 'Are all (workers of) miracles?' (ver. 29). We find him, in like manner, in Gal. iii. 5 referring to him 'that worketh miracles among you,' where the word is the same. In these passages, we venture to affirm, the meaning is sufficiently plain, and would never have been seriously questioned, except for dogmatic and apologetic purposes of a negative character. There is no adequate ground whatever for holding that Paul uses the Greek word under consideration[3] in a different sense from what it bears in the New Testament and early writers of the Church. According to New Testament usage, it means either miracles, or the power of working miracles, which comes to the same

[1] Greek, ἐνεργήματα δυνάμεων.
[2] Greek, δυνάμεις.
[3] Viz. δυνάμεις.

thing. The passages which may be adduced in proof of this are sufficiently numerous and plain. We find the 'mighty works' which our Lord had done in Chorazin, Bethsaida, and Capernaum denoted by the very word employed by Paul (Matt. xi. 20–23). We find it used in exactly the same sense in Mark (vi. 2, 5), in Luke (x. 13, xix. 37), in Acts (viii. 13, xix. 11), and in Hebrews (ii. 4). From this we see that the word is commonly used in the New Testament as signifying objective or external miracles. In a few passages it may perhaps be taken rather as meaning miraculous powers, as, for example, in Matt. xiv. 2, where Herod is represented as saying of Jesus that 'mighty powers work in Him' (cf. also Mark vi. 14; Matt. xiii. 54). But in either case, the result is substantially the same, and points to objective miracles. And, as we have said, there is no sufficient reason for supposing that Paul used the word in an entirely different sense from the other New Testament writers. He uses the singular in the same way as they do; he uses the plural once in the sense of governments,—just as they also do,—in a context where the meaning is plain (Rom. viii. 38); and therefore in the other passages, which are in contexts plainly dealing with the miraculous, we must conclude that he uses it in the sense which it generally bears in the New Testament, that is, miracles, or powers of working miracles. Indeed, we may affirm that in every passage in the New Testament, outside of the four Epistles with which we have to do, where the word under consideration is used with verbs of working, it means miracles or miraculous powers, and there is no valid ground for interpreting it otherwise in the writings of Paul. We maintain, accordingly, that the expression 'working of miracles' or 'miraculous powers,' in the passages adduced, must refer either directly or indirectly to objective miracles. The apostle therefore bears his testimony to the existence of such miracles or powers of working miracles in the Christian Church, and refers to them as notorious and undeniable.

We come, last of all, to examine another and most important passage. In 2 Cor. xii. 12, Paul says to the Corinthians, 'Truly the signs of an apostle were wrought among you in all patience, *in signs, and wonders, and mighty deeds*.'[1] It is necessary to observe the connection in which this verse stands. His apostleship had been questioned by certain opponents at Corinth,

[1] Greek, ἐν σημείοις, καὶ τέρασι, καὶ δυνάμεσι.

It may be expected that we should add here, as a second passage in which the apostle explicitly refers to his own miracles, Rom. xv. 18, 19 (cf. Revised Version); but as the last two chapters of this Epistle are rejected by both Baur and the author of *Supernatural Religion*, they are excluded from our consideration. At the same time, it is right to say that these chapters are accepted by Hilgenfeld and Renan, and, to use Alford's expression, can only be rejected by the 'very insanity of hypercriticism.' Accepting them as unquestionably genuine, we see that Paul therein bears explicit testimony to the facts *that he himself wrought miracles*, and *that the other apostles wrought them also*.

and in the preceding verse he says, 'In nothing am I behind the very chiefest apostles.' Then he goes on in this verse to give the proof; for 'truly the signs of an apostle were wrought among you,' etc. There is scarcely any need to say that past interpreters have unanimously understood this verse to mean that Paul, or God through Paul, wrought among the Corinthians visible miracles in attestation of his apostleship. We may venture to affirm that this is the only natural meaning of the verse, and that no other would ever have been wrested out of it unless it had been necessary for the support of dogmatic unbelief. The verse, we believe, unquestionably means that Paul claims to have wrought miracles himself at Corinth, and on no other ground can his argument have the slightest force.

The question which we have first to look at here is, What is the meaning of the accumulated expression, 'signs, and wonders, and mighty deeds'? It is the strongest and most emphatic expression for external miracles known in the New Testament, and in ancient scriptural Greek. We have already considered the meaning of the word rendered 'mighty deeds.' We have now to consider the meaning of the other two words, 'signs and wonders,' and we take them together for the sake of brevity, and because they are frequently used together. The question then is, What do the words so translated [1] habitually mean in Scripture Greek? The answer is by no means difficult.

The apostle may have derived the formula from the Septuagint, or Greek translation of the Old Testament. He used this translation habitually, it was his Bible to a large extent, and hence we naturally ask, what is the meaning of the words there? The formula is used altogether between twenty and thirty times in the Septuagint, and there can be no doubt whatever about its meaning. It is the highest expression which this version knows for miracles. It is found three times in Exodus, applied to the 'signs and wonders' performed by God through Moses in the land of Egypt (vii. 3, xi. 9, 10). It is used ten times in Deuteronomy, and in seven it is applied to the same miracles in Egypt (Deut. iv. 34, vi. 22, vii. 19, xi. 3, etc.); once in Nehemiah (ix. 10), thrice in the Psalms (lxxvii. 43, civ. 26, cxxxiv. 9), twice in Jeremiah (xxxii. 20, 21), all with the same explicit reference. In these passages, therefore, it means miracles, beyond a doubt. Of the remaining passages, in one it refers to the 'curses' which God would bring upon Israel for disobedience (Deut. xxviii. 46), where the idea of the supernatural is also apparent. In two passages (Isa. viii. 18, xx. 3) Isaiah uses it of himself as being a sign and a wonder to Israel, where it is true the miraculous is not so obvious. In three

[1] Viz. σημεῖα καὶ τέρατα.

other passages the miraculous is clearly meant—Deut. xiii. 1, 2, and Dan. iii. 33, vi. 27,—the last two passages referring to the miraculous incidents in the life of Nebuchadnezzar and Daniel. In every case where the formula is used with a verb of action, it signifies *external and visible miracles,* and we see that it is especially applied to the miracles of Moses. In short, the Septuagint knows no higher form of words to denote miracles, and it was the Bible which Paul used, and from which he probably derived the expression.

We find the continuity of meaning between the Old Testament and the New Testament age kept up in the Apocrypha. The expression occasionally occurs there, and evidently with the same general force. In Baruch ii. 11 it is used explicitly of the signs and wonders in the land of Egypt. It occurs twice in the Wisdom of Solomon, which was written about 100 B.C., and was possibly known to Paul (cf. Rom. ix. 21 with Wisd. xv. 7). In one of these passages it may mean unusual natural events (viii. 8), yet in the other (x. 16) it again has its usual reference to the miracles in the land of Egypt.

Turning to Josephus, who was not only a Jew, but also a contemporary, to a certain extent, of Paul, we find the expression used occasionally in his writings, and distinctly in the sense of something miraculous or supernatural. We do not refer to the fact that he uses both words separately, and generally 'sign' in reference to the miracles of Moses, but to his use of both words together, as in the verse at present before us. We find him applying them to the regression of the shadow on the sun-dial of Ahaz, the sign given to Hezekiah (*Antt.* x. 2. 1); to miracles which impostors pretended should be wrought by the providence of God (xx. 8. 6); and again, to the signs and wonders which preceded the destruction of Jerusalem (*Wars*, Introd. 11). There can be no doubt that Josephus, the contemporary of Paul, uses the words as denoting miracles.

We now come to the New Testament, and the meaning of the words there. The expression occurs about fourteen times outside of those Pauline Epistles to which we are at present restricted. It is applied in three passages to miracles which impostors professed to work (Matt. xxiv. 24; Mark xiii. 22; 2 Thess. ii. 9); eight times to miracles wrought by the apostles or apostolic men (Acts ii. 43, iv. 30, v. 12, vi. 8, xiv. 3, xv. 12; [Rom. xv. 19]; Heb. ii. 4); once to the miracles performed by Moses in the land of Egypt (Acts vii. 36), and twice to the miracles performed by our Lord (Acts ii. 22; John iv. 48, more generally), in all of which the meaning plainly is external, visible miracles. The addition of the word 'mighty deeds' to these two words only increases the force of the expression, as in other passages (Acts ii. 22; Heb. ii. 4; [2 Thess. ii. 9]).

Surely it is plain from these texts what is the meaning of the expression in the New Testament. Beyond all reasonable contradiction, it refers to visible miracles or supernatural events. It is the strongest New Testament expression for miracles; and if it does not mean miracles, then what other stronger word or expression can be used for them? If Paul adopted the expression from the Gospels, written or oral, it is clear that he can have meant only visible miracles in the highest sense. When we find that the expression means 'miracles' both in the Septuagint and the New Testament (written or oral), from one or other of which sources Paul must have taken it, can it mean anything else than 'miracles' in the writings of the apostle? Surely not. We are therefore forced to the conclusion, that the apostle used the formula in its accepted sense as the highest expression for real, objective, visible miracles. The verse, accordingly, contains a plain statement by the apostle that he himself wrought miracles; and clearly, unless he was insane, he could not be mistaken in his testimony. Is not this direct, personal testimony to miracles?

But may not the phrase which we have been discussing refer to moral effects of a striking nature wrought within the minds of the Corinthians, akin to reformation, new impulses, increase of moral strength, and the like? Is not this proved by the fact that the Greek for 'among you' is really 'in you'?[1] Certainly not. For, first of all, in no case whatever is the phrase 'signs and wonders' used of merely moral effects wrought in the soul, but only of *objective events visible to the eye.* And secondly, while the words rendered 'among you' may mean 'in you,' they are the common Greek for 'among you,' and no other preposition than that employed could have expressed 'among' more perfectly. To show that the preposition used habitually means 'among' when joined to a plural noun, we might adduce numerous passages from the New Testament. Let the following out of many from the four Epistles suffice: 'That He might be the first-born *among* many brethren' (Rom. viii. 29); 'I say to every one that is *among* you' (xii. 3); 'I determined not to know anything *among* you' (1 Cor. ii. 2); 'We speak wisdom *among* them that are perfect' (ii. 6); 'Is it so that there is not a wise man *among* you?' (vi. 5), etc. As expressions exactly akin to that under consideration, we may quote the following: 'If I had not done *among* them the works which none other man did' (John xv. 24); 'By the hands of the apostles were many signs and wonders wrought *among* the people' (Acts v. 12); 'Stephen did great wonders and miracles *among* the people' (vi. 8). In these expressions the preposition is used with reference to external miracles, exactly as

[1] Greek, ἐν ὑμῖν.

in the verse we have been discussing. In short, the preposition used regularly means 'among' when joined with a plural noun, and is so used in the Greek, and translated in the English Testament, upwards of a hundred times. There is therefore nothing in all this to shake the reference to physical miracles, but everything exactly as if such miracles had been meant.

It is sometimes adduced as a fatal objection to Paul's testimony, that he only makes general statements, and does not narrate any one particular case in which he wrought a miracle. This is true, but the reason is plain. The miracles referred to were notorious,—well known to the Corinthians as wrought amongst them, and not denied apparently by any of them. It would therefore have been quite out of place to have given detailed cases, and quite foreign to the apostle's manner. Accordingly, it is utterly groundless to affirm that because he gives no detailed case, but only general references, therefore he did not really work any miracles. As well might we argue that because he does not give any fully-detailed cases of conversion in the Epistles to the Corinthians and Galatians, but only general statements, therefore no one in these churches had been converted by Paul. No individual miracles of our Lord are narrated in detail in the Acts of the Apostles, and yet no one can doubt that His miracles were well known to the speakers and the writer.

Once more, it is very natural to object that we have not the opportunity of cross-examining the witness. This, of course, is literally the case, and it cannot be helped. Still, we have what is very much equivalent to a cross-examination. There were many men in the churches of Corinth and Galatia, and in other churches, bitterly opposed to Paul, who were ready to scan with eager eyes any flaw in his character, his reasoning, and his testimony, and expose it to the utmost. Yet, in addressing such men, he boldly and categorically refers to miracles as existing facts,—to his own miracles as notorious and undeniable facts, so undeniable that he refers to them as a matter of course, and admitting of no doubt even on the part of his enemies. To have done this, had the whole thing been a delusion or a hoax, would have been sheer madness on the part of Paul; and his opponents would soon have shown up the hollowness of his pretence, overwhelmed him with infamy and ridicule, and hurled him for ever from his position as an apostle. It is certain, however, that they did no such thing, and that the opposition to the apostle soon died out of the Corinthian church. In other words, the statements of the apostle in reference to his own working of miracles in particular, and the existence of miracles in general, bore the test of hostile scrutiny and cross-examination. We accept, therefore, the testimony of Paul to miracles as of the highest possible kind.

We can now go a step further. Looking at 2 Cor. xii. 12, we see that Paul says, in the verse immediately preceding, 'In nothing am I behind the very chiefest apostles.' He does not say he is ahead of them in regard to miracles, but only that he is at least abreast of them. Surely this naturally implies that the other apostles wrought miracles as well as himself. Again, he goes on in ver. 13 to say, 'For what is it wherein ye were inferior to other churches?' The Corinthians were not inferior to other churches in regard to the miracles which had been wrought among them, but he does not say they were superior, and surely this implies that miracles had been wrought in other churches also. In short, just as Paul had wrought miracles, so also had the other apostles; and as miracles had been wrought in Corinth, so had they also been in other churches. In other words, we have here the distinct testimony of Paul to the fact that miracles were wrought not merely by himself and in the church at Corinth, but by the other apostles and in the other early churches.

It should likewise be distinctly noted that the testimony of Paul is practically the testimony of the early Church. To speak of it as the testimony of a solitary and perhaps peculiar man, is evidently absurd. He spoke as the representative of the Church, and gave utterance to what was the universal belief of the Church.

These Epistles bear positive testimony to the fact, that he had the closest relationship with the churches in Jerusalem and Judæa, Syria and Cilicia, Galatia, Ephesus, and Asia Minor in general, Macedonia and Greece, and even indirectly with Rome,—in short, with the churches in almost all the Eastern world (2 Cor. xi. 28). This, too, was in the first generation of Christians, before the year 60, when the Church was fully able to criticise and correct his statements, had that been possible and necessary. Accordingly, when we find that this testimony to miracles is that of a man who was so widely and vitally connected with the Church, and that it was accepted and endorsed by the whole Church, when the work of refuting it, if at all assailable, was very easy, we may reasonably accept it as practically the testimony of the universal Church.

We now conclude our investigation, and the general result is this. We have had before us a witness of the very highest character and veracity, a man of the best education, who had been a bigoted Jew and a furious persecutor, but under the force of irresistible evidence became a Christian ; who, both as persecutor and Christian apostle alike, had every opportunity of examining into the truth of the Christian miracles, and who was prepared to seal, and did seal, his testimony with his blood. He declares that the apostles and other early Christians with whom he came into the closest contact had seen the risen Lord ; he declares that he himself had seen Him ; he bears testimony to the existence of various kinds of miracles in the Church as a notorious fact ; he declares that he himself wrought miracles, and speaks of it as a thing well known, undenied, and undeniable even by his bitterest enemies. Surely, unless he was positively insane, he could not be deceived as to the testimony of his own senses, and as to that which he actually did himself, and for which he had the testimony of his own consciousness. Accordingly, we venture to affirm that the conclusion to which our investigation has led us is, that in the New Testament we have direct personal testimony to miracles, and that of the highest kind ; so that if we regard miracles as provable by testimony at all, we have the most powerful reason for still accepting them as belonging to those things which are to be 'most surely believed among us.'

IX.

THE RESURRECTION OF CHRIST, AND WHAT IT IMPLIES.

'It is said that the theo-philanthropist Larevellière-Lépeaux once confided to Talleyrand his disappointment at the ill-success of his attempt to bring into vogue a sort of improved Christianity, a sort of benevolent rationalism which he had invented to meet the wants of a benevolent age. "His propaganda made no way," he said. "What was he to do?" he asked. The ex-bishop politely condoled with him, feared it was a difficult task to found a new religion, more difficult than could be imagined, so difficult that he hardly knew what to advise! "Still,"—so he went on after a moment's reflection,—"there is one plan which you might at least try: I should recommend you to be crucified, and to rise again the third day."'[1]

This statement so tersely put contains within it an all-important double-edged truth. It contains the explanation of the failure of mere man-made systems

[1] *Natural Religion*, p. 181.

of religion. They fail to a large extent because they want the divine credentials of miracles like our Lord's resurrection, and the spiritual power contained in such a supernatural fact. But it also contains the explanation of the success of Christianity. It is to be found in the fact and power of our Lord's resurrection. We may sometimes meet with those who profess to be Christians, and yet affirm that the truth of Christianity depends but little upon the reality of the resurrection;[1] but Strauss, from his position of determined antagonism, is acute enough to perceive that it is 'the centre of the centre, the real heart of Christianity,' and says, that 'it can scarcely be doubted that with it the truth of Christianity stands or falls.'

It is clear from the New Testament that the apostles attached the profoundest importance to the resurrection of Christ. In their estimation it was the crowning test in regard to His divine mission and propitiatory work. If it was false, then His mission was a delusion, His teaching no less a delusion, and His death that of an impostor, or at best that of an amiable enthusiast. If it was true, then He is the divinely-appointed Messiah, His teaching the eternal truth of God, and His death the propitiation for the sins of the world. Hence it is that the apostles were required, as an important part of their work, to bear personal testimony to the resurrec-

[1] See Appendix, Note XIII.

tion. Hence it is that we find them in their early sermons, as recorded in the Acts, always giving a foremost place to this grand truth. Hence it is that we find it not only laid down as a fact, but taken for granted in all the leading books of the New Testament. And hence it is that we find Paul very explicitly declaring, 'If Christ be not risen, our faith is vain, and we are yet in our sins' (1 Cor. xv. 17). Indeed, we might almost say that the resurrection of Christ is the keystone in the arch of the Christian evidences. If it be removed or broken to pieces, the arch collapses: if it holds, the arch is strong and safe, and able to bear upon it the weight of the whole system of Christian truth.

In endeavouring to establish the fact of the resurrection, it is of importance at the outset that we clearly see what is the kind of proof which we have a right to expect. It is an event of the past, an historical event, and that determines at once that the proof must be mainly historical. We cannot expect mathematical proof; for it is not a mathematical truth. We cannot expect the proof of our own senses; for it is a past and not a present event. We cannot expect the proof of intuition; for that is restricted to necessary and axiomatic truth. It is an historic event belonging to the past, and therefore, from the nature of the case, we must be content mainly with historic proof.

In approaching the consideration of the evidence, it may be well to observe, that there is a distinctly-felt fitness and consistency between the person and character of Christ and the fact of His resurrection. He is represented as the Incarnate Word, as God manifest in the flesh, as the Holy One of God, holy and harmless and undefiled and separate from sinners. Our Christian instinct at once sees that it falls in with the nature of things that such a Person should not see corruption. We can scarcely think of Him becoming the prey of ordinary decomposition in the grave, without a feeling of the utmost incongruity. It may be very natural for man, whose body has been poisoned and permeated with sin, to become the prey of corruption; but it is quite otherwise with the body in which God became incarnate, and which knew no taint of sin. 'It was not possible that He should be holden of death.' Furthermore, it is very obvious that the resurrection was a most natural pledge that He had completed His appointed work, that the conditions of the covenant had been fulfilled, and that the Father had fully accepted His propitiation. In short, it fits, with the utmost consistency, into the New Testament doctrine in regard to the person and work of Christ, and therefore has all the force which the argument from natural congruity can give.

We find that our Lord distinctly foretold the fact that He should rise again. He did so repeatedly, and utterances to this effect are recorded in all the evangelists. He declared that, 'as Jonah was three days and three nights in the whale's belly, so shall the Son of man be three days and three nights in the heart of the earth' (Matt. xii. 40),—a prophecy this all the more likely to have been vividly remembered from its peculiar and memorable form. We find another explicit statement in Matt. xvi. 21, in connection with the strong rebuke to Peter, 'Get thee behind Me, Satan,' a circumstance well calculated to impress it deeply upon the minds of the apostles. It is to be noted that this prophecy is also related by Mark (chap. viii. 27–33), and that he wrote his Gospel from the recollections of Peter, who could not possibly have forgotten the circumstance. Again, He charged His disciples after the transfiguration, that they should 'tell the vision to no man, until the Son of man be risen again from the dead' (Matt. xvii. 9; Mark ix. 9). It is to be noticed that this announcement is not only given in two Gospels, but is also connected with an incident which must have helped to fix it indelibly in the minds of the apostles. Once more, we find Him saying in John ii. 19, 'Destroy this temple, and in three days I will raise it up,' in which He refers, as John declares, to His resurrection. That this statement was actually made by Christ is rendered certain in the highest degree by the fact, that it is brought up in Matthew and Mark in connection with His crucifixion (Matt. xxvi. 61, xxvii. 40; Mark xiv. 58, xv. 29). Here again the prophecy is bound up with a statement which made a deep impression on the minds of those who heard it. We pass over other prophecies of a more general kind, such as Matt. xvii. 22, 23, Mark ix. 30, 31, and John xii. 24, and confine ourselves to the above. We would only draw attention to the fact, that they are to be found in all the evangelists, and are connected with incidents or utterances so striking that they were sure, apart from any theory of inspiration, to have been correctly remembered.

We now come to the fact itself and the historical proof of it. It is natural, first of all, to inquire what the Roman guards had to say; for they were the only persons present. They were not men likely to be easily deceived or frightened, and had no friendly feeling towards Jesus; not to speak of the stern severity of the Roman discipline. Yet they reported to the chief priests that an earthquake had taken place, that a strange apparition had appeared and rolled away the stone. It is not said that they actually saw Jesus come forth from the tomb, and probably this may not have been the case. But overwhelmed though they were with terror, it is certain that they knew that the tomb was opened and that the body had disappeared. They reported so much to the chief priests, and agreed on the reception of a bribe to keep silence in regard to the miracle, and to declare that 'His disciples came by night, and stole Him away while they slept' (Matt. xxviii. 2–4, 11–15). In other words, we find that the Roman soldiers who acted as guard over the sepulchre by night, bear their testimony, as far as could be expected, to the fact of our Lord's resurrection.

We next come to the testimony of the apostles. And here let it be observed that we have no reason to believe that we have a record of the whole of our Lord's appearances after the resurrection. Indeed, we have good reason for believing that we have not, just as we have not a full record of His miracles before the resurrection. At all events, when Luke says that to His apostles He 'showed Himself alive after His passion by many infallible proofs, being seen of them forty days, and speaking of the things pertaining to the kingdom of God,' there is room to believe that other appearances and conversations took place besides those recorded in the sacred books.

We find the fact that the resurrection took place on the third day recorded by all the evangelists and the Apostle Paul, and that in the most explicit terms. We have distinct notice in the New Testament of at least ten separate appearances. It is a little difficult to determine the exact order of these, but the following is probably correct: — I. The appearance to Mary Magdalene, Mark xvi. 9; John xx. 16: II. To the other women, Matt. xxviii. 9, 10: III. To Peter, Luke xxiv. 34; 1 Cor. xv. 5: IV. To the two disciples on the way to Emmaus, Luke xxiv. 13–33: V. To the apostles, Thomas being absent, Luke xxiv. 36–44; John xx. 19–23: VI. To the eleven apostles, John xx. 26–29: VII. To the disciples at the Sea of Tiberias, John xxi.: VIII. To 'more than five hundred brethren,' probably including the eleven apostles, on a mountain in Galilee, Matt. xxviii. 16; 1 Cor. xv. 6: IX. To James, 1 Cor. xv. 7: X. To the apostles at the Mount of Olives immediately before the ascension, Acts i. 4–12. In short, we have two appearances recorded by Matthew, three by Mark, four by Luke, four by John, and five by Paul.

We cannot enter into a detailed discussion of those different appearances; but a few remarks are necessary. They are numerous, sufficiently numerous to attest the fact beyond a doubt. They were made to numerous witnesses of different classes, at different times, in different places and circumstances. Some of the cases are fully detailed, as that to the two disciples on the way to Emmaus, that to the seven disciples at the Sea of Galilee, and that to the eleven at the ascension. They had not merely the testimony of their eyesight, but of their ears, and even their hands as well (Matt. xxviii. 9). They had this witness, not merely in the dark or twilight, but in the daylight; not merely for a passing moment, but for a length of time. They not only saw the Lord, but heard Him speak; and they not only heard Him speak, but carried on lengthened conversations with Him. The apostles could not possibly be deceived in regard to the matter, and they had no reason to tell lies about it. They showed the depth of their conviction by devoting their lives to the proclamation of the truth, in spite of loss, of toil, of shame and persecution, and finally in many cases they sealed their testimony with their blood. If ever there was sufficient testimony to the real appearance and identity of a person, we may reasonably say that we have it here.

When we pass from the direct testimony of the four evangelists to the other books of the New Testament, we find that the fact of the resurrection runs through them all. It formed one of the grand fundamental themes of the preaching of the apostles as recorded in the Acts. Peter dwelt on it at great length on the day of Pentecost in Jerusalem, where the event had taken place only seven weeks before, and when the imposture, had it been such, could easily have been detected and exposed (Acts ii. 22–33). He not only declares the resurrection of Christ, but affirms that he and all his fellow-apostles were witnesses of the fact. He boldly declares the same truth in the Sanhedrim, the very council which a few weeks before had condemned Jesus; and it is plain that, instead of producing the dead body and exposing the delusion, they quailed before the dauntless witnesses, as they affirmed, 'We cannot but speak the things which we have seen and heard' (Acts iv. 10, 15–20). We find the same truth fully proclaimed by Paul in the synagogue at Antioch in Pisidia (Acts xiii. 29–37), in Athens, the very centre of ancient culture and philosophy (xvii. 31), and before Festus and Agrippa at Cæsarea (xxvi. 23, 26).[1] Clearly, if we are to accept the testimony of the Acts at all, it is certain that the Church was founded on the fact of our Lord's resurrection.

We next proceed to consider the testimony of Peter as recorded by himself in his First Epistle.[2] This, as we have seen, is one of the fully-accredited books of the New Testament, and continued unquestioned down to the days of modern unbelief. We must bear in mind, as we discuss the testimony of Peter, that he was an apostle, an eye-witness of the risen Saviour, and even had a special appearance granted to himself. Now as to his testimony there can be no doubt. He declares that God the Father 'hath begotten us again unto a lively hope by the resurrection of Jesus Christ from the dead' (i. 3). Again he says, 'God raised Him up from the dead and gave Him glory, so that your faith and hope might be in God' (i. 21). And once more, at the close of the difficult passage in the third chapter, he

[1] Cf. also Acts i. 21, 22, iii. 15, iv. 33, x. 40, 41.

[2] I leave the Second Epistle out of consideration, because of the doubts which long existed in regard to its authenticity, and which are still entertained even by some Christian authors.

declares that 'baptism doth now save us through the resurrection of Jesus Christ' (iii. 21). It is as certain as language can make it, that Peter, the frequent eye-witness of the risen Lord, in his First Epistle testifies explicitly to the resurrection, and everywhere takes it for granted as an understood and fundamental fact.

From the testimony of the eye-witness Peter, we pass to that of the eye-witness John, as given in the Revelation. And we have a very special reason for laying stress upon this testimony; for it will be remembered that this is one of the five books of the New Testament accepted by the extreme school of negative criticism in our day. On their authority we may certainly accept it as genuine, and as written about the year 68. We ask then, Have we any testimony to our Lord's resurrection in this book, which our opponents accept as the genuine work of John? We have, beyond all reasonable possibility of doubt. In chap. i. 5 he speaks of Jesus Christ as 'the first-born of the dead,' which, in spite of all ingenious and special pleading, can only mean that He was the first who had risen from the dead to resurrection-life. In the same chapter (ver. 18) he represents the glorified Christ as saying, 'I was dead, and behold I am alive for evermore, and I have the keys of death and of Hades.' In like manner we read in chap. ii. 8, 'These things saith the first and the last, which was dead, and lived again.' There can be no reasonable doubt that these passages distinctly state, as much of the book distinctly implies, the fact of our Lord's resurrection. In other words, John, the beloved apostle and eye-witness, in this book, which is accepted as genuine by the most hostile scholars, bears clear testimony to the resurrection.

In considering the testimony of Paul, we restrict ourselves to that contained in his first four Epistles, already shown to be accepted as incontestably genuine by the extreme school of negative criticism in Germany, France, and England. It is not at all necessary to adduce general references to the fact; for from the beginning of Romans to the end of Galatians such references are numerous, both implicit and explicit.

The passage which chiefly claims our attention is the well-known statement contained in 1 Cor. xv. 3–8, 'I delivered unto you first of all that which I also received, how that Christ died for our sins according to the Scriptures; and that He was buried, and that He rose again the third day according to the Scriptures; and that He was seen of Cephas, then of the twelve: after that, He was seen of above five hundred brethren at once; of whom the greater part remain unto this present, but some are fallen asleep. After that, He was seen of James, then of all the apostles. And last of all He was seen of me also, as of one born out of due time.'

Now the testimony of this passage is very explicit

and very much to the point. Paul had the most abundant and direct means of communicating with these apostles and disciples. He tells us in Galatians (chaps. i. and ii.) that he came into the closest contact with Cephas, James, and John, and those 'which were of reputation' at Jerusalem, and compared his Gospel with theirs. But as the resurrection was the keystone of the whole, it is certain that it must have formed a central question for consideration. Accordingly, there can scarcely be the slightest doubt that the apostle here relates the testimony which he had received from the apostles and early disciples. 'It cannot be doubted,' says the author of *Supernatural Religion*, 'that Paul was told that such appearances had taken place.' And Strauss declares no less emphatically, 'There is no occasion to doubt that the Apostle Paul had heard this from Peter, James, and perhaps from others concerned; and that all of these, even the five hundred, were firmly convinced that they had seen Jesus who had been dead, and alive again.'[1] It ought also to be remembered that the apostle had himself been a persecutor, accustomed to examine and cross-examine the Christian martyrs and confessors, so that he knew all about the resurrection from the side of the enemies as well as of the friends of Christianity. And once more, it should be remembered that the apostle is here dealing with

[1] *New Life of Jesus*, vol. i. p. 400.

opponents who denied the doctrine of a real resurrection, and who would only have been too eager to refute his statements, had that been possible. Here then we have the statement of an undoubted contemporary, a man who knew the facts both as a persecutor and as an apostle, a statement made to opponents, a statement by a witness of the very highest character, who forsook all for his testimony, was ready at any moment to die for it, and at last did die for it. What higher testimony can we have or even conceive?

But it may be said that we have even higher and more direct testimony than this. The apostle says: 'Last of all He was seen of me also, as of one born out of due time' (1 Cor. xv. 8). We have already dwelt at some length on this appearance in a previous study, and it is not necessary to do so again. As we then saw, there can be no doubt that the apostle here refers to a real external view of the risen and glorified Lord; to no spectral illusion, but a true objective appearance of Christ in His resurrection-body as it continues in heaven. As such it was really a proof of the resurrection. Still, as several years, perhaps six or seven, had passed since the event, this appearance, to many minds, may not seem so powerful a proof. It may be said that if Moses could appear with a glorified body in the mount of transfiguration, without a previous resurrection, so also may it have been with Christ. Yet even in this view it was a miraculous appearance of Christ, which implied the truth of His resurrection. We say that it implied the reality of His resurrection; for, like other miracles, it must have been at least a 'sign' in attestation of truth, and very particularly, as appears from the connection in which Paul introduces it and the stress which he lays upon it, in attestation of the fact of Christ's resurrection. In either case, therefore, directly or indirectly, the appearance to the apostle was a proof of the event.

Another powerful argument is to be found in the extraordinary change which took place in the minds of the apostles at the supposed date of the resurrection, It was a change, sudden, deep, thoroughgoing, and abiding. Before this date they were entangled in narrow, worldly views of Christ's Messiahship; immediately thereafter, they broke through into a clear perception of its spiritual nature and world-wide bearing. Before it, they were overwhelmed with unutterable sorrow and depression, almost with helpless despair; immediately thereafter, they burst forth into exultant assurance and joy, and inextinguishable hope. Previously, they were feeble, timid, almost cowardly, so that the boldest among them denied the Lord when questioned by a servant-maid; all at once they became fearless and unflinching in their confession of Him, and in testifying to His resurrection. Previously, they were small and selfish in their aims, quarrelling about the most lucrative and honourable places in the expected worldly kingdom; immediately thereafter, they have trampled out their selfishness, and are ready to sacrifice, and do sacrifice, all things, even life itself, for Christ. Such a change as this could have been produced only by a firm belief in the fact of the resurrection. This is admitted even by negative critics themselves. Baur, for example, says: 'Only the miracle of the resurrection could dispel the doubt which appeared necessarily to dismiss faith itself into the eternal night of death.'[1] It is no doubt true that Baur might try to explain away 'the miracle' here as being only something mysterious and mental, though by no means supernatural. But he holds that the disciples had the 'most firm and immovable faith' in the resurrection. This, however, in their case almost necessarily implies that it was a real fact; for they had the best means of knowing, and could not be deceived as to what they saw, and heard, and felt.

Closely connected with the above, is the argument derived from the early planting and remarkable success of the Church in Jerusalem. Of this we have the narrative at length in the opening chapters of the Acts. The apostles did not go away to Samaria or Antioch, Ephesus, Corinth, or Rome, to preach the resurrection and make the first beginning of the Church. They

[1] *Kirchengeschichte d. drei ersten Jahrhunderte*, p. 39.

began at Jerusalem, where the event had taken place, and just seven weeks after it had taken place, when the memory of the past must have been quite fresh and minute. If it was an utter delusion, it would still be easy to extinguish it. The priests might still produce the dead body, and that would settle the matter. Or they might bring forward the soldiers of the Roman guard and have them examined on oath. Instead of doing that, however, they bribed them to keep silence in regard to what had actually taken place. Some at least of the disciples might have been frightened by persecution and the terror of death, to become informers and expose the deception. But no such thing ever took place. On the contrary, three thousand were added to the Church in one day; very soon after, we read of five thousand Christian men in Jerusalem, not to speak of women and children; and we are expressly told that 'a great company of the priests were obedient to the faith.' And all this was accomplished by the preaching of the resurrection, in the very city where it was declared to have taken place, and only seven weeks thereafter. If it was an utter delusion and a myth, surely it is impossible reasonably to account for the planting and rapid progress of the Church, as described in the Acts and in Paul's Epistles. In other words, the early planting and the rapid success and continuance of the Church, form a very substantial proof of Christ's resurrection.

The Church is indeed the monument of His resurrection, and a monument reaching back to the very date.

It may not be amiss to draw attention to the fact, that the existence of the Lord's day as the special worship-day of the Church, is also a proof possessed of no small force. It is an institution running back without interruption to the very resurrection. In the Revelation of John (i. 10), one of the books accepted by negative critics, we have explicit mention made of it, under the name of 'the Lord's day,' in such a way as to indicate that it was familiarly known. We find mention made of it under the name of 'the first day of the week' in 1 Cor. xvi. 2, another of the books accepted by negative critics, and written about A.D. 57. In the Acts, we find that the disciples 'came together on the first day of the week' (Acts xx. 7). In the Gospel of John we find them assembled on the first Lord's day after the resurrection (John xx. 26). And why was the worship-day changed from the seventh to the first day of the week? No other reason worth notice has been given, or can be given, than the fact that it was the day on which the resurrection took place. When we can trace a commemorative institution back to the very time of the event commemorated, as in the present case, it becomes a most powerful proof of the event.

We may now proceed to look at some of the hypotheses suggested by opponents to explain away this to them very troublesome fact of Christ's resurrection. We need only to mention the earliest of these methods. It was that adopted by the priests, as recorded in Matthew, viz. that the disciples stole away the body by night. The text which records it also refutes it, by declaring that it was, and was known to be, a device for explaining away a most damaging truth. Furthermore, if the disciples stole the body, they must have known that Christ remained dead, and saw corruption. But this supposition, in view of their conduct afterwards, is utterly incredible, and may be at once dismissed.

Another hypothesis which has been propounded is, that Christ was never really dead; that He only fell into a temporary swoon through suffering and the loss of blood; and that in course of time animation was restored, perhaps through the influence of the fragrant spices. But in view of this, what are we to make of the great wound in His side from which the blood and water flowed? What are we to make of the fact that the Roman soldiers, who had some experience in such matters, and those who took part in His burial, clearly regarded Him as dead? What are we to make of the statements of the New Testament, which everywhere regards His death as a most certain fact? Also, what became of Jesus after He recovered from the swoon? Did He hide Himself from His disciples and retire to some desert cave? Did He live and die in utter obscurity, and quietly allow His disciples to go on preaching the great lie of the resurrection, and to suffer martyrdom for it? Surely this also must be utterly incredible.

In view of the above hypothesis, we may also well ask how we are to explain the many recorded appearances. They must have been fatal to the belief in a true resurrection; for the appearance of a poor, feeble, wounded, ghastly man never could be mistaken for a triumphant resurrection from the dead. But perhaps we cannot do better than let Strauss sweep away this hypothesis in his usual trenchant way: 'It is impossible that a being who had stolen half-dead out of the sepulchre, who crept about weak and ill, wanting medical treatment, who required bandaging, strengthening, and nursing, and who yet at last yielded to His sufferings, could have given to the disciples the impression that He was a conqueror over death and the grave, the Prince of Life, an impression which lay at the basis of their future ministry. Such a resuscitation could only have weakened the impression which He had made upon them in life and in death, but could by no possibility have changed their sorrow into enthusiasm, have elevated their reverence into worship.'[1]

[1] *New Life of Jesus*, vol. i. p. 412. Compare a passage of equal vigour and to the same effect in Keim, *Geschichte Jesu von Nazara*, vol. iii. p. 576; and Fairbairn, *Studies in the Life of Christ*, p. 339.

There yet remains the third, and for the present the favourite explanation, namely, that by means of spectral illusions. It is known by the name of the 'vision hypothesis.' That is, the appearances of the risen Lord were not real objective appearances. They were spectral illusions, mere inward visions, having their seat in morbid nerves, and souls full of sorrow, of eager desire, of enthusiasm and expectation. This is the view adopted by Strauss, Renan, and the author of *Supernatural Religion.* It is, however, more especially Renan who has brought it into notice in our country. According to him, it is mainly to the love, the strong imagination, and peculiar nervous system of Mary of Magdala that we owe the resurrection. She had a spectral vision of the Lord, and from that illusion arose the myth of the resurrection. 'Divine power of love!' he exclaims in a way quite characteristic, 'sacred moments, when the passion of a woman under hallucination (*d'une hallucinée*) gives to the world a God restored from the dead!'[1]

But very slight reflection will enable any one to see that this view is quite as absurd and untenable as either of the preceding. If there had been only one appearance, and that to Mary Magdalene, it might not have seemed so unreasonable; although, of course, there would still remain the certain fact of the open and

[1] *Vie de Jésus*, p. 434, 12th edition.

empty grave to be explained. But the multitude and variety of the witnesses, and the number and the circumstances of the appearances, place this explanation beyond the bounds of all probability. The apostles and the early disciples were not all crazy, or men of feeble and diseased nerves, the kind of subjects for seeing spectres and illusions. Furthermore, they do not appear to have had any expectation of the resurrection, and were not looking for it in the least. They were utterly surprised by the fact, and did not believe in it until they were overwhelmed with the evidence. They were not therefore in a state predisposing them to see such visions. In any case, spectral illusions are extremely rare occurrences, and it is infinitely more rare that the very same spectral illusion should occur to different individuals. But what have we here? We have the same form appearing to men of different temperaments and in perfect health, which is not the case with spectral illusions. We have the risen Lord appearing at different times, and in very different parts of the country, which is not the case with mere illusions. We have Him appearing not to one or two merely, but to groups of ten or eleven, and even to a company of more than five hundred, which is not the case with spectral illusions. We see Him not only appearing, but even being touched and held fast, which is not the case with mere illusions. We see Him not only appearing to the disciples, but holding long conversations with them, speaking and being spoken to, and surely that is not the manner of spectral illusions. Why also did these visions cease at the end of forty days, and not reappear at the excitement of the first Pentecost? It is not necessary to proceed further. Such spectral illusions as this hypothesis requires are plainly contrary to all 'experience,' and utterly inadequate to explain the facts. The very desperateness of the hypothesis is one of the best proofs that the reported facts are real facts. In short, the only method of explanation, which is simple with all the simplicity of the truth, is that which accepts the resurrection as a certain fact.[1]

We now conclude our present study. And what is the natural outcome of the whole? It is that the resurrection of our Lord is an historical reality. The Church is not founded on a spectral illusion, still less on deception or a deliberate lie, but on a fact, the fact of Christ's resurrection. And who does not see at a glance the supreme importance and wide sweep of this conclusion? It gives us new reasons for believing in God, proving His existence as a free Person above and behind nature; for 'He raised Him up from the dead, so that our faith and hope might be in God.' It proves the divine commission of the Lord: He was 'declared to be the Son of God with power, by the

[1] See Appendix, Note XIV.

resurrection from the dead.' It proves that His propitiatory work was perfect, and that God fully accepted it as such. It is the divine seal set upon all His teaching, so that we may now accept His revelations of truth above the reach of human reason as being fully authoritative and certain. It affords the highest assurance which we could possibly conceive that He will carry on the work of salvation to completion, both in the individual and in the world: 'For if when we were enemies we were reconciled to God by the death of His Son, much more, being reconciled, we shall be saved by His life.' It is a proof that He 'hath abolished death,' and 'destroyed him that hath the power of death.' It is a pledge of a coming judgment-day, when Christ will sit as Judge: for of this 'God hath given assurance unto all men, in that He hath raised Him from the dead.' It is a proof and earnest of our own resurrection to a glorious immortality; for 'Christ is risen from the dead, and become the first-fruits of them that slept.' Yes, when the stone was rolled from His sepulchre, the crushing weight of hopeless despair was rolled from the bosom of humanity. When the resurrection morning broke, there dawned a day of brighter hope, of purer life, of sweeter light upon the benighted world. When the sepulchre was opened, it proved a fountain whence a stream of heavenly grace and blessing flowed forth for the quickening, refreshing, and cleansing of a dead, and sad, and sinful world. That stream has flowed on, the strong central artery of the world's history, during the eighteen Christian centuries; it is flowing on in the present day; and, as we look down the future, we see it still flowing on from age to age, until at last, far off on the dim horizon, where the earth and heaven seem to meet in a circle of uncreated light, we behold it blending with the eternal ocean. Looking, then, into this empty grave, we may well take up the doxology of Peter: 'Blessed be the God and Father of our Lord Jesus Christ, which according to His abundant mercy hath begotten us again unto a lively hope by the resurrection of Jesus Christ from the dead, to an inheritance incorruptible, and undefiled, and that fadeth not away.'

X.

The Argument for Christianity from the Unique Personality of Christ.

No one can deny that the results produced by Christ in history have been of the most extraordinary kind. He is the fountainhead from which not merely the Church, but all the river of modern history has flowed. He was at once thc solvent which silently disintegrated the mighty power of ancient religion and civilisation, and the constructive spiritual force which built up a new civilisation and religious life. And, indeed, it is not merely Christianity and modern civilisation which owe their origin to Christ, but even such an antagonistic system as Mohammedanism as well; for if Christianity and the Bible had not previously existed, it is certain that Mohammedanism would never have appeared.

But in all this it is evident, that it is Christ Himself who is the living heart, the fountain of spiritual power and energy. The current of modern Christian history received its original impulse directly from Him. If we think of those men who throughout the ages have been the powerful actors and the leading forces therein, we may see at once that it was from Him they drew their inspiration. These men were such as Paul and John, Athanasius and Augustine, Luther and Knox, not to mention hundreds of less famous names. But these men were and would have been nothing without Christ. It was not they, but Christ in them. Their torches were kindled at the heaven-descended fire that burned in Him, and but for Him would have remained for ever dark. At the very first sight, we see that there is evidently something quite unique and extraordinary in Christ.

Looking at the matter in another aspect, we readily see that Christ stands to Christianity in a very different relation from that in which the founder of a philosophy stands to his system. We may have a very complete knowledge of the systems of Aristotle or Epicurus, of Kant or Hegel, of Reid or Herbert Spencer, without any reference whatever to the person and character of their respective authors. But we cannot so separate between Christ and Christianity. In fact, Christ is Christianity. Every doctrine in it of fundamental importance runs up into Him and ends in Him. If we speak of the doctrine of sin, it was that dark fact that brought Him into the world and to the cross; if of the Trinity, it is around His person that the doctrine of the Trinity has always turned; if of atonement, He is the sacrifice. If we think of Christian faith, He is the explicit object of it; if of justification, He is the ground of it; if of sanctification, He is both the pattern of it and the source of all sanctifying power. If we speak of the resurrection, He is the Resurrection and the Life; if of judgment, He is the divinely-appointed Judge; if of heaven, it is because He lives there that His people live there also. As in some of the old ecclesiastical cities of the Continent, the chief streets all lead up to the cathedral at the centre, so all the chief doctrines of Christianity lead up to Christ, and find their centre of system and order in Him. He is the Christian system, the living centre in which all things in it consist. We can no more separate Christ from Christianity, than we can separate the soul from the body without producing instantaneous death.

Nothing shows more convincingly that the personality of Jesus is felt to be something wonderful, than the many attempts which are constantly made by unbelievers to account for it on mere natural principles. They feel instinctively that it is a terrible stumbling-block to them, and that they must explain it away if their systems are ever to succeed. They are fain to ask with Pilate of old, 'What shall we do with Jesus, who is called Christ?' Hence they weary themselves with the vain problem, how they may best dissolve Him into mythic haze, or resolve Him into natural elements. But they have not yet succeeded, and they themselves feel that they have not succeeded. For no sooner has one come forward with his explanation, than brother unbelievers show themselves to be conscious that it is not quite satisfactory. Accordingly, they set themselves anew to the task, only to meet with a similar fate. Paulus explains Jesus on the grounds of the old rationalism; the miracles were only natural events, but mistaken as miraculous through the stupidity of the apostles. Strauss arises and demolishes Paulus, and explains Christ by the hypothesis of myths. Baur, and especially his more extreme followers, prefer to explain Him by modified forgery. Renan finds his explanation in the legendary, not without a decided element of intrigue and intentional deception on the part of Christ. This course of action shows that even the opponents of Christianity consciously feel that the stone of stumbling has not yet been removed. They rush against the Rock of Ages at the risk of dashing themselves to pieces upon its eternal adamant: but it remains firm and immovable as ever,—

> 'As some tall cliff, that lifts its awful form,
> Swells from the vale, and midway leaves the storm;
> Though round its breast the rolling clouds are spread,
> Eternal sunshine settles on its head.'

In considering the person and character of Jesus, we

are confined mainly to the four Gospels as the source of our materials. It is held, indeed, by some that the Christ of the three so-called Synoptics, Matthew, Mark, and Luke, is quite a different person from the Christ of John. That there is a difference between the portraits is true. It is not, however, the difference between two distinct persons, but only between two different views of the same person. The Synoptists show us Jesus teaching among the peasants of Galilee; John, the same Jesus discussing with the priests, rabbis, and learned Jews of Jerusalem. The former show us Jesus in His more public, outward life; the latter, largely, Jesus in His inner life and intercourse with His disciples, and revealing the higher truths of faith. The former show us Jesus speaking mainly in the sunshine; John shows us Jesus speaking when He is already under the shadow of the cross, and in the strange other-world light of His eventide. 'The Christ of the fourth Gospel is the Word of God; but He is still the Son of man. He utters no Sermon on the Mount; but still He preaches the kingdom of heaven. The sheep scattered abroad find in Him still the Good Shepherd. There is no exorcism, but the prince of this world is cast out. There is no transfiguration, but His glory is throughout beheld; no agony in the garden, but His soul is troubled. Mary and Martha reappear, but attended by Lazarus. He does not say,

"This is My body," but He gives His flesh to eat; and words as heavenly and in fuller measure soothe the parting meal. He has the same night watches. He sheds the same tears. He walks the same waters, and ascends up where He was before. His prayer in all the Gospels is intercession—in the last most prolonged and tender. He returns from the grave to breathe the Holy Ghost, and to connect that name with the Father's and His own. His presence is the final hope of the earlier Gospels; His coming, of the last; and the closing charge but repeats all former calls, "Follow thou Me."'[1]

Perhaps the difference between the Synoptics and John may have some light cast upon it by an example. There was no more original and lofty character in ancient Greece than Socrates, none that at a distance more resembled Christ. We have two portraits of him preserved to us, one by Xenophon, and another by Plato, and these not a little different the one from the other. On the ground of this difference some have rejected one or even both as fictitious, just as some critics have done with the portraits of Christ in the Gospels. But this is acknowledged by the ablest thinkers to be a mistake; and it is rightly held that the portraits are of the same real man, only from

[1] Principal Cairns, *Christ the Central Evidence of Christianity*, p. 10. Cf. Row, *The Jesus of the Evangelists*, c. xii.

different points of view. Xenophon, the clear, practical, objective narrator, gives us one view, in which he photographs what suited his taste and stuck to his mind, while he leaves out or even misapprehends the greater heights and depths in his master. Plato again, a man of a much more exalted type, presents boldly and abundantly those higher and deeper reaches of the character and teaching of Socrates which fell in with his philosophic taste and mind, to the exclusion largely of more superficial elements and traits. Sometimes he even interfuses his own personality with that of Socrates in such a degree, that Plato and Socrates imperceptibly blend in thought and style of language. Yet, after all, the representations of Xenophon and Plato are only two different aspects, the outer and the inner, of a rich and varied personality, each author having treasured up that for which he had a special receptivity. And so is it in great measure with the Jesus of the Gospels. The two representations are the outer and the inner, the simpler and the deeper aspects of the character and teaching of Jesus, with here and there innumerable points of contact between them, which show that the two streams ever and anon run braided into one another, and are therefore one and the self-same river of life.[1]

Now the Gospels present to us Jesus as unique in

[1] See Appendix, Note XV.

His sinlessness. While the Old Testament and the New alike represent all men as tainted with sin and guilty of sinful acts, the Gospels represent Jesus as the Holy One of God. They tell us that He explicitly claimed to be sinless. 'I am the Truth;' 'Which of you,' saith He, 'convicteth Me of sin?' And He not only made the claim, but His whole life and conduct were consistent with His claim. The Gospels contain no acknowledgment at any time of sin on the part of Jesus, and record no word of confession that ever escaped His lips. His friends who knew Him best, and His enemies who hated Him most, alike unite in their testimony to His stainless character. Peter, a constant, close, and favoured eye-witness, declares that He was 'without blemish and without spot,' that 'He did no sin, neither was guile found in His mouth.' Pilate and Herod find no fault in Him, and alike declare Him innocent. The Jews never bring forward any charge of sin or wrong-doing against Him, not even at His trial. The very traitor himself, the miserable Judas, who no doubt would have been glad to soothe his conscience with the excuse that Jesus was just a sinner like other men, and deserved to die for His pretensions, declared, 'I have sinned in that I have betrayed innocent blood,' and went and hanged himself. The Gospels, like the Epistles, represent Jesus as 'holy, harmless, undefiled, and separate from sinners.'

But the idea of a sinless man was something quite new and uncommon among the Jews, and not likely to have occurred to a forger. The Old Testament contains the strongest expressions in regard to the universal sinfulness of man: 'There is not a just man upon the earth, that doeth good and sinneth not.' The doctrine of the New Testament is the very same. It takes up and repeats the saying of the Old Testament, 'There is none righteous, no, not one,' and adds its own strong statement thereto, 'All have sinned, and come short of the glory of God.' From this we see that the idea of a sinless man was quite foreign to Jewish modes of thought, and not likely to have been ventured on by a mere forger.

But what is of far more importance, is the fact that the Gospels do not merely affirm Jesus to be sinless, but consistently depict Him as always living, speaking, and acting as the sinless One. This is just the rock on which the forger would have gone to pieces. It was easy to declare Jesus sinless, but a very different and difficult thing to represent Him naturally all through as leading a sinless life. Yet this is exactly what we find in the Gospels. They exhibit to us the real living Jesus. They show Him to us in all departments of life: in public and in private; in quiet, and in sudden and trying crises; in the midst of applause and success, and in the midst of bitter opposition and persecution; in the enjoyment of social intercourse and friendship; in the agonies of Gethsemane and the cross; in short, in all conceivable circumstances. Yet in them all, He is still the same sinless One. He is never overtaken in a fault, never loses His self-possession for a moment, ever maintains the most complete equilibrium and presence of mind. Yea, His self-possession and stable holiness only shine out more clearly as the circumstances are more trying, just as the stars shine out most distinctly in proportion as the night is dark.

Without condescending to further details, it may be well to look for a little at the way in which He faced and went through death. It was altogether wonderful and strange. He went on towards it knowingly, under an awful inward impulse; so awful that His very manner, when He was consciously under it, filled the disciples with fear. When He set His face stedfastly to go to Jerusalem to suffer, 'they were amazed, and, as they followed Him, they were sore afraid.' It is clear that He might have escaped His death, humanly speaking, at any moment up to the last. There was no outward necessity compelling Him to go up to Jerusalem, or, once there, to remain there; no necessity for continuing in the garden of Gethsemane, or for surrendering Himself to Judas and his band. It was all a matter of pure free-will on His part. Then what divine dignity and calm self-possession during all His unrighteous and insulting trial! What divine self-forgetfulness and compassion as He toils under the weight of the cross along the way to Calvary!—'Daughters of Jerusalem, weep not for Me, but weep for yourselves, and for your children.' What divine self-forgetfulness and compassion even in the agonies of the cross! Though in the intensest suffering, He thinks of all others before Himself; of them first, and of Himself last of all. He prays for His murderers: 'Father, forgive them, for they know not what they do.' He answers the prayer of the penitent thief: 'Verily I say unto thee, To-day shalt thou be with Me in paradise.' He tenderly makes provision for His widowed mother, as He says to John, 'Behold thy mother.' Only after His murderers, the penitent malefactor, and His mother, does He think of Himself, and say, 'I thirst: it is finished; Father, into Thy hands I commend My spirit.' Surely such a death is not after the manner of men; and as we reverently behold afar off, we may well confess with the centurion, 'Truly this was the Son of God.'[1]

In short, when we compare Jesus with the ordinary sons of men, even when ennobled and sanctified by the Spirit of God, we find that He gathers up into Himself, as into a perfect flower, all the moral beauty and fragrance that can adorn humanity. In Him we find meekness greater than that of Moses, meekness that never fails; firmness greater than that of Elijah, a firm-

[1] See Appendix, Note XVI.

ness that never falters; a nature more kingly than that of David, and which never stoops to a single act of meanness; wisdom greater than that of Solomon, a wisdom never at fault; patience greater than that of Job, a patience that never murmurs; a zeal and an activity which were greater than those of Paul; and a love most pure and lofty, of which that of John was but the shadow. Every grace is found in Him in its own proper place and setting, every grace at its best and fairest, every grace without a flaw.[1]

In thorough keeping with His moral perfection, we can also see at once that the personality of Christ is one of transcendent power. Nothing shows its singular power more overwhelmingly than the effect which it produced upon His apostles. They were very ordinary men, humble fishermen for the most part, who but for Him would have lived and died utterly unknown. It was not they who made Jesus, but Jesus who made them what they afterwards became. It was He who awakened, quickened, ennobled, transfigured their common earthly natures. He put into them a new life, was indeed the very life of their life. He inspired them with an all-consuming love and devotion to Himself, so that they were willing to live, to work, to die for Him, even 'rejoicing to be counted worthy to suffer shame for His

[1] See Appendix, Note XVII.; cf. Kennedy, *Christian Evidences*, Part II. c. iii.

name.' It was He who delivered them from their carnal views, and enabled them to rise up to the conception of an intensely spiritual religion and kingdom of God. He freed them from the galling chains of a proud and narrow Judaism, and possessed them with the sublime idea of a universal religion and a holy brotherhood of man. He inspired them with His own bravery and firmness, so that they who were previously timid and feeble were able to suffer persecution, to stand undaunted before kings and magistrates, and to face a martyr's death with a heroic dignity hitherto unknown. He filled them with that irrepressible and inexhaustible energy which made them known as the men who turned the world upside down, and enabled them to inaugurate the most wonderful revolution and movement that the world has ever seen. When we consider that He produced such marvellous effects on such commonplace materials, and made out of them such noble and powerful personalities, we must see herein a proof of the supreme power of Christ's own personality. 'The faith, the enthusiasm, the constancy of the first generation of Christians can be explained only by supposing at the origin of the movement a man of colossal proportions;'[1] yea, One who is more than man.

When we pass from His character and person to His teaching, we perceive the same uniqueness and

[1] Renan, *Vie de Jésus*, p. 448.

originality. We observe this in the very manner of it. To a large degree it assumes the outward form of the parable. It is not meant that Jesus was the first and only teacher who used the parable, for we have some specimens in the Old Testament and the Talmud; but He is the one great Teacher who made a supreme use of this method. Further, and looking a little more deeply into His manner, He teaches not by reasoning out His truths from previous premises, as is the case with man. He does not gather up facts and evidence by laborious study, and then by ordinary processes of logic draw His conclusions from them. He sees and knows the truth directly and intuitively. He does not reason it out, He reveals it. He teaches by direct and authoritative revelation: 'Verily, verily, I say unto you, We speak that We do know, and testify that We have seen.' He speaks directly to heart and conscience, as one who knows exactly what is the state of each individual man. He frequently replies even to the unuttered thoughts, doubts, and feelings of the hearer—a fact which explains much of the difficulty and many of the sudden transitions that we have in His utterances. 'He taught as one having authority, and not as the scribes.'

Another grand characteristic of Christ as a teacher, was the fact that He aimed at the inmost soul. His great and immediate aim was to reach the essential man, and to implant there the potent germ of a new principle and life. This method was not indeed altogether peculiar or original, for it had been largely the method followed by the ancient prophets. But it was almost if not entirely unique in that age in Palestine—an age in which religion had crystallized into external, punctilious ritualism. He alone had the divine originality, the strength and the courage, to break through the method of mere ritualism, to break away from it and to break it up. He taught men that religion was not merely an outward church etiquette or conventionality, but an intensely inward, real thing of the heart and spirit. The man whose religion is a matter of mere rites and ceremonies is like the whited sepulchre, whose exterior may be beautiful enough, but which within may be full of rottenness and dead men's bones. There must be a new heart within; a man must be born not merely of water, but of the Spirit, if he is ever to enter into the kingdom of God.

When we come to the material of His teaching, we see no less clearly His divine originality. To exhibit this in full, however, would be to give a statement of all the characteristic doctrines of the Christian system. It will be enough to flash the fact upon the mind if we touch upon a few main points. We see this originality in His revelation of God. He revealed Him as Father, as well as King. By this is not meant Father in the general sense of being the origin of our existence, or as a mere title of respect, which was almost all that the Greeks and the Romans meant when they spoke of Zeus under this name. We mean Father in the highest sense, all that the ideal Father ought to be, raising us as He does to the status, and conferring on us the privileges of sons, both here and hereafter. He reveals Him as a God of mercy and love, as well as a God of justice and judgment. He teaches the doctrine of regeneration by the Spirit, and gratuitous justification on the ground of His own blood. He teaches that personal faith in Himself is the saving state of the soul —that true faith which identifies the soul with Him, and contains within it 'the potency and promise' of all the Christian graces and virtues. When a man enters into this relationship to Him, then salvation is his that instant, full and free, as a gift of God. He declares love to be the ruling principle, the grand energetic motive power of the Christian life, and Himself as the incarnate law to be the rule and ideal of that life. The whole is fresh and original—fresh with all the freshness of the breezes that blow from the eternal hills; original with all the originality of God. Well might the people be 'astonished at His doctrine.'

Another quite unique and unparalleled feature in the teaching of Christ, is the place which He gives to His death. It is, no doubt, true that He does not develop the doctrine of His death as a sacrifice and propitiation to the same extent as His apostles do. This, of course, was to be expected, for His death had not yet taken place, and therefore the time had scarcely come for revealing the fulness of its significance. Nevertheless, He does assign an all-important and most singular place and power to His death. It was one grand object of His incarnation; He 'came to give His life a ransom for many.' It was a divine necessity: 'the Son of man must be lifted up' on the cross. His blood was a true atonement; it was 'shed for many for the remission of sins.' It sealed and ratified the covenant of redemption with God the Father: 'This cup is the new covenant in My blood.' His body and blood sacrificed in death, are, through the great truths and forces which underlie them, the life of the world: 'Except ye eat the flesh of the Son of man and drink His blood, ye have no life in you.' Yea, His death is the sowing of the seed which is to spring up in the spiritual harvest of a glorious Church; He is the corn of wheat which falls into the ground and by dying brings forth much fruit. Then, to crown the whole, how unique, how significant the institution of the Supper—an institution which, beyond all contradiction, goes back to the time of Christ, and which was designed to represent and commemorate through all ages the supreme importance of His death!

Again we see the unique originality of Christ when

we contemplate the peculiar kingdom which He purposed to found and actually did found. He entered on His ministry, declaring it to be His mission to found a spiritual society or kingdom, which He called the kingdom of God, or the kingdom of heaven. This was both His first and last message; for He refers to the same subject in His trial. By this expression He meant a kingdom which should have God as King, which should be founded on the truth, which should be governed by moral and spiritual laws, and exist for moral and spiritual ends. It was a kingdom not of this world, but one in which men were to unite for mutual help in moral and spiritual things, and for spreading the reign of truth and righteousness throughout the world. It was a kingdom which was to interpenetrate all earthly kingdoms like a heavenly leaven, as the life permeates the body, or as the summer warmth and fragrance are diffused throughout the air. It was a kingdom of which the world and time are only an outlying province, and heaven and eternity the true home-country and capital. Now, this was an entirely new and original idea. It was not a mere duplicate of the ancient Jewish theocracy. At the most it was only related to that as the spirit of the glorified saint is to his earthly body. It was in direct antagonism to the gross worldly views of the Messianic kingdom entertained by the Jews of that age, who looked for a kingdom after the type of imperial Rome rather than the New Jerusalem. It was a conception which had never dawned upon the Greek or Roman mind, even in its highest flights of speculation. There can be no doubt that the kingdom of God as taught by Christ was a new and original idea in the world, and, like the holy city in the vision of John, it descended from God out of heaven.

We see also the originality of Christ in the universality of His purpose. Beyond all cavil, His aim was to unite all mankind as members or brothers on equal terms in His great spiritual kingdom. It mattered not to what people or rank they belonged. Whether they were white or black, cultured or uncultured, rich or poor, Pharisee or Sadducee, publican or sinner, bond or free,—all were equally welcome to citizenship in His kingdom, and to its privileges both here and hereafter. He required His disciples, no doubt, to begin the spiritual conquest of the world at Jerusalem; but they were to carry the banner of the cross to Samaria and the ends of the earth. The field was the world, and they were to go into all the world and preach the gospel to every creature. And in this universal purpose we have something sublimely new. It was far beyond the conception of the contemporary Jews, who regarded the Gentiles as dogs, as unclean animals, with whom they would not even so much as eat. It was in direct contradiction to the spirit of the Greek, who looked upon all other nations in a manner as barbarians. It was beyond even the farthest stretch of Roman thought; for the Roman citizen fondly regarded himself as a very superior being compared with the conquered nations who did homage to the imperial senate and people. Yet here we have a peasant from the mountains of Galilee, into whose native glens the tide of the world's great ocean had never flowed, who had scarcely heard its confused roar even from afar, coming forward at once with this universal, world-wide conception fully matured! Surely this is something grandly original and strange.

Another very peculiar feature in Christ's plan is the fact that He puts Himself forward as the corner-stone of this spiritual temple, the very heart and centre of this new body. Men were to be admitted to its membership, not by any adherence to an abstract creed or code of rules, but by personal trust in Christ and loyalty to Him. He knew the weakness and need of man, knew that nothing reaches and takes his heart like real, brotherly humanity. While men have no enthusiasm for a dry code of laws, however excellent, perhaps even shrink from it, they are powerfully drawn by the mystic cords of human sympathy, and deep, tragic, loving self-sacrifice. By His divine wisdom He at once transcended that fatal weakness of all Greek and Roman philosophy—the want of an incarnation of God's law and will in a loving, pure, sympathizing life, and its culmination in a tragic, self-sacrificing death of heroic martyrdom. Having provided in Himself a powerful centre of spiritual attraction and energy, He put Himself forward with the astounding claim that men should rest themselves on Him as the one Saviour, build themselves upon Him as the one Foundation, and join themselves to Him as the one Head and Centre of the new spiritual body or society. In short, loyalty to Himself was the condition of membership in His kingdom—a feature in which He totally differed from all ancient philosophers.

We see not less clearly the wonderful originality of His plan, when we consider the special means which He adopted to bring men into His kingdom. The weapons of His warfare were not carnal. He did not use the power of mere physical omnipotence to force them in. He did not use the arts of human diplomacy or intrigue. He did not bribe men by the hope of wealth and power and fame. Still less did He seduce them by pandering to their lower tastes. He did not even take the method of beating down men's reason by crushing argument. He took a much more new and wonderful and Godlike way. It was the method of subduing men's opposition and melting their hearts by love. He knew that if any power could accomplish this and make them truly willing, it would be the power of self-sacrificing love.

He shows this love for men in all His life, and especially in His suffering for them on the cross. He shows this love to them even when dead in trespasses and sins, and ignorantly and thoughtlessly treading Him under foot. He shows it to them to the very uttermost. This love was that mighty power by which He sought to break down, and does break down, yea, even melt, the hard and stony heart. The heart which can resist arguments and threats and physical pain, and even grow harder under them, yields to love. He conquers by the power of His love, especially as expressed and exhibited upon the cross, and draws and binds the heart of man to Him by its everlasting bonds. His kingdom is the only great kingdom or society in the world whose grand secret is the power of pure, self-sacrificing love; and surely here again we have something divinely new and strange.

Once more, it is worthy of notice that Jesus came forth from His mountain home in Galilee, certainly from His temptation in the wilderness, with the idea of His plan complete. It is extremely rare to find a man who appears and plays a large part in the scene of history, whose plan is perfect from the very first, and followed out without alteration. Still more rare is this when the plan is something new and original; and most rare of all, when it meets with much opposition on every side. But all this was the case with Jesus. Plainly

He came forth from the wilderness with His plan finished and fixed. Just as plainly He adhered to it all His life through; and not less plainly did He adhere to it in His death. His life was a straight line through the world leading up to the cross, and through the cross and the darkness of death to the establishment of His spiritual kingdom. How different from the lives of men in general, which rather resemble the motion of the empty boat upon a troubled sea than the straight pathway of a firm purpose leading up to a fixed and glorious termination!

Let it be clearly noticed also, that all these unique and original elements are not heaped up together about Christ in a heterogeneous mass. They unite and harmonize in Him in a real personality and life. Indeed, one of the grand peculiarities of Jesus is just the fact that in Him the most opposite virtues are not merely present, but blend into an harmonious and well-balanced whole. In Him we have the utmost strength united with the utmost gentleness; the extreme of firmness with the extreme of tenderness; the loftiest ideal with the intensest practicalness. He has a hand so powerful that it can wield the mightiest worlds, and yet so gentle that it can bind up the wounds of the broken heart. In Him we see the purest truth going hand in hand with the purest love, the highest justice glorified by the sweet light of the highest mercy. In Him the closest unity with God co-exists harmoniously with the utmost sympathy with sinful, sorrowing man. While He follows on His pathway straight to His sublime aim amid the strain of opposition and persecution, He has yet time to notice the flower by the wayside, to take up the children in His arms and bless them. He puts forward claims the most extraordinary, such as would be ridiculous and blasphemous in the mouth of any mere man, and yet His is clearly the most modest and humble of natures. There is something in Him that overawes the hypocrite and hardened sinner; something that draws to Him the children, the penitent, and broken-hearted. In Him mercy and truth meet together, righteousness and peace kiss each other. Just as the different colours seen in the rainbow unite to form the pure, colourless light; so the different virtues and graces in the character of Christ blend harmoniously together to give us the pure, colourless light of perfect holiness. His personality is not only real and rich, but of the most harmonious balance and blending.

In view of what we have seen, it is clear that we cannot possibly regard the personality of Christ to be the evolution of merely natural forces and ordinary historical elements. Every attempt to explain Him satisfactorily by mere natural evolution has hitherto been baffled. No chemistry has ever yet succeeded in analysing Him into mere earthly elements. What is true of man is infinitely more so of the Son of man. Materialists may resolve the human body into its component parts, so much oxygen, so much hydrogen, so much nitrogen, so much carbon, so much lime, so much phosphorus, and the like. They may present us with the mixture all right in regard to weight and measure; and as we look at the heap, they may triumphantly say, 'There is the man; that is the whole; and there is no mystery about it.' But a thousand times, No. The life is wanting, the co-ordinating soul, the man. The heap of dust is not even a human body. And just as no mere earthly chemistry can account for man, much less can it do so for Christ. No theory of mere natural evolution can explain Him; He refuses to be expressed by any mere earthly equation. Unbelieving critics may try to explain Him by showing that there is in Him so much drawn from Jewish monotheism and morality; so much from Greek culture and sunshine; so much of the universal, suggested by the world-wide empire of Rome, and the like. They think that when they have said so much they have explained Him away, and deprived Him of all title to 'the Wonderful.' But after all, the grand and divine personality stands up before us as unsolved and unexplained as ever, baffling the utmost efforts of human ingenuity to analyse Him into mere natural elements, or account for Him by mere natural evolution.[1]

[1] Comp. Principal Rainy, as quoted in Stalker's *Life of Christ*, p. 141.

But may not this wonderful personality be an utter fiction and forgery? The supposition, as indeed we have already seen, is inadmissible. It is clearly not a fiction, but history. Had it been a fiction, it must have been the production of one great mind; but instead of this, we see it represented by different writers of very different types, all of whom contribute some traits which are distinct but which nevertheless harmonize into one whole. Besides, the humble followers of Jesus were quite unable of themselves to devise, and most manifestly unable to carry out, such a fiction. It would have required a greater genius than Scott or Shakespeare to do so, and there was no Scott or Shakespeare there. 'It is more inconceivable,' says Rousseau, 'that several men should have united to forge the gospel, than that a single person should have furnished the subject of it. It has marks of truth so great, so striking, so utterly inimitable, that the inventor of it would be more astounding than the hero.'[1] 'It takes a Newton to forge a Newton,' says Parker. 'What man could have fabricated a Jesus? None but a Jesus.'[2] 'Who among His disciples,' says J. S. Mill, 'or among their early proselytes, was capable of inventing the sayings ascribed to Jesus, or of imagining the life and character revealed

[1] *Émile*, Livre iv. p. 370 (Firmin-Didot).

[2] Quoted by Bushnell, *Nature and the Supernatural*, p. 279 (Strahan, 1861).

in the Gospels? Certainly not the fishermen of Galilee; as certainly not St. Paul, . . . still less the early Christian writers.'[1] We must give up the idea of forgery and fiction as utterly untenable.

But if it is not a fiction, then the perfect moral character of Christ must force us to the conclusion that His claims were thoroughly well founded. He must be all that He really claimed to be, for any other supposition is morally impossible. When He who is the truth, who everlastingly inculcates truthfulness, and who was the very essence of humility, claims to be from heaven, the Son of God, the divinely-commissioned Messiah, possessed of all power in heaven and in earth, surely His claim must be well founded. Surely the supposition of deliberate deception is utterly impossible and inconceivable. Is it conceivable that One whose moral character is the highest the world has ever seen, even the opponents of Christianity being judges, should have lived a life of thoroughgoing and uninterrupted deception? Is it conceivable that a deceiver would have planned and proclaimed and established a system of such pure, high, uncompromising morality as we have in the teaching of Christ? Is it conceivable that He should have practised all manner of intense deceit and hypocrisy in order to drive deceit and hypocrisy and sin in every form from the face of the earth for ever? If

[1] *Three Essays*, p. 253.

so, then the point of Schwab's epigram[1] must be true, and Jesus, throughout the Christian ages, must have been driving out the devil through Beelzebub. But it cannot be. Nothing can act habitually in a way directly contrary to its essential nature. Heat cannot freeze water, nor gravitation make the stone ascend, nor can a man of perfect truth live a life of habitual deceit and hypocrisy. The tree is known by its fruit. In short, the unquestionable moral excellence of Christ carries with it that He was all that He really claimed to be.

We would very particularly emphasize the fact, even at the risk of repetition, that the unique personality and character of Christ demand something more than the merely human to explain them. They point explicitly to the scriptural doctrine of His true divinity. For it cannot fairly be doubted that the Gospels and the Epistles alike represent Him as more than man, as, indeed, very God. It can scarcely be doubted that He Himself calmly claims to be divine—the Son of God in the highest sense; so that if not really divine, He must either be an impostor or a deluded enthusiast.

[1] On the Tübingen hypothesis in regard to the origin of the fourth Gospel:—

'Hat dieses Buch, das ewige Wahrheit ist,
Ein lügenhafter Gnostiker geschrieben,
So hat seit tausend Jahren Jesus Christ
Den Teufel durch Beelzebub vertrieben.

See Schaff, *Apostolic Christianity*, vol. ii. p. 724.

No other view, indeed, will carry us through the New Testament than that of His true divinity. It will not read intelligibly on the supposition that He is only a mere man. Even thoroughgoing Unitarians and unbelievers are at times frank enough to admit this fact. 'The orthodox are right,' says a leading American Unitarian, 'in interpreting the Scriptures as they have done and are doing.'[1] And, as we have just said, the personality, character, life, influence of Christ harmonize with His real divinity, and demand it for their explanation. In contemplating them with thought and sympathy, we feel instinctively that they are just such a character, life, and influence as we could naturally suppose to belong to God incarnate. When we hear Jesus saying, 'I and My Father are one,' 'He who hath seen Me hath seen the Father,' and the like, we feel that there is a perfect harmony and consistency between His life and His claims. Apart from any array of separate proof texts, His character, life, and influence all alike lead us up to the doctrine of His divinity. We feel that Rousseau was right when he said, 'Yes, if the life and death of Socrates are those of a sage, the life and death of Jesus are those of a God.' And if Christ is divine, then so is Christianity; for its heart and essence is Christ.

[1] Cf. even Matthew Arnold, *Literature and Dogma*, p. 178 (Popular Edition).

In Christ then, such is our conclusion, we have a truly supernatural personality. In the very fact of His perfect holiness itself we see this demonstrated. For perfect holiness is not a thing found in the sphere of nature.[1] It is something that distinctly comes from above, it is supernatural in the highest sense. It is even a higher type of the supernatural than superhuman knowledge or power, the power of working physical miracles. It is higher than these, in proportion as the moral is higher than the merely intellectual and physical. But this perfect holiness we have in Jesus, and not that alone. We have such originality, such a completeness and fixity of plan from first to last, such insight into man and the future, as to betoken a wisdom and knowledge more than human, just as His miracles betoken a power more than human. In other words, we see united in Him the threefold supernatural—supernatural power, wisdom, holiness, which betoken, at the root of them, His supernatural essence. Accordingly His unique personality can be the result of no mere earthly chemistry or evolution. A spring that rises so very high must have its origin beyond the highest summits of earth, in the very heaven of heavens itself. As the chemist can, from the slightest analysis, deduce that a stone is meteoric, and has descended upon the earth from a higher sphere; so the analysis of the

[1] See Appendix, Note XVIII.

Person of Jesus shows that He, the second Adam, is the Lord from heaven. As the sun demonstrates his existence, surpassing splendour, and power by his light, heat, and attraction; so Christ demonstrates Himself to be the Sun of Righteousness by the surpassing heavenly light and splendour, and the mighty, attractive power of His Person. 'His Θεοπρέπεια or God-becoming impress of majesty, sovereignty, omniscience, independence, holiness, justice, goodness, wisdom, and power, is not only a sufficient and real, but in very deed the greatest objective light and evidence imaginable.'[1] In the very act of looking at Him, we see Him to be not only a reality, but a supernatural, yea, a divine Person. In fine, Christ as seen in the Gospels is His own best proof, and the best proof of the supernatural and divine character of His religion.

[1] Halyburton, *Nature of Faith*, chap. iii.

XI.

Some important Converging Lines, and the Argument therefrom.

The object of the present study is to adduce some important facts and elements not yet discussed, and show how they converge on and in Christianity; to prove that, according to the Theory of Probabilities, they cannot well have united in Christianity by mere chance, but only by intelligent design; and to draw the reasonable conclusion therefrom, that its origin must be supernatural and divine.

The general principle of the argument is very simple. It resolves itself very much into the commonplace question, How can we distinguish whether an object or event is the outcome of mere chance or of intelligent design? It may be that the discovery of a single element in it which looks like the adaptation of means to an end, may not exactly prove it to have been the product of intelligence. But when two such elements, and still more when three or four, are plainly discovered, the likelihood that intelligence was present becomes vastly increased. When ten or twenty or more singular elements, all converging to the same end, have been discovered, the case becomes certain. Without any doubt we take it out of the category of mere chance, and set it down as the outcome of intelligence. In what follows we mean to adduce a number of singular facts, which converge and focus in Christianity, all contributing to one and the same end, and to conclude therefrom that Christianity cannot reasonably be supposed to be the outcome of mere drift and chance, but must be regarded as the product of a divine intelligence coming down upon history from above, and working within its current.[1]

We have now to look at the genesis and history of Christianity, to adduce some of the suggestive features and peculiarities referred to, and to consider their natural bearing and reading.

One of these peculiarities is the monotheism of the Jewish race in which Christianity emerged. We do not enter into any discussion as to whether monotheism was the primary religion of man or not. It is plain that if it was, it did not long continue to be so. Hume holds that 'polytheism and idolatry was and naturally must have been the first and most ancient religion of mankind.' Rawlinson says, 'It seems impossible to maintain that men are instinctively monotheists.' 'If we are

[1] See Appendix, Note XIX.

asked,' says Max Müller, 'how it was that Abraham passed through the denial of all the gods to the knowledge of the one true God, we are content to answer that it was by a special divine revelation.' Here, then, is how the matter stands. Of all the thousand or more tribes and nations of antiquity, the Jews, and the Jews alone, possessed and held fast in the central current of their history and life the doctrine of the 'one living and true God.' Amidst multitudes of temptations from idolatrous nations around them, and even in the midst of their own country, in spite of a powerful tendency, even among themselves, constantly to apostatize into polytheism, their monotheism remained the grand peculiarity, the palladium, the life and reason of the national existence. This is a very striking and undeniable fact, however we may choose to explain it.

Another very important fact in the Christian line of history is our collection of sacred books. In this expression we are to include at present the Old Testament as well as the New. These sacred books form a progressive organic religious unity, such as is found in the literature of no other nation. They begin with the germs of a religion which goes on developing by a gradual but supernatural growth, like that of some sacred tree, for a period of fifteen hundred years, until we arrive at the blossom or fruit in the form of Christianity. They form a unity with one spirit and life running through them all. However different the authors, and however distant from each other in time or place, their contributions, instead of coming into collision, harmonize, and fall into their proper place in the organic growth and whole, until the culmination is reached in the New Testament. This is something extremely singular, quite unique in the history of nations. We find no such consistent, organic religious unity in the literature of any other people. We do not find it in that of ancient Greece; on the contrary, it has almost no unity except that of language. We find thinker standing up against thinker, and philosophers denouncing and opposing the systems of each other with the utmost freedom and determination. In like manner, we find no such religious organic growth and unity in the literature of our own country. It is impossible to regard its multifarious productions, its warring literary, philosophic, scientific, and theological schools, as forming any organic unity. It presents, indeed, a perfect contrast to the Bible literature. Accordingly, when we contemplate the literature of the Jews as we have it in the Holy Scriptures, and see that it is a unity, a religious unity and growth, the organism of one religious life and spirit, we discover that this forms another and an essential characteristic in the Christian line of history.

Another extremely striking element is the wonderful preservation of the Jewish nation itself. This is also quite a unique phenomenon. This singular people maintained their separate existence in the iron furnace of Egyptian bondage. In Palestine they contrived to survive, though ground between the upper and the nether millstones of Assyria and Egypt. They were carried away captive into Babylon, but their nationality was not destroyed—was only intensified thereby. They were dispersed still more widely under the sway of the Syrian kings, during the four centuries between the Old Testament and the New, so that at the advent of Christ they were found in every large town of the Roman Empire; but in spite of it all, they tenaciously preserved their national distinction. They continued during the dark ages, scattered throughout Christendom, everywhere exposed to furious persecution and the most fearful barbarities and massacres; yet the stubborn people still maintained their independent existence. After thousands of years have passed away, they exist at the present day dispersed among all nations, but separate from them, and likely to remain separate for an indefinite time to come. This is a fact quite unparalleled in history. There is no case on record of a people driven from their native country, scattered among all nations, and speaking their respective languages, and yet, in spite of the most powerful inducements to the contrary, continuing quite distinct from them for millenniums. This, whatever we may make of it, is a most singular and instructive fact.

It is said that Frederick William I. of Prussia once asked one of his chaplains for a proof of Christianity, adding that he must be short with it, for business was pressing. The chaplain answered instantaneously, 'Sire, the Jews.' And there is a large amount of truth in the reply; for the unique history of the Jews is in itself a very striking proof of Christianity.

But what makes this wonderful truth more wonderful still, is the fact that it was distinctly prophesied. It was distinctly and repeatedly foretold that the Jews should be scattered amongst all nations, and yet not be annihilated or absorbed. We find this clearly prophesied in the books of Moses. We do not require to consider at present the question of their date. It is certain that they were written before the year 400 B.C., and that is clearly enough for our purpose. We read in these books statements like the following: 'I will scatter you among the heathen, and will draw out a sword after you: and your land shall be desolate, and your cities waste. . . . And yet for all that, when they be in the land of their enemies, I will not cast them away, neither will I abhor them, to destroy them utterly, and to break My covenant with them' (Lev. xxvi. 33, 44). Again, in Micah (v. 7) we read that 'the remnant of Jacob shall be in the midst of many people as a dew from the Lord.' Our Lord, in His prophecy of the destruction of the Holy City, declares that the people 'shall be led away captive into all nations; and Jerusalem shall be trodden down of the Gentiles, until the times of the Gentiles be fulfilled' (Luke xxi. 24). The Apostle Paul takes it for granted that the separate existence of the Jews in their dispersion will continue until the complete Christianization of the Gentile world, an event obviously as yet far enough off. He says, 'Blindness in part is happened unto Israel until the fulness of the Gentiles be come in; and so shall all Israel be saved' (Rom. xi. 25, 26). From all this it appears that it was a matter of distinct prophecy that the Jews should be scattered among the nations, and yet maintain their separate national existence. This was a most unlikely event, the prophesying of which no astute impostor would have dared to venture. But after all, we find that this most unlikely prophecy has been, is being, and is likely to be wonderfully fulfilled to the very letter. Surely such a strange coincidence could not possibly happen by any mere chance.

Another very striking truth is this, that just in this singular race Jesus Christ actually came—'Of them, as concerning the flesh, Christ came.' We do not say anything at present concerning His divine nature and mission, but only accentuate the facts just mentioned, which all will admit. A unique Person did appear among this people, more than eighteen hundred years ago, whose character must be admitted to be peculiarly noble, powerful, and original. He revolutionized the religion of the world, and that too in a way quite unparalleled. However great a man's capacity for scepticism may be, no sane man can deny that Jesus of Nazareth has produced a greater effect upon the world than all Greek and Roman sages, statesmen and generals, with all their mighty appliances. Surely it is very strange, that just in this wonderful stream of history, and nowhere else amid the thousand tribes of the earth, the Founder of the great world-religion should have appeared. Surely it must begin to dawn upon the mind that so many singular elements could not drift together by mere wild chance.

But what increases the wonder a thousandfold, is the fact that such a Messiah was distinctly prophesied in the Old Testament as destined to arise in the Jewish race. Not to mention the suggestive symbolism of the law, we find an almost unbroken current of prophecy, clearly Messianic in its spirit, pointing to some great Messiah, or Anointed One, who was to come. 'The testimony of Jesus is the spirit of prophecy.' Sometimes the utterance is more dim; sometimes it is very clear; but it meets us everywhere. He is the Seed promised to Abraham, in whom all the families of the earth are to be blessed; the Shiloh who was to come; the Prophet like unto Moses. He is David's Son and David's Lord, who was to be King on Zion, whose dominion was to extend from sea to sea, and endure as long as the sun and moon. He was to be the Wonderful, the Counsellor, the mighty God, the Father of Eternity, the Prince of Peace, the Rod out of the stem of Jesse; who was to be wounded for our transgressions, to make His soul an offering for sin, and on whom the Lord was to lay the iniquity of us all. He was the Branch of righteousness who was to grow up unto David; the Lord our Righteousness; the Son of man who was to come in the clouds of heaven; the Messiah who was to be cut off, not for Himself, but for the sins of the people. All this is admitted in his own way even by Strauss. 'The expectation of the Messiah had become a peculiar national idea.' It was 'the expectation of a sovereign of David's sort, of the lineage of David;' and 'the name of Messiah, or the Anointed, was adopted for the expected Deliverer.'[1] Surely this current of antecedent prophecy, which even unbelievers are compelled in some measure to admit, makes the strange fact of the advent of Christ in the Jewish race yet more strange and striking.

[1] See *New Life of Jesus*, pp. 225 ff. Renan, *Vie de Jésus*, chap. i. 'Lord Bolingbroke asserts Jesus Christ to have brought on His own death by a series of wilful and preconcerted measures, merely to give the disciples who came after Him the triumph of an appeal to the old prophecies!'—Chalmers, *Evidences of the Christian Revelation*, Book ii. chap. vii. 3. Surely this implies that Bolingbroke believed very strongly that the death of the Messiah was explicitly prophesied in the Old Testament.

But this wonder is still more intensified by the fact that the Jews universally expected the Messiah about the time at which He actually did appear. If scepticism should try to explain away the so-called prophecies as mere poetry or happy guesses, yet here is a stubborn fact that cannot be denied. At the time of Christ's advent, the Jews were on the very tiptoe of Messianic expectation. We see this from the New Testament. Not only was it the assured expectation of the devout, like Simeon and Anna, but also of the Jews in general. When John the Baptist began his ministry, they sent a deputation to him, to ask if he was the Christ; and the coming of the Messiah was also a foremost thought even in the Samaritan mind, as we learn from our Lord's conversation with the woman at Jacob's well. But we know of this widespread expectation among the Jews not merely from the New Testament; we know it also from their own books—their Targums and apocryphal literature.[1] The air of Judæa was perfectly electric with feverish hope and expectation that the

[1] Thus even Josephus: 'But now, what did most elevate [the Jews] in undertaking this war [which ended in the destruction of Jerusalem], was an ambiguous oracle that was also found in their sacred writings, how "about that time one from their country should become governor of the habitable earth." The Jews took this prediction to belong to themselves in particular, and many of the wise men were thereby deceived in their determination.' He characteristically adds: 'This oracle certainly denoted the government of Vespasian, who was appointed emperor in Judæa.'—*Wars*, Book vi. chap. v. 4.

Messianic day was just about to break. This is frankly acknowledged even by negative thinkers. Keim testifies that 'the times of Jesus were full of a restless expectation of the salvation that was to come.' 'The old prophetic watchwords — the Messiah, Christ, the kingdom of the Great King, the kingdom of heaven, the throne and seed of David—were, in the days of John the Baptist and Jesus, on every man's lips in Judæa and Galilee, and even in Samaria.' And the still more negative Renan witnesses to the same effect: 'In Judæa expectation was at its full. Men felt that the age was travailing with mighty events; they felt the approach of something unknown. Revolution, or, to use another word, Messianism, set all heads working. People believed they were on the eve of seeing the advent of the great renewal.'[2] Nothing can be plainer than the fact that the Jewish people were full at this very time of Messianic expectation, and by this same fact they bore their testimony that this was the age in which Jesus was to come. And when we consider that the Messiah not only came, but came in the very age in which He was expected, surely this must seem so passing strange that we cannot reasonably regard it as the outcome of mere

[1] Keim, *Geschichte Jesu von Nazara*, vol. i. pp. 244 f. Compare the whole section, 'Die messianische Hoffnung,' vol. i. pp. 239–250.

[2] Renan, *Vie de Jésus*, pp. 18, 63.

chance, but only of a gracious Providence guiding the current of history.

Another consideration which is very strange and striking, is the fact that the advent of Christ took place at what is well called 'the fulness of the time.' The Jewish people still existed as a nation under one government, and the sceptre had not quite departed from Judah; and yet only forty years elapsed after the crucifixion until Jerusalem was destroyed, the nation broken up and dispersed, and the Jewish religion in its true ceremonial at an end for ever. Furthermore, the Jews were now scattered over all the civilised world, and had a community and synagogue in every large city. These formed so many hearths for receiving the sacred fire of Christianity, and hence as a rule the apostles sought out and preached the gospel first of all to these communities, and met with their first converts there. We also find that, through the conquests and colonization, the culture and the commerce of the Greeks, their language had in this age become a kind of common tongue. A knowledge of Greek was almost enough to carry the early preachers of the gospel over the length and breadth of the civilised world. Once more, it was an age in which the world-wide empire of Rome, by its vigorous rule, maintained practically universal peace. Under its imperial canopy the missionary of the cross had at first no hindrance or difficulty in passing from province to province, from country to country, from tribe to tribe, in a way which would have been utterly impossible had they all been in a state of mutual hostility, or even isolation. The inscription on the cross, written in Hebrew, Greek, and Latin, was a suggestive symbol that the three great lines of ancient history—the Hebrew, the Greek, and the Latin—converged to prepare the fulness of the times, and met as in a focus at the cross. In this convergence of historic lines we see another very strange phenomenon connected with Christianity.

We find another singular fact in the establishment of the Church by Christ. He established it in the world, humanly speaking, by the most unlikely means, as we have already seen in a previous study. He not only established it, but caused it to make rapid and wonderful progress. As we look at the tiny barque of the Church setting sail, we see that it begins at once to move up the stream against all the opposition of moral and social currents and forces, and in spite of political storms and waves. Steadily but surely, propelled by no mere human power, we see it moving against stream and wind and tide, contrary to all the laws of earthly navigation. The Church encountered even the most fearful persecution on the part of kings and governors, who did their very utmost by the prison, the sword, and the stake, to sweep it from the face of the earth. But by and by, in spite of Jewish bigotry and hatred; in spite of Greek culture, philosophy, and contempt; in spite of Roman pride, determination, and imperial power, it conquered the very Empire itself, and sat down upon the throne of the Cæsars. It remains unto this day able and eager for further conquests; for it is founded upon the Rock, and the gates of hell cannot prevail against it. Here then is another wonder. Out of this same Christian line of history, out of Christ springs that religion which, in spite of all opposition, has won the sovereignty over the flower of the nations, has organized itself in the Christian Church, and alone promises to be the ultimate religion of the world. This is another of those singular elements which unite in the line of the Christian history, and take it out of the realm of blind chance, and the grinding of mere unintelligent laws and forces.

But we have further to remark, that the planting and spread of the Church was also an explicit subject of prophecy. It was from the earliest ages a theme of Old Testament prophecy. It was pointed to in the promise made to Abraham, and already quoted, that in his seed all families of the earth should be blessed. It was referred to in the Messianic prophecies: 'I shall give Thee the heathen for Thine inheritance, and the uttermost parts of the earth for Thy possession; He shall have dominion also from sea to sea, and from the river unto the ends of the earth.' The Jews of Christ's day understood these and similar prophecies as implying universal dominion on the part of the Messiah. And this line of prophecy is taken up by Christ Himself when He declares: 'Upon this rock I will build My Church, and the gates of Hades shall not prevail against it; all power is given unto Me in heaven and in earth; go ye into all the world and preach the gospel to every creature.' The same truth is clearly taught in the apostolic writings: 'He must reign till He hath put all enemies under His feet.' And in the Revelation of John, Messiah is represented as going on conquering and to conquer, until at last 'the kingdom of the world is become the kingdom of our Lord, and of His Christ.' Obviously the universal dominion of the Church is the theme of clearest prophecy; and when we reflect that, so far as man could foresee, this was one of the most unlikely events, we may safely conclude that such prophecies are no mere lucky guesses, but genuine prophecies with a real fulfilment which is being actualized from age to age.

Over against this we may look at another very singular fact, viz. the prophecy of the great corruption of the Church, followed, alas! by a fulfilment only too literal. This was a kind of prophecy not likely to be indulged in by a mere forger. Such a writer would have portrayed the future in the most brilliant colours, and would never have spoiled the dramatic effect by dashing the picture with dark shades and discordant elements. But we find that the New Testament explicitly foretells the fearful degeneracy and corruption of even the Church of Christ. Our Lord distinctly does so Himself in the parable of the Tares (Matt. xiii. 24 ff.). The Apostle Paul does so once and again, and very particularly in Second Thessalonians, one of his very earliest Epistles, of which the second chapter has a very distinct bearing on the present point. The same is true of the Apostle Peter. In his Second Epistle (ii. 1, 2) he says: 'There shall be false teachers among you, who privily shall bring in destructive heresies, and many shall follow their pernicious ways.' And not to mention the Apocalypse, the Apostle John speaks once and again of the Antichrist who was to come. These and other similar prophecies were not only made, but, as all history declares, were literally fulfilled. No one can glance at the multitudes of heretics and sectaries in ancient and modern times without seeing that this is true. No one with an unbiassed mind can contemplate the Romish Church, especially in the dark ages, and compare it with the Church of the New Testament, without feeling the vast change that has taken place in spirit, in doctrine, in ritual and practice. Nevertheless, it was the distinct burden of other prophecies that the Church would surmount and survive such inward corruption, as well as all outward hostility. And this also has been realized in history. These prophecies, and their fulfilment, we may well regard as another singular fact, though perhaps not of the same high rank with most of the others mentioned, pointing to the conclusion that Christianity is not of chance, nor of man, but of God.[1]

There is one very special prophecy by our Lord, referring to a singular event occupying an important place in the line of Christian history, to which it may be well to refer in this connection. We mean the complete destruction of Jerusalem and the Jewish temple, and the consequent termination of the Jewish dispensation. This event has special significance when viewed alongside of the prophecies referring to the beginning and perpetuity of the Christian Church and dispensation. That our Lord actually uttered such a prophecy, there is no well-founded reason to doubt. It is strongly and literally declared in the utterance to which He gave expression when He wept over the city, an incident so remarkable that the utterance connected therewith could not easily be forgotten. It is implied in His words to the daughters of Jerusalem on His way to Calvary; another incident and utterance not likely to be forgotten. But above all, it is fully detailed in Matt. xxiv., Mark xiii., and Luke xxi. Of these, the first two narratives were certainly written before the event took place; for

[1] Cf. Cairns, *Success of Christianity*, p. 39.

not only do they refer to it as future, but they contain a parenthetic note apparently meant for the timely warning of their readers: 'Let him that readeth understand;' a note which has no point whatever unless the events be still future. The early Christians rightly understood those prophecies as referring to the destruction of Jerusalem, and when the thunder-brooding clouds began to lower over the city, they fled to Pella beyond Jordan, and so escaped the ruin. We do not need to dwell on the fact that Josephus, though no Christian, testifies to the literal fulfilment of our Lord's prophecies in the utter destruction of the city and temple—an event which formed the end of the Jewish dispensation, and implied that it had given way to the Christian age. This is another singular event which falls in with the current of the Christian history.

Another line of evidence, both interesting and important, which may well find a place here, is that which we possess in the continued existence of the Lord's Supper. We know as a most certain fact that the Lord's Supper has existed, and been the central ordinance of the Church, from the days of the apostles and the other contemporaries of Christ. We do not require to trace its observance back, step by step, until we arrive at the Apostolic Age; for we know directly and most certainly that it existed then. It will be remembered that we have very full references to this sacrament in the tenth and eleventh chapters of First Corinthians. We may especially refer to the words of institution as they are delivered to us by Paul in the latter chapter in a passage familiar to every Christian (vv. 23–29). But it will also be remembered that First Corinthians is one of those Epistles of Paul which, as we have seen in a previous study, are incontestably genuine, — undisputed, and indisputable, according to the great representatives of the unbelieving schools of criticism in Germany, France, and England. We know, then, for a certain fact, acknowledged even by the most thoroughgoing opponents of New Testament Christianity, that the Lord's Supper was a common ordinance at the meetings of the faithful on the Lord's Day from the very beginning of the Christian Church.

Now this sacrament may be regarded as a monument or memorial ordinance of the very highest class. Every one can see at a glance that an almost contemporary monument, memorial, or memorial ordinance must be the very best evidence possible in regard to a past event. Narratives may be forged, but monuments and memorials cannot be so easily forged, and memorial ordinances least of all. The monument upon the field of Waterloo is an excellent witness to all succeeding ages of the great battle there. A coin with the head and name of Aretas is the very best proof that there existed princes of that name, though we find little mention made of them in history. The arch of Titus at Rome is an incontrovertible proof of the capture of Jerusalem. The celebrated Moabite stone is an irresistible witness to the historical reality of Mesha, king of Moab. But while such monuments and memorials as these are very high evidence, memorial ordinances are higher still. The observance of the fourth of July by the Americans, as the anniversary of their independence, must continue for ever an unassailable proof of the event. The celebration of the Passover is, independently of the narrative in Exodus, an excellent proof of the deliverance of Israel from Egypt. Memorial ordinances like these are the very highest kind of evidence, because it is scarcely possible that they can have been forged. Any wealthy man who takes the whim may raise the monument, any coiner may forge the coin, but it is next to impossible to fabricate a memorial ordinance to commemorate an event which is alleged to have just taken place, but which every one knows to be a pure myth. People will not allow such an observance to be palmed off upon them; they will not readily lend themselves to such a gross public deception; and hence it follows that a memorial ordinance, reaching back to the age of the event commemorated, is evidence of the very highest kind.

Now all this holds good in regard to the sacrament of the Supper. It is a very characteristic memorial ordinance. It reaches back, beyond all contradiction, as we have seen, to the New Testament age. We can trace back the regular observance of it until within a few years of Christ's death, along with the observance of the Lord's Day, on which it was celebrated. It is impossible that it could have been forged and foisted in upon the early Church; for not only were the apostles themselves alive at the time, but multitudes besides, who knew whether Christ had actually lived, and died, and risen again from the dead. We may accept the regular celebration of the Supper on the Lord's Day as testimony of the very highest order.

What, then, does the Lord's Supper, taken along with the Lord's Day on which it was held, testify? We see that it testifies to the historical reality of Jesus. There was such a person. It testifies to His real humanity, for it symbolizes and mentions His body and His blood. It testifies to His divinity. It does so not merely by its name—the LORD'S Supper, but by the fact that the whole ordinance is a service of the highest worship to the Saviour. It testifies to His death: for, not to speak of its explicit design, and the breaking of the bread, the separation of the bread and wine distinctly symbolizes the separation of the body and blood; in other words, a violent death by blood-shedding. It testifies to His death as a true atonement: 'This is My body which is [broken] for you;' 'This cup is the new covenant in My blood.' It testifies to His resurrection very especially, because of its celebration on the first day of the week, the day set apart from the very first in commemoration of our Lord's resurrection. It testifies to the need of personal appropriating faith in Christ and His atoning death: 'Take, eat;' the cup is 'the communion of the blood of Christ;' the bread is 'the communion of the body of Christ.' It testifies to the idea, existence, and unity of the Holy Catholic Church: 'For we being many are one bread and one body; for we are all partakers of that one bread.' In other words, restricting ourselves entirely to First Corinthians, we see that in the Lord's Supper we have a memorial ordinance going back to the time of Christ, an ordinance which could not be forged, and which testifies most explicitly to the grand facts and doctrines which form the basis and substance of Christianity. It furnishes us, in short, with a separate and independent line of proof of the very highest order, which cannot be explained by mere chance.

Such are a few lines and elements of importance that converge in the sacred history of which Christianity is the flower and crown. Their number might easily be increased; but the preceding are enough to indicate the nature and the point of our present argument It is this: that such a multitude of very striking and special elements and lines, many of them distinctly prophesied, and all converging to one and the same great end, cannot have originated and met together by blind chance. It must have been the result of a guiding intelligence somewhere. It is quite obvious that it cannot be explained as the result of intelligence merely human; for the continuity of the Jewish race, the coming of Christ, the spread of the Church, and the antecedent prophecies in regard to these wonderful events, are obviously beyond the reach of man. Accordingly, it follows that here we have a current of history which is under special divine guidance, in which God manifests Himself in a positively miraculous and supernatural way. In short, mere chance is out of the question, and therefore we must recognise in it the hand of God.

But to many minds nothing gives so vivid and firm a grasp of a result as figures. Let us consider, then, how we might approximately express the possibility of all this happening by mere chance in virtue of the mathematical Theory of Probabilities.[1] It is a simple and easily demonstrable mathematical law, that 'the probability of the joint occurrence of any set of independent events is the product of their separate probabilities.' To make this plainer by an example:—If we have a bag with a hundred balls, of which ninety-nine are black and only one white, the probability of drawing the white ball at the first trial is only 1 to 100 ($\frac{1}{100}$); the probability of drawing it twice in succession is not 1 to 200, but one to 10,000 ($\frac{1}{100} \times \frac{1}{100}$); the chance of drawing

[1] Compare Appendix, Note XIV.

it thrice in succession is only 1 to 1,000,000 ($\frac{1}{100} \times \frac{1}{100} \times \frac{1}{100}$), etc. In other words, the ultimate chance or probability is the product of the separate chances or probabilities; so that to find the ultimate probability we have simply to multiply the separate probabilities.

Now it is not difficult to apply this in a general way to the case before us. The main difficulty is to estimate the chance or probability of each individual instance; but as our object is a *practical illustration* rather than mathematical exactness, we shall content ourselves with a general estimate of the probabilities, which in most cases will fall far within the mark. We take up the elements in the order in which they have been given in the previous pages.

The first of these was the unique monotheism of the Jewish race. It was the only ancient race that possessed and held fast to monotheism. There were probably a thousand different tribes existing in the ancient world; but let us say that there were only 100. The probability, therefore, that just this race out of 100 should alone be monotheistic, is only as 1 to 100 ($\frac{1}{100}$). The uniqueness of the sacred literature was the next point. There is no other sacred literature like it in existence. The chance that it should have been found in the Jewish race is again only 1 to 100 ($\frac{1}{100}$). Accordingly, by the Theory of Probabilities, the chance that the two elements mentioned should have been found in the

Jewish race, and there alone, is the product of the above, *i.e.* $\frac{1}{10,000}$, or 1 to 10,000. Again, the very wonderful preservation of the Jews, quite singular among the supposed 100 nations, gives a chance of 1 to 100 ($\frac{1}{100}$). That this unique historic fact should have been distinctly prophesied and exactly fulfilled, is a thing so unlikely to have resulted by blind chance, that it is hard to express the probability by mere figures; but let us put it down as also 1 to 100 ($\frac{1}{100}$). In like manner, we might go on through all (let us say) the twelve special elements which we have adduced, estimating the probability that each one should take place at all, and take place just in this line and nowhere else, as 1 to 100 ($\frac{1}{100}$). To find the resultant probability that all these should have happened to converge by chance, we must multiply the separate probabilities. The result is $\frac{1}{1,000,000,000,000000,0,000,000,000}$. That is to say, the probability that the above elements should have taken place and united in the Christian line of history by mere chance is only as 1 to 1,000,000,000,000,000,000,000,000, a probability in itself so infinitesimal, that it is impossible to have any clear idea of it. In other words, it is improbable in the highest conceivable degree that Christianity can be the result of mere blind chance and not of divine intelligence. At all events, the probability of its being the outcome of chance is so excessively small, that in all ordinary cases it would be considered as practically equal to nothing, and would be totally disregarded.

The method commonly adopted to break down such cumulative evidence as we have adduced above, is the method of special pleading. The advocate of unbelief takes up the different lines of proof one by one, shows how there is nothing in them separately; how they are found elsewhere separately in other systems; and how they can all be accounted for by mere nature and historical evolution. After doing this, he thinks his task triumphantly accomplished, and practically he turns round and says to the bewildered inquirer, 'Behold how the entire mass of evidence has vanished!' But after all, he has scarcely touched the heart and strength of the argument, which consists not merely in so many separate, independent lines, but in the fact that *so many singular lines should converge to one and the same end.*

Perhaps we may make the matter clearer by a simple illustration. Let us take the case of a jury trial, in which the prisoner at the bar is clearly guilty. The evidence consists, let us say, of a dozen strong converging lines. The advocate in defence is a skilful special pleader, and addresses himself to the task in detail. He takes up the first line of evidence fastening the crime upon the prisoner, and shows that it may have happened quite naturally, and yet the man be innocent. He takes up the second converging line, and shows that it has happened in such and such a case before and yet meant nothing. And so he goes over the whole twelve lines, explaining each of them away, and showing how they really prove nothing. But by this method he does not move a common-sense jury in the least. They will reply that it is very skilful pleading, but it does not touch the heart of the matter. It is possible that one, or even two, of the lines may hold good, without proving the prisoner necessarily guilty. But the fact that six such lines should converge upon him, makes his guilt practically certain; while the convergence of twelve such lines places his guilt beyond all possibility of a moment's doubt. The advocate with all his cleverness fails to account for the convergence of so many lines upon the same person, and it is just in this that the strength of the evidence lies. The jury see this by their practical logic and common sense, and with the utmost confidence they convict the prisoner, and bring in a verdict of guilty, though it is certain to cost him his life.

Now the course of procedure adopted by the advocates of unbelief is very much the same, and the cause of its weakness very much the same. They take up one by one the elements of the evidence bearing on Christianity, and attempt to dispose of them as best they can by showing that there is in them nothing supernatural or even uncommon. If we speak of the monotheism of the

Jews, they will adduce dim and lingering indications that monotheistic views were secretly held by the priests of Egypt. If we point to the peculiarity of our sacred books, they will point to those of the ancient Parsees. If we mention the marvellous preservation of the Jews, they will place over against it the case of the gipsies. If we adduce the wondrous character of Christ, they will affect to parallel it with that of Socrates, who himself declared that he had in his heart the germs of all evil inclinations. If we speak of His matchless moral teaching, they will sing the praises of Buddha, of Epictetus, or Marcus Aurelius. If we bring forward His miracles, they will talk of the fictitious wonders of Apollonius of Tyana. If we point to the marvellous spread of the Church, they will point to the marvellous spread of Mohammedanism. By thus taking up the different elements of proof one by one, and trying to parallel them by something brought from the north, or south, or east, or west, they think that they have destroyed the force of the argument. But they have scarcely even touched it. Their parallels only need to be looked at in order to see that, for the most part, they are no real parallels at all, and some of them more properly cases of conspicuous contrast than of parallelism. But even though they were ten times more apt than they are, the essential point is yet untouched—the fact that all those lines of evidence should converge upon and unite in Christianity. The problem is not,

Can we explain away this or that element by mere chance or natural causes? but, How do the elements all come to meet in one and the same centre? Was it by chance that all the military roads led to ancient Rome, or was it because it was the imperial city?[1]

What, then, is the natural outcome of the whole? What is the inference most reasonably to be drawn from the many converging lines, some of them strange and unique, which unite in and around Christianity? Is it not that there must have been presiding over it a great Intelligence, 'the King of the ages,' watching and working on throughout the weary centuries, and graciously directing all for the highest good of man? Or are we to suppose that this wonderful convergence is only the result of a happy, or rather of an unhappy, and delusive chance? Surely it must require no small capacity of faith to believe this latter. We cannot imagine that the noble ship riding in all its stateliness at anchor in the river, with its freight of hopeful emigrants bound for a new world, is the result of mere chance. We cannot suppose that its planks and cordage and other material kept floating up and down all oceans, until at last they were wrought into proper shape and size by tossing and friction; and then were luckily drifted together by a thousand different winds and currents from all seas and all directions of the compass, so as to meet at last in

[1] Compare Davison, *Discourses on Prophecy*, p. 31.

some secluded Highland loch. We cannot suppose that, on a night of mysterious darkness and storm, the different materials were luckily washed and jolted and lifted up into their proper places and there fixed, by the play of wild winds and waves, so that when the morning broke the completed ship floated upon the water in all its queenly pride. And just as little can we reasonably suppose that the wonderful elements of which we have spoken in this and the preceding studies, after tossing hither and thither for ages as flotsam upon the surface of human history, were wrought by the tossing into proper form,—were wafted at last by a thousand different storms and currents and counter-currents from all possible quarters into the little troubled bay of Jewry; and that there, by some strange conjunction of blind chances, they were united and built up into that noble Ark of our common Christianity, which rides so triumphantly upon the surging sea of time, freighted with the highest destinies of man, with all the noblest hopes of the future, and with many happy pilgrims bound for the world beyond.

XII.

Christianity proving itself by the Principle of the 'Survival of the Fittest.'

In the seventh chapter of Exodus we meet with a singular and suggestive miracle. We see Aaron in the presence of Pharaoh confronted with the wise men of Egypt. We are told that he cast down his rod, and it became a serpent; and that the wise men did the same with their rods, and these became serpents also. But the end of the scene was, that 'Aaron's rod swallowed up their rods;' and we read that afterwards it budded, and blossomed, and brought forth almonds.

The miracles of Moses and Aaron, like those of Christ, were not mere wonders to gratify man's empty curiosity, but are habitually called 'signs.' They are 'signs,' that is, significant or symbolical of some truth. They are what we would nowadays call a kind of object-lesson. And it is not difficult to discern what is the lesson taught, or at least suggested, by the present miracle. The rod is the symbol of authority, power, office. It is, in short, the sceptre. Aaron, as the future high priest, is the representative of the true God and His heaven-descended religion. Accordingly his rod or sceptre is the symbol of the power and dominion of God and His religion. The wise men of Egypt, on the other hand, are the representatives of mere man-made religions, human speculations, and earth-born systems. Their rods or sceptres are the symbols of the power and dominion of those human religions and systems. But Aaron's rod swallowed up their rods, and this fact teaches by a very vivid symbolism that the dominion of the divine religion is destined to supersede all man-made systems and mere nature-religions, to overturn their thrones and set up in their place its own eternal throne.

Of course, living in the Christian Age, we naturally apply the truth taught by this symbolism to the Christian religion. As the heaven-born, ultimate world-religion, it is demonstrating its power and final destiny by superseding all other religions.

The science of the present age speaks much about a great principle that determines and regulates the continuity and upward progress of life on the earth. That principle is the 'Survival of the Fittest' in the struggle for existence. The means of supporting life on the earth are of necessity limited, and hence arises a constant struggle for existence. In this struggle it is only the most powerful, 'the fittest,' and best adapted to the circumstances, that survive. And there is, without doubt, a large measure of truth in the principle. We see that this is the case in the vegetable kingdom. It is the plants that are best adapted to the soil, climate, and general environment that survive and spread. We see the same thing in the animal kingdom. It is those animals that are most powerful, and are the best adapted to the special surroundings and circumstances, that survive and prevail. We see it in the human species itself. When a more vigorous race comes into collision with a race possessed of less vitality, then, unless the moral power of Christianity intervenes to prevent it, the more vigorous race tends to push the feebler off the face of the earth. We see the same thing still more in human systems of science, philosophy, government, and the like. It is the one with the most power of truth in it, the one best fitted to the age, the people, the general environment and circumstances that survives. It is, in short, the fittest that survives in the struggle; and the fact that it does survive is, as a rule, a tolerably good proof that it is the fittest.

Now this principle just enunciated tells in favour of Christianity. It has been, and still is, superseding other systems in the struggle for existence. Its rod swallows up their rods. It survives in the struggle, and by its very survival it shows itself to be possessed of greater power of truth, greater vitality and fitness for humanity.

We see the fact of this survival very clearly demonstrated when we contemplate the early spread of

Christianity. When it entered on the scene of history, eighteen centuries ago, it found the world already possessed by various religions. It was at once launched into a life-and-death struggle for its existence. Every one sees from the New Testament that it had a terrible contest to maintain at first with the hard and narrow Judaism of the age. As it passed beyond its first stage, it had to enter on a much more formidable struggle with the old paganism of Greece and Rome. At a later period it was launched into a similar struggle with the strong and wild religion of our old Teutonic ancestors. And what was the result? It was that in each case Christianity showed itself to be the fittest by its survival in the struggle. So complete was its victory in the contest with Greek and Roman and Teutonic paganism, not to mention many other less known systems, that it drove them out of existence altogether, just as the animals of our present geological age have superseded the inferior animals of the previous ages. In the present day, we know about these obsolete forms of heathenism only from ancient literature or the remains of their idolatrous service preserved in our museums, just as we know about the remains of those earlier but now obsolete animals from their remains in the rocks of the earth. Clearly Christianity, in its struggles with these ancient systems, has triumphantly approved itself by the principle of the survival of the fittest.

But it may be said, Are not the original power and vitality of Christianity now spent? Is it not waxing old, and becoming ready to vanish away, like some of the ancient plants and animals referred to? By no means. The fact is, that, since the centuries of its youth, Christianity has never shown its aggressive power and vitality to such a degree as in the present century. This is especially demonstrated by the wonderful advance that it has made in mission work throughout the length and breadth of the world. Within the last fifty years or so, we have seen whole groups of islands in the South Seas Christianized; such, for example, as the Fiji and the Sandwich Islands. We have seen Madagascar furnishing converts by tens of thousands every year to the Church, so that there are now in that island upwards of 250,000 professing Christians, and the progress is still going on. In India proper, in 1851, there were only 103,000 native Protestant Christians, whereas in 1881 there were 453,000.[1] Sixty years ago, probably there were not ten native Christians in China, and now there are 80,000 who bear that sacred name. At the beginning of the century there were not more than 50,000 converts from modern heathenism, and now there are about 3,000,000. That is to say, the Christian Church during the present century has reclaimed from

[1] *Statistical Tables of Protestant Missions in India, Burma, and Ceylon* (1881), p. xiii.

heathenism, and much of it of the grossest type, a number nearly equal to three-fourths of the entire population of Scotland, and the work is going on at the present time with greater rapidity than at any previous portion of the century.[1]

We have reason to believe that the spread of Christianity in heathen countries, in the present age, compares not unfavourably with that of the early centuries. It is, of course, difficult to bring this to the test in the form of statistics; still an approximation may be made which may be instructive and interesting. Of course, so far as the ancient Church is concerned, we cannot possibly attain to exactness, and can guard against error only by leaving a sufficiently large margin. We do not descend into details, but only give results. What, then, are some of the results at which competent men and special students of the early Christian ages have arrived? Lange, at the close of his Commentary on Matthew, estimates that the number of professing Christians at A.D. 100 was 500,000, and that at the time of Constantine, say A.D. 320, it was 10,000,000.[2] Uhlhorn estimates that at the latter date they formed less than one-twelfth of the population of the East, and less than one-fifteenth in the West; that is, perhaps

[1] *Report of Centenary Conference on Protestant Missions held in London*, in June 1888, vol. i. p. 153.

[2] *Bibelwerk*, Matt. xxviii. 16–20.

about eight or nine millions.[1] Schaff gives a similar general estimate. At the close of the first century, 'the estimate of half a million among the one hundred millions or more inhabitants of the Roman Empire is probably exaggerated. At the time of Constantine the number of Christians may have reached ten or twelve millions, that is, about one-tenth of the total population of the Roman Empire.'[2] Gibbon also enters into a lengthened discussion of the question, and he comes to the conclusion that at the latter period the Christians formed about one-twentieth of the population of the Empire; in other words, they amounted to about six millions.[3] Dean Milman thinks that Gibbon is 'perhaps inclined to underrate' the relative number of the Christians, but believes that 'with regard to the West he is clearly right.'[4] Let us agree with Milman that Gibbon's estimate, and even all those given above, are too low, and set down the number of Christians at the year 320 as 16,000,000. Let us also accept 500,000 as the estimated number at A.D. 100, and the result is that their number *doubles every forty-four years.*

Let us now consider how this increase compares with

[1] *Kampf des Christenthums*, p. 367.

[2] *Apostolic Christianity*, vol. i. pp. 196–197; *Ante-Nicene Christianity*, vol. i. pp. 22 f.

[3] *Decline and Fall*, chap. xv. Cf. also Renan, *Marc-Aurèle*, c. xxv.; Charteris, *The New Testament Scriptures*, pp. 53 ff.

[4] *History of Christianity*, vol. ii. p. 276, note.

the spread of Christianity in the mission field at the present day. We select one important field, viz. India, including Burmah and Ceylon, partly because it is one whose case is somewhat parallel to that of the ancient Roman Empire, and partly because we have the most trustworthy statistics in regard to mission work in our Indian Empire. How, then, do the statistics stand? Confining ourselves solely to the work of Protestant missionaries, we find that the number of professing Christians brought over from heathenism amounted in the aggregate in 1851 to 103,000; in 1861, to 213,000; in 1871 to 318,000; and in 1881 to 528,000.[1] And what is the rate of increase indicated by these figures? It is, that the Protestant Christians of our Indian Empire are *doubling every thirteen years* or so; and we have the best reason for believing that other fields, such as Madagascar, and not a few of the South Sea Islands, could show an equally satisfactory result. Surely this compares not unfavourably with the increase during the second and third centuries, when the Christians doubled not in every thirteen, but in every forty-four years. In other words, modern missions demonstrate that Christianity has lost nothing of its ancient regenerating power and energy, and is still proving its divinity as much as ever by the principle of the survival of the fittest.

[1] *Statistical Tables of Protestant Missions in India, Burma, and Ceylon* (1881), pp. x. and xiii.

We might even say that we get a more vivid proof of the wonderful regenerative and elevating power of Christianity in modern mission work than in that of the ancient Church. In the early ages it came into contact only with the comparatively high civilisation of the Roman Empire, and for centuries encountered no such degraded peoples as the Esquimaux, the Australians, and many of the tribes of Southern and Central Africa, of the South Seas, and even of India. But it has encountered such tribes in its modern advance, and has demonstrated that it has the capacity of descending to the very lowest depths, of meeting the wants of the most degraded nations, and of raising them up to the platform of Christian life and civilisation. Of this the thrilling story of mission work in many of the above-mentioned fields, as detailed not merely by missionaries, but by other intelligent observers, furnishes a most interesting and satisfactory proof. Surely this shows us that the vitality and elevating energy of Christianity, far from being spent, are as fresh and vigorous as in its early dawn, and that it is still possessed of all its youthful power of adaptation.

But in estimating the energy of modern Christianity we must also bear in mind that it has not been contending merely with low and feeble systems of superstition and idolatry. It is engaged in close and deadly contest with systems that are among the very highest in the scale of mere human religions. It is face to face in India and Japan with Buddhism, which is perhaps the most powerful system of idolatrous religion that the world has ever seen, and yet it is winning its converts every day from its mighty grasp. It is in direct conflict with the religion of China, one of the most civilised and conservative of heathen nations, and even in China it is receiving converts by hundreds every year within the Christian fold. It has begun to attack Mohammedanism,—a religion sprung in no small measure from itself; and notwithstanding the mortal hatred which Mohammedans bear to Christianity, and the most barbarous and sanguinary laws which visit the convert to the Cross with persecution and death, it has won not a few noble trophies from the religion of the Crescent. Besides, nothing can be more certain than the fact that the days of Mohammedanism as a mighty aggressive force are numbered, and that both as a religion, a civilisation, and a world-power, it is destined to hopeless disintegration and collapse in the face of Christianity and Christendom. The Crescent of Mohammed is beyond all doubt a waning Crescent. In conflict with such modern systems, some of them much more powerful than any of the ancient world, Christianity is demonstrating itself more fully every year to be the fittest and most powerful by its survival in the struggle.

But we may see still more vividly the regenerative

power of Christianity when we contemplate the moral transformation which it has effected wherever it reigns. It is extremely difficult to conceive, and utterly impossible to represent in books to be read by Christian eyes, the unspeakable change which it has produced in the moral state of the human race. For the sake of greater definiteness we may fix our mind more especially on the ancient Roman world. Of course, as a rule, the ordinary eye sees only the best of ancient heathenism, the results of its high culture, its noble edifices, its peerless works of art, its better and purer literature. But every one who has looked behind the veil, knows what a hideous spectacle lies there concealed. There meets his horrified gaze a festering mass of pollution and abomination the most unspeakable. Chastity is almost unknown; self-indulgence of the most sensual kind everywhere prevails; lying and deception in trade, bribery and corruption, cruelty and oppression, suicide and the reckless waste and contempt of human life, leaven the whole community. This is not merely the picture drawn by Paul in the first chapter of the Romans, but it is the very picture portrayed by the satirists and by the more sober historians of the ancient world; the picture preserved for modern eyes by a singular but awful providence in the revelations of buried Pompeii. The very gods themselves were sunk in vice, and a man cannot well be expected to be better than his god. In short, the heathenism of ancient Rome in its more degenerate age, shows us just such a deplorable mass of reeking corruption as that which our missionaries find rampant in heathendom at the present day. And yet Christianity succeeded in effecting a radical and incalculable moral change. It was not merely the salt which preserved the race from further corruption and from rotting off the face of the earth, but the vital power which put a new spiritual life into the carcase, which first stopped the leprosy, then mastered it, and finally made the healthy 'flesh come again like the flesh of a little child.' No doubt the morality of Christendom is still far short of the Christian ideal; but as compared with that of ancient Rome, not to speak of modern heathendom, it is high as the heaven is above the earth; and this is a fact which is substantially admitted by men without as well as by men within the circle of catholic Christianity, by men like Lecky as well as men like Loring Brace.

But we see the transcendent moral power of Christianity not less in national life and government and international relations. We see it in the abolition of slavery. In ancient Greece and Rome alike, slavery prevailed to an almost incredible extent. In Athens, it is said that out of 400,000 inhabitants only 100,000 were free citizens. And the case of Rome was somewhat similar, for it is calculated that about one-half of the population of the Empire consisted of slaves. But Christianity slowly remedied the terrible evil and let the oppressed go free. The gladiatorial shows fed the Roman thirst for blood with tens of thousands of wasted lives every year; but Christianity stepped into the arena, and put an end to the horrid cruelty. Woman occupied a most degraded position in most parts of the ancient world; but Christianity took her by the hand, raised her up, and set her by the side of man. Marriage was in the later Roman age a matter of mere temporary and sensual convenience; divorce was so easy and so frequent that women, it was sarcastically said, counted the years by their husbands; but Christianity uttered its blessing over the marriage bond and made it sacred. Infanticide was a custom common even in Greece and Rome; for had not parents an absolute right to do what they liked with their own? But Christianity took the little children up in her arms and blessed them. War was the natural state of things, the most honourable life for a man to follow, and it was generally carried on with bloody barbarity; but Christianity has not only infused its own merciful spirit into it; it has greatly lessened the frequency of war by means of diplomacy and arbitration, and by declaring peace and honest toil to be in the highest degree right and honourable. But why enlarge? Even Plato, the noblest of ancient philosophers, in his ideal republic, admits such things as slavery, the community of women, the exposure of infants, and the like. How very different from all this the religion of Jesus! How much higher its morality! How mighty its spiritual power, which has succeeded in crushing out these and similar evils, and in supplanting them by their opposite virtues!

But another consideration, which shows that Christianity is in our day as much as ever the support and energetic power of all high morality, is the sad fact that the decline of the former sooner or later means the decline of the latter. Mere culture or education or æsthetic taste, yea, all of them together, are quite inadequate for this purpose. Christianity alone suffices. It may no doubt be true that a nation for two or three generations may maintain a fairly high morality after positive religion has lost its hold on the faith and heart of the people, just as the train may continue to move for some time after the engine has been detached, or the twilight remain for a while after the sun has set. But by and by the train comes to a stand without the engine; and so with the continuance of morality after the motive power of Christianity has been withdrawn. By and by, after the sun has set, the twilight darkens into night; and so with morality after the sun of Christianity has gone down. It takes, of course, two or three generations to enable us to demonstrate this fact by statistics; but such statistics as we have point distinctly in this direction. Luthardt, a distinguished German writer, in one of his late volumes, shows very clearly the sad results of the prevalence of pantheism and materialism in modern Germany. He adduces statistics which demonstrate a rapid and fearful increase of crime, especially crimes against chastity, and a terrible advance in the deepening darkness and intensity of the 'social evil.' His statistics are certainly enough to show that where gross materialism prevails, mere culture can no more sustain genuine morality and virtue, as distinguished from the outward semblance thereof, than it could in the declining days of Rome or in the age of the first French Revolution. The mighty spiritual power of Christianity is as necessary for this purpose now as ever. It and it alone has the strength to support, and the motive energy to propagate, true morality in the average run of men of which nations are mainly composed.[1]

The question even admits of being seriously discussed, whether a nation or people can continue to exist without a religion. Certainly no such people of any historical importance has ever yet existed on the surface of the earth. In proportion as religion has declined in any nation, morality has decayed; and in proportion as morality has decayed, the nation has become rotten, honeycombed, and ready to collapse on the first vigorous assault from without, or even in course of time from

[1] See Appendix, Note XX.

internal decay and hollowness. Past history affords us numerous illustrations of the fact from the time of ancient Babylon downwards, and, as we have just seen, modern history and statistics point in the same direction. If it be too much to affirm that 'there cannot be a second generation of an infidel state, for society would fall to pieces,' we may safely maintain that Professor Flint speaks forth the words of truth and soberness when he says, 'The prevalence of atheism in any land must bring with it national decay and disaster. Its triumph in our land would bring with it, I believe, hopeless national ruin.'[1]

Nor does it militate against our present argument to object that Christianity has been the cause of not a little misery in the world. It could not possibly overthrow hoary systems of evil, or tear up ancient and deep-rooted vices and customs, without violence and suffering. And just as little does it tell against the substance of our argument, that many cruelties have been committed in the name of our most holy faith. We refer particularly to the fearful persecutions and massacres carried on by Christians against Jews, infidels, and heathens, and even fellow-Christians. These horrible crimes were not the outcome of Christianity, but of fallen human nature as yet imperfectly Christianized. They were directly contrary to the spirit and the teaching of our religion; and it is

[1] See the whole passage, *Anti-Theistic Theories*, pp. 36 ff. Cf. also Drummond, *Natural Law in the Spiritual World*, pp. 167 ff.

even a powerful argument in favour of its divinity, that though it took Christendom eighteen centuries to learn the doctrine of religious toleration, yet all the time it was there in the New Testament as clear as the sun. The crimes referred to sprang not from full Christian faith, but from the want of it; and therefore they do not prove, as is sometimes supposed, that Christian faith is and has ever been only a well-spring of evil. On one occasion some one remarked in the hearing of Carlyle, that *belief* had done immense evil in the world. 'True,' he replied with vehemence, almost with fury; 'true, belief has done some evil in the world; but it has done all the good that ever was done in it, from the time when Moses saw the burning bush, and *believed* it to be God appointing him to be deliverer of His people, down to the last act of belief that you or I executed. Good never came from aught else.'[1]

From such considerations as the preceding, we see that Christianity has been and still is proving its divinity, its moral power, and final destiny, by its triumphant survival in the struggle for existence. In this respect it differs as much from modern speculative systems of religion as from those of the past ages. These new and rival systems may seem very logical and ingenious; but they are earth-born, with nothing but human authority to support them. They may do well enough for the study, the

[1] Froude's *Life of Thomas Carlyle*, vol. ii. p. 331.

easy-chair, the lecture-room, or summer weather; but they fail when they come to practical matters of life and death. They want the inherent spiritual power of making their adherents willing to consecrate themselves to works of self-sacrifice, and, if necessary, to martyrdom, for the spread of their cause and the welfare of humanity. We hear little or nothing of them undertaking benevolent and mission work amid the slums at home, or among the still more degraded heathen abroad. We never hear of any heathen tribes which they have civilised, not to say Christianized. They have scarcely even the power of organization and self-support, and are more at home in trying to break down the walls of Christianity than those of vice and heathenism. In decided contrast to them, the persistent aggressive energy of Christianity shows that the future, the survival in the struggle, and the final triumph as the fittest religion for man, belong to it and not to them. In the words even of Renan: 'The world will be everlastingly religious, and Christianity, in a large sense, is the last word of religion. Christianity alone remains in possession of a future.'[1]

It may be well for us briefly to inquire what are some of those elements in Christianity which give to it its mighty power and make it 'the fittest.' We mean to touch on only a few of the more important points.

One powerful element is to be found in the practical

[1] *Revue des deux Mondes*, Oct. 15, 1860, pp. 790, 770.

certainty which Christianity affords us in regard to those matters which are of paramount importance to man. The soul which is in earnest cannot do otherwise than yearn anxiously and intensely after reasonable assurance in reference to those matters which may concern its welfare for eternity. Is the soul mortal, or is it immortal? Is there a heaven? Is there a hell? Does God forgive sin, or does He not? If He does, then on what terms? Is there any way by which we may be delivered first from the guilt, and then from the power and bondage of sin? In regard to questions such as these, human philosophies have no certain answer to give, or they give answers diametrically opposed to one another. In such a state of doubt and dissension Christianity offers a real, a well-founded, and a reasonable certainty; and to earnest souls seeking agonizingly after the truth, this certainty gives it, of necessity, a vast power over mere human speculations, which can only attain at the utmost to a 'perhaps.' This reasonable certainty produces in the mind of the Christian a true, energetic faith, which is always a mighty power in itself; for, as J. S. Mill says, 'One person with a *belief* is a social power equal to ninety-nine who have only interests.' One element of the power of Christianity is found in the reasonable certainty which produces well-assured faith.

Another source of its power is to be found in the fact that it reaches down into the eternal, and has its wellsprings in God. It brings souls into the most direct contact with the Fountain of life and power. Human systems at the best are only like mere surface wells, which penetrate but a little into the ground, and do not reach the perennial springs. They do well enough in favourable seasons, but in times of burning, withering drought they become utterly dry, and fail altogether just when they are needed most. But Christianity is like the Artesian well, which penetrates away down through the layers of rock to the inexhaustible supplies of water beneath, and which accordingly keeps springing up with undiminished force and abundance at all seasons and in all weathers. In other words, Christianity reaches down into God, connects the soul with God, and draws its life and power and supplies of grace from Him. These supplies keep gushing, welling up from the infinite ocean beneath, through the ordinances of the Church and the means of grace. In the devout Christian who is united to Christ by faith, the Spirit is as a well of water springing up unto everlasting life, quickening, refreshing, cleansing, strengthening the soul with all might in the inner man. Assuredly another cause of the conquering might of our holy religion is to be found in the Spirit of life and power which it draws from the eternal source, and which is the river the streams whereof make glad the city of our God.

We must also emphasize the fact that much of this power of which we speak arises from the person of

Christ, from the incarnation of God and of the moral law which we have in Him. The ordinary mind has a difficulty in thinking about a God who is a pure, invisible, formless Spirit; but the incarnation exactly meets this need. In Jesus Christ we have one who lives and moves before us, and on whom it is easy for us to fasten our minds and think. Because of His real humanity, we are drawn to Him by the mysterious bonds of human sympathy. By means of His holy and beautiful character and life, we are strongly attracted to Him by all the magic power of holy beauty. In virtue of His unselfish love, His exquisite tenderness, grace, and mercy, our heart is taken wholly captive. On account of His painful and tragic death, borne for the noblest purpose and with the divinest dignity, the soul is drawn to Him with the deepest and most romantic interest. In Him everything meets which can captivate and fill the mind, the heart, the imagination, and make them rest on Him with ease and delight. But He is God; He is the moral law. That God, that moral law, of which we found it difficult to think in the pure, colourless, abstract form, we now find it easy and delightful to think of and love as brought before us in the person of Christ. The incarnate Son is indeed the very power of God, because He meets man's want of a real incarnation of the invisible God and the abstract moral law. Accordingly, Christianity derives much of its power from Him. He is its very fountainhead of spiritual power and life. All the grand movements in its history throughout the ages are but the throbbings of His heart. All the great Christian reformers and workers have drawn their inspiration, enthusiasm, and spiritual force from Him.

But another fact which gives much of its mighty power to Christianity, is its adaptation or fitness to meet the moral and spiritual wants of man. Human nature is a perfect bundle of spiritual wants, and Christianity girdles it all round and exactly fits into it on every side. When a true soul has been really awakened and sees its guilt, it sighs for pardon; and Christianity presents it with a pardon, full and free and righteous. The God-awakened man, in his deepest nature, yearns not only for pardon but for inward holiness: and Christianity meets this want by working in us a new and holy nature which enables us to love and practise all the Christian graces and virtues freely, and to find our true delight therein. We have a natural yearning for a genuine friend, around whom our affections and esteem may twine, and who may fully satisfy all the insatiable longings and desires of our heart; and such we have in Jesus, who is the Friend that sticketh closer than a brother. And not to enlarge, we have an instinctive desire for immortality; and Christianity meets this desire by assuring us of a glorious immortality of intellectual and spiritual perfection and blessedness in the very presence of the Lord for ever. Just as the crystal water flows into all the intricate corners of the intricate vessel and fills them up, so Christianity exactly fits into and fills up all the manifold wants of our spiritual nature. And herein is another secret of its blessed power, and not only that, but another proof that it is of God, and the one true religion.

Another source of the overmastering might of Christianity consists in the motive power with which it fills and possesses the soul. No other religion can supply or bring such motive power to bear upon the soul. We are not to think at present of that motive power which arises from a healthful dread of hell, or from a strong desire after the blessedness of the Christian heaven. We are rather to think of the enthusiastic love and devotion awakened in the Christian's heart by the Lord Jesus, which form indeed the distinctive motive power of our religion. When the faithful soul realizes how much it owes to Jesus, it becomes filled of necessity with a perfect storm of grateful feeling. When we contemplate Jesus leaving glory for us, bearing privation, shame, and suffering for us, dying a felon's death upon the cross for us, seeking out us His lost sheep in our wayward, wandering days, how can Christian hearts be otherwise than consumed with love for Him? When we think that He saved us of His own grace, bought us and washed us with His own blood; when we think of the awful hell from which He has rescued us, of the glorious heaven to which He has brought us, and that He Himself is to be our inheritance for ever, how can Christian hearts do otherwise than glow with a holy enthusiasm of gratitude to Him? Surely such considerations, when we realize them, must kindle the fire of an unquenchable love in the soul. And who does not see that this love is not only a fire which purifies and burns away all that is low and mean in us, but a grand motive power 'in our heart, as a burning fire shut up within our bones, so that we become weary with forbearing, and cannot stay'? It moves us to shun sin because it crucified the Lord, to grow holy like Himself because it pleases Him, to work our little best for Him who did His great work so willingly for us. The enthusiasm of a holy love to Christ, which Christianity awakens and feeds, is another secret of its marvellous power.

Nor must we omit to state that the joy with which true religion fills the soul as with a heavenly light, is another element in its mighty spell. Men sometimes speak of Christianity as a gloomy, morose, melancholy thing. There never was a greater mistake. From its very nature, where it is real it is a religion of peace and joy and hope. The soul which has been delivered from hell, reconciled to God, and made an heir of heaven, and which knows it as it ought, cannot help living in an atmosphere of peace and joy and hope. Nay, Christianity inculcates joy as an abiding habit of mind, for it commands us to rejoice in the Lord alway, to rejoice evermore. It is not Christianity but atheism that is the deeply hopeless, melancholy system. Let Professor Clifford, who wandered into the dark and lonely and dreary wilderness of the latter, speak: 'It cannot be doubted that theistic belief is a comfort and solace to those who hold it, and that the loss of it is a very painful loss. It cannot be doubted, at least, by many of us in this generation, who received it in our childhood, and have parted with it since with such searching trouble as only cradle-faiths can cause. We have seen the spring sun shine out of an empty heaven to light up a soulless earth; we have felt with utter loneliness that the Great Companion is dead.'[1] There we see the spirit of atheism, full of sadness and of wailing. But Christianity gives us a Father, a Saviour, a Brother, a blessed immortality, and a glorious home. Its spirit is a spirit of hope and joy; and the hope and joy which it inspires add to its divine power in the world. 'The joy of the Lord is its strength.'

Another element in the power of Christianity is its wonderful capacity of self-adaptation and assimilation. It is essentially a constructive and conservative system, and only destructive with a view to be truly constructive and conservative. It adapts itself alike to all men of every clime, of every degree of civilisation, of every form of

[1] *Lectures and Essays*, vol. ii. p. 247. See Appendix, Note XXI.

government. It stoops to raise from their degradation the Australian and the Hottentot. It meets the case of the learned and philosophic sons of India and China. It finds itself equally at home under the paternal government of the African chief, the autocracy of the Russian Czar, the constitutional monarchy of Britain, and the republicanism of America. Whatever it finds peculiar, but right and healthful, in national life and civilisation, it not only conserves, but works up into itself, and assimilates, so as to form a new and special type of Christianity particularly adapted to the nation. And there can be no doubt that herein lies much of its power as compared with Judaism, Mohammedanism, and other religions. Every one knows the story of Winfrid, the Apostle of Germany, and the sacred oak of Geismar, hallowed by dim ages of pagan rites. The mighty spell which the tree cast like an awful shadow over the minds of the heathen people, proved a powerful entanglement to keep them back from embracing Christianity. Winfrid saw this, and determined on the bold stroke of hewing it down by the root. He did so, and with the material he built a little Christian chapel; so that by his wise action he not only removed the obstruction and broke the spell, but made use of the material and even the spell itself for Christian purposes. And this is the true spirit of all healthy Christianity. It hews down the old and sacred trees, but only to use them for Christian chapels. It takes care not to lose anything that is good and healthful in ancient religions, civilisations, and nationalities, but preserves it, works it up into the national type of Christianity, and turns it to a new and noble use. Nay, it even gathers fresh life and strength and fruitfulness from the assimilation, as Aaron's rod after the absorption of the rods of the Egyptians budded and blossomed and brought forth almonds. There can be no doubt that this capacity for adaptation and assimilation contributes largely to the fitness of Christianity for becoming the ultimate religion of the world.

But once more, and to crown the whole, the irresistible power of the Christian religion arises from the fact that God is on its side. In the fourth chapter of Revelation, the King of kings is represented as sitting on His exalted throne, which is surrounded with an emerald rainbow, the well-known symbol of covenant grace and mercy. As He looks forth upon the affairs of men, He looks at them through the emerald rainbow. That is, He looks out upon the course of history through the covenant of grace and mercy, and directs it all in the interests of this blessed covenant. In other words, He regulates history and the current of events in the case of the individual, the Church, the world, with a view to the interests of grace and Christianity. He overrules even persecutions, schisms, and heresies in the Church with a view to a purer life, greater emulation and activity, a simpler, clearer, and better-balanced theology and teaching. He directs the spread of education, science, and commerce in the world, and even revolutions and wars, with a view to make crooked places straight and rough places plain for the advancement of Christianity, and to open up the way for the Church to enter in and possess the land for Christ. With God upon its side Christianity must survive and prevail, until at last it is completely triumphant, and the shout ascends from a redeemed humanity, 'Alleluia! for the Lord God omnipotent reigneth.' As we look down the future and strain our eyes to behold the vision of the latter days, we see the world in the summer evening of time lying wrapt all round in the light and glory of a universal Christianity, and a banner floating in the breeze and waving blessings over the nations: but that banner is not the blank flag of a know-nothing scepticism; not the black flag of a hopeless, materialistic atheism; not the Crescent of Mohammed, but the CROSS OF CHRIST.

In drawing to a close, I wish in parting to say a respectful word to the reader. My aim, dear friend, throughout these studies has been supremely practical; not to exercise or satisfy merely your logical understanding, but, if possible, to prepare the way and lead you up to a living faith and trust in Christ; and unless this is accomplished in some degree, their object is lost. In other words, it has been my devout wish to take you by the hand and lead you up to the gate of the City of God. And now I would leave you there alone to knock for yourself, with the assurance that the Lord of the City will open to every true and honest seeker, and with the prayer that you may enter in through the gate into the City.

Let me respectfully but earnestly remind you that there are other capacities in your mind which have to do with religion besides the logical intellect. One of these is your moral nature, including especially conscience. It has to do with God and religion even more directly than the pure intellect has. It is much more sensitive towards God and divine truth, and can feel in the dark where the intellect cannot see. Accordingly, in matters of personal religion, it is safer, as a rule, to trust your moral nature and conscience than mere logic; for the former will often guide you aright when the latter stands bewildered and dumb, or even leads astray. The conscience is, indeed, the highest summit of the soul,—the one which raises itself up farthest towards God and heaven, and is freest from clouds and vapours. And just as the loftiest Alpine peak retains the light of the setting sun long after the plain land and the lower ridges are enveloped in the dusky twilight, so conscience often retains the light of God when the gloomy night of scepticism is setting in upon the intellect. But just as the same sublime Alp also receives the light of the rising day long before the lower hills and plains, and even while they are as yet lying covered with darkness and mist; so the conscience, as a rule, receives the rising light of God and religion before the intellect, and even while the latter is yet in the mists and clouds and glimmering twilight of scepticism. While intellect 'in the valley stumbles through the mist,' conscience 'on the mountain top beholds the morn.' I pray you to recognise this fact. Consult your conscience, your moral nature, and not your logical intellect alone. It will respond, if only you will honestly listen; and it will reply that you, even you, are a sinner in the eyes of the All-holy—a sinner guilty and helpless, and it will impel you to cry, 'What must I do to be saved?'

Let me say that the only satisfactory answer to that question must still be that of the Apostle Paul: 'Believe in the Lord Jesus Christ, and thou shalt be saved.' In other words, the one divinely-authorized way is the way of personal faith in the Lord Jesus Christ. Even supposing that other ways might *perhaps* save you, if you believe in the possibility of salvation at all you must believe that the Christian way, when honestly followed out, will *certainly* save you. But in such a matter no wise man ought to peril his all on a mere *perhaps*, when he can find, and find at hand, a method of salvation which is *yea and amen*, the way of personal faith in Christ.

Do you ask what this faith is? What is the distinctive nature and feature of saving faith? It is simply this, that it rests on Christ as its object, on Christ as set before you in the Gospel, on Christ for your personal salvation. You renounce all trust for salvation in self or in any arm of flesh, and rest solely, consciously, intentionally, abidingly on the Lord Jesus, His person, work, and word. When your mind settles down in this state as its final attitude, it enters into the condition of saving faith. It has that faith which accepts Christ as your Covenant Head, Saviour, and Lord; which identifies you with Him in His life, and death, and righteousness, so that you become a sharer in the blessing of full and free and instantaneous justification for His sake. You have now that faith which unites you with Christ as the branch with the vine, with Christ the source of all spiritual life and power, holiness and activity. This faith puts you into possession first and at once of pardon and acceptance, thereafter of increasing holiness and spiritual energy, and finally of a blessed immortality with Him in heaven.

But you also ask how you can awaken and produce this saving faith towards Jesus in your soul. You cannot work yourself up into it by mere bodily exercise or excitement. You cannot get yourself translated into it by any mere outward ritualistic charm or spell. You cannot vault into it by any grand volition or transcendent effort of mere human will. You can enter it only by the reasonable and scriptural way of turning your mind towards Christ, while you pray for His Spirit to open your eyes and incline your heart to the truth. It is the very nature of Jesus and the truth as it is in Him, when properly contemplated, to produce faith in the soul. Look therefore at Him. Keep Him persistently before your mind. Try to understand Him. Dwell, think, and meditate upon Him, and the different features of His life and character, teaching and work. Give them the time and the opportunity to bear and tell upon your heart. Then, as you do so, you will feel, you cannot tell how, your obstinacy giving way, your hard heart melting, your interest awakening, faith and trust arising, and your soul finally settling down, gently, naturally on the Lord Jesus, as your own personal Saviour. And in that blessed moment you will enter into the position of a justified man, a pardoned and accepted son and heir of God, and a citizen of the Holy City. A new day will begin to break in upon your soul, a day of light and life, of hope and joy; and thereafter, amid the changes and troubles, the bereavements and heart-aches of life, you will find that Christ meets all the wants and experiences of your many-sided nature. He will turn for you at last the shadow of death into the morning; and, alike in time and eternity, He will prove Himself to be all your Salvation and all your Desire.

APPENDIX.

NOTE I. p. 3.

STATE OF RELIGION IN ENGLAND IN THE EIGHTEENTH CENTURY.

'ALTHOUGH a brilliant school of divines maintained the orthodox doctrines with extraordinary ability, and with a fearless confidence that science and severe reasoning were on their side, yet a latent scepticism and a wide-spread indifference might be everywhere traced among the educated classes. There was a common opinion that Christianity was untrue but essential to society, and that on this ground it should be retained. . . . Butler, in his preface to his *Analogy*, declared that "it had come to be taken for granted that Christianity is not so much a subject for inquiry; but that it is now at length discovered to be fictitious." . . . Addison pronounced it an unquestionable truth that there was less "appearance of religion in England than in any neighbouring state or kingdom," whether it be Protestant or Catholic; Sir John Bernard complained that "it really seems to be the fashion for a man to declare himself of no religion," and Montesquieu summed up his observations on English life by declaring, no doubt with exaggeration, "that there was no religion in England, that the subject, if mentioned in society, excited nothing but laughter, and that not more than four or five members of the House of Commons were regular attendants at church."'—Lecky, *History of England in the Eighteenth Century*, vol. ii. pp. 529 ff. (chap. ix.).

'The utter depravity of human nature, the lost condition of every man who is born into the world, the vicarious atonement of Christ, the necessity to salvation of a new birth, of faith, of the constant and sustaining action of the Divine Spirit in the believer's soul, are doctrines which, in the eyes of the modern evangelical, constitute at once the most vital and the most influential portions of Christianity, but they are doctrines which during the greater part of the eighteenth century were seldom heard from a Church of England pulpit.'—*Ibid.* p. 545.

NOTE II. p. 15.

THE SCIENTIFIC SPECIALIST NOT NECESSARILY AN AUTHORITY IN THEOLOGY OR CRITICISM.

'When the human mind has achieved greatness and given evidence of extraordinary power in any domain, there is a tendency to credit it with similar power in all other domains. Thus theologians have found comfort and assurance in the thought that Newton dealt with the question of revelation, forgetful of the fact that the very devotion of his powers, through all the best years of his life, to a totally different class of ideas, not to speak of any natural disqualification, tended to render him less instead of more competent to deal with theological and historic questions.'—Tyndall, *Fragments of Science*, vol. ii. p. 150.

The above principle surely applies to scientific men in the present day, who set themselves up for metaphysicians and theologians, as well as to the case of Newton. At any rate, it finds an admirable illustration in the late controversy between Professor Huxley and Dr. Wace in the *Nineteenth Century* (1889).

NOTE III. p. 20.

RELIGIOUS TRUTH BEYOND THE REACH OF PHYSICAL SCIENCE.

'The mere study of physical nature does not carry us beyond matter and its processes. Its most elaborate methods can give us no apprehension of God, or soul, or moral sense. So far as mere physical science can discern, "if God had slept a million years, all things would be the same." No telescope or microscope can enable us to detect free-will or any other attribute of mind. Physical science can only tell us of physical objects, physical properties, and physical laws.'—Professor Flint, *Anti-Theistic Theories*, p. 106. Cf. *The Unseen Universe*, sect. 221; Harris, *Basis of Theism*, p. 337.

'In the preceding portion of these remarks, we have adverted only to that class of truths which are connected with external nature, reduced to laws,—and the evidence of sense elaborated by reason into science. But no extent of physical investigation can warrant the *denial* of a *distinct order* of impressions and convictions, wholly different in kind, and affecting that portion of our compound constitution which we term the moral and the spiritual.'—Baden Powell, *Order of Nature*, p. 276. Compare also *Essays and Reviews*, p. 152, 12th edition. So far Powell is correct, but he limits the principle far too much in its application.

NOTE IV. p. 23.

THE BIBLE NOT A REVELATION OF SCIENCE.

'From a very early period in the history of scientific inquiry, it has been more or less clearly recognised that the Bible is not a science-revelation, but a revelation of religious truth and duty, discovering the true ideal and destiny of man in fellowship with God. Let us have it kept clear on both sides that there is no divine revelation of scientific truth. Nature is its own revelation.'

'But what we most need in these days to keep conspicuous, is the true view of the Bible as a professed revelation from God. It does not profess to be a revelation of facts such as scientific appliances are adequate to ascertain, while it does profess to discover facts, both as to the universe and as to man, which science cannot approach. It is not a history of the earth, but it includes within it historical records of events closely connected with man's moral and spiritual wellbeing.'

'From these few statements it may readily appear what is the attitude of the Bible towards science. It leaves man to his own research for the structure of science in all its divisions; it proffers no help in such work, but has a range of application quite beyond the area traversed by science.'—Professor Calderwood, *Science and Religion*, pp. 76, 77, 78.

NOTE V. p. 26.

EVOLUTION NOT NECESSARILY INCONSISTENT WITH THEISM.

'Some of the profoundest theologians and ablest defenders of religion in the early Church were believers in the doctrine of spontaneous generation—which may be consistently held in modern times by believers in natural and revealed religion. There is really no ground for the fears of the timid on the one hand, nor on the other hand for the arrogant expectation of the atheist, that he will thereby be able to drive God from His works. Spontaneous generation is not to be understood as a generation out of nothing, an event without a cause, an affair of caprice or chance. It is a production out of pre-existing materials by means of powers existing in the materials,—powers very much unknown, working only in certain circumstances, and requiring, in order to their operation, favourable conditions, assorted by divine wisdom.

'It is now admitted that Christians may hold, in perfect consistency with religion and Genesis, that certain layers of rock were formed, not at once by a fiat of God, but mediately by water and fire as the agents of God. And are they not at liberty to hold, always if evidence be produced, that higher plants have been developed from lower, and higher brutes from lower, according to certain laws of descent, known or unknown, working in favourable circumstances? There is nothing irreligious in the idea of development properly understood.'—M'Cosh, *Christianity and Positivism*, pp. 36, 37. Cf. Row's Bampton Lectures, p. 134 f.; Harris, *Basis of Theism*, pp. 504 ff.; Temple's Bampton Lectures, pp. 108, 122.

'That the doctrine of evolution is gaining ground over the doctrine of special creations we will not deny, but the much more general doctrine of a finality[1] in things is not at all impugned thereby. For the rest, the learned and acute defender of evolution under its most recent form, Mr. H. Spencer, seems himself to recognise the truth of this, when he tells us: "The genesis of an atom is no easier to conceive than that of a planet. Indeed, far from rendering the universe less mysterious than before, it makes a much greater mystery of it. Creation by fabrication is much lower than creation by evolution. A man can bring a machine together; he cannot make a machine that develops itself. That our harmonious

[1] M. Janet uses this word, of course, in the common French meaning of 'final cause or purpose.'

universe should formerly have existed potentially in the state of diffused matter, without form, and that it should gradually have attained its present organization, is *much more wonderful than its formation, according to the artificial method supposed by the vulgar, would be.* Those who consider it legitimate to argue from phenomena to *noumena*, have good right to maintain that *the nebular hypothesis implies a primary cause as superior to the mechanical God of Paley as that is to the fetish of the savage*."'[1]—Janet, *Final Causes*, p. 223 (Clark). See also pp. 268 f.

'It follows that theism is completely disinterested in the properly scientific question (of evolution), as moreover it ought to be; for, as we have often said, so far as science contents itself with verifying facts, grouping them together, and drawing from them the consequences required by its methods, it is sovereign. Let Darwinian evolution be demonstrated or not, theism has nothing to lose thereby: let the conditions of existence be determined as we may wish, the question of cause and origin remains intact. Darwinism has been accepted by men who believe in spirit, as is shown by the capital work of Mr. A. R. Wallace on Natural Selection. It is well known that Mr. Wallace, who had arrived, by his own investigations, at a solution identical with that of Darwin, even before the latter had formulated and systematically expounded his view, has not less established in the most categorical manner that natural selection implies finality, at least as much as the theory of successive creations.'—Pressensé, *Les Origines*, p. 180.

[1] The italics are mine. Perhaps it may be well for me to give the footnote appended by M. Janet to the above extract: 'Let us remark in passing that the God of Paley is not a mechanical God. As it is impossible to speak without a metaphor, it is certain that when one compares the machines of nature to those of man, we are apt to speak of God as a mechanician. So, at other times, one talks of the divine Poet, the great Geometrician, the great Lawgiver, the sovereign Judge, etc. These are modes of expression, and if they are forbidden, we must cease to speak of these things.'

'The present disputes *concerning the origin of the human species* we regard with indifference. Once we have grasped the fact that every operation in nature, down even to the most minute, takes place only under divine assistance, the greater dignity of man and his nearer relation to God can be injuriously affected by no method of origination of the race which the testimony of experience may compel us to adopt. It is therefore, from the religious point of view, a matter of indifference what the investigation of nature may educe on this point.

'The development of simpler organisms into higher is without doubt indisputable, though the more exact mode of this may be perhaps beyond our reach; but the irreligious tendency, so industriously propagated, to regard this development only as a series of *chances*, is utterly untenable. It is *theoretically* untenable.'—Lotze, *Grundzüge der Religionsphilosophie*, p. 78.

As it may be interesting to see what was one of Darwin's latest utterances on the consistency of evolution with theism, I append the following letter, written in May 1879 to Mr. John Fordyce, and printed by him in his *Aspects of Scepticism*, p. 190:—

'It seems to me absurd to doubt that a man may be an ardent theist and an evolutionist. You are right about Kingsley. Asa Gray, the eminent botanist, is another case in point. What my own views may be is a question of no consequence to any one except myself. But, as you ask, I may state that my judgment often fluctuates. Moreover, whether a man deserves to be called a theist depends on the definition of the term, which is much too large a subject for a note. In my most extreme fluctuations I have never been an atheist in the sense of denying the existence of a God. I think that generally (and more and more as I grow older), but not always, an agnostic would be the most correct description of my state of mind.'

NOTE VI. p. 28.

EVOLUTION ONLY AN HYPOTHESIS AND NOT AN ASCERTAINED TRUTH OF SCIENCE.

The following extracts bearing (1) on the statement that evolution is as yet only an hypothesis, (2) on the descent of man from the ape by mere natural evolution, and (3) on the time requisite for the development hypothesis, are taken from authorities of the first rank.

(1) That evolution is as yet only an hypothesis and not an ascertained scientific fact:—

Professor VIRCHOW, Berlin:—'This *generatio æquivoca* [by which is meant spontaneous generation], which has been so often contested and so often contradicted, is nevertheless always meeting us afresh. To be sure, we know not a single *positive fact* to prove that a *generatio æquivoca* has ever been made, that there has ever been a case of procreation in this way, that inorganic masses —such as the firm of Carbon & Co.—have ever spontaneously developed themselves into organic masses. No one has ever seen a *generatio æquivoca* effected; and whoever supposes that it has occurred is contradicted by the naturalist, and not merely by the theologian. . . . We must acknowledge that it has not yet been proved.'—Virchow, *The Freedom of Science in the Modern State*, pp. 36 f. (2nd edition).

LOUIS PASTEUR, Member of the Academy of Sciences, Paris:—'There is no case known at the present day in which we can affirm that microscopic creatures have come into existence without germs, without parents like themselves. Those who pretend that they do have been the dupes of illusions, of experiments badly performed, vitiated by mistakes which they have failed to perceive, or which they have not known how to avoid.'—*Revue des Cours scientifiques*, 23 Avril 1864, p. 265; Article, 'Des Générations spontanées.'

Professor TYNDALL:—'I here affirm that no shred of trustworthy experimental testimony exists to prove that life in our day has ever appeared independently of antecedent life.'—*Nineteenth Century*, March 1878, p. 507. 'Every attempt made in our day to generate life independently of antecedent life has utterly broken down.' —*Fragments of Science*, Preface to the 6th edition, p. vi.

Professor HUXLEY:—'Not only is the kind of evidence adduced in favour of abiogenesis [spontaneous generation] logically insufficient to furnish proof of its occurrence, but it may be stated as a well-based induction, that the more careful the investigator, and the more complete his mastery over the endless practical difficulties which surround experimentation on this subject, the more certain are his experiments to give a negative result.' Again, he says: 'The fact is, that at the present moment there is not a shadow of trustworthy direct evidence that abiogenesis does take place, or has taken place, within the historic period during which existence of life on the globe is recorded.'—*Encyclopædia Britannica*; 9th edition, article on 'Biology.'

(2) On the descent of man from the ape by mere natural evolution:—

Professor VIRCHOW, Berlin:—'You are aware that I am now specially engaged in the study of anthropology, but I am bound to declare that every positive advance which we have made in the province of prehistoric anthropology has actually removed us further from the proof of such a connection [of man with the ape] . . . When we study the fossil man of the quaternary period, who must, of course, have stood comparatively near to our primitive ancestors in the order of descent, or rather of ascent, we find always a *man*, just such men as are now. . . . The old troglodytes, pile-villagers, and bog-people, prove to be quite a respectable society. They have heads so large that many a living person would be only too happy to possess such . . . Nay, if we gather together the whole sum of the fossil men hitherto known, and put them parallel with those of the present time, we can decidedly pronounce that there are among living men a much larger number of individuals who show a relatively inferior type than there are among the fossils known up to this time. . . . Not a single fossil skull of an ape or an "ape-man" has yet been found that could really have belonged to a human being. Every addition to the amount of objects, which we have attained as materials for discussion, has removed us farther from the hypothesis propounded.'—Virchow, *The Freedom of Science in the Modern State* (2nd edition), pp. 60, 62, 63.

His conclusion is: 'WE CANNOT TEACH, WE CANNOT PRONOUNCE IT TO BE A CONQUEST OF SCIENCE, THAT MAN DESCENDS FROM THE APE OR ANY OTHER ANIMAL.'—*Ibid.* p. 62. In the Preface (p. vi.), he says: 'With a few individual exceptions, this protest has met with a cordial assent from German naturalists.'

A. RUSSEL WALLACE:—'The few remains yet known of prehistoric man do not indicate any material diminution in the size of the brain-case. A Swiss skull of the stone age, found in the lake dwelling of Meilen, corresponded exactly to that of a Swiss youth of the present day. The celebrated Neanderthal skull had a larger circumference than the average; and its capacity indicating actual mass of brain, is estimated to have been not less than 75 cubic inches, or nearly the average of existing Australian crania. The Engis skull, perhaps the oldest known, and which, according to Sir John Lubbock, "there seems no doubt was really contemporary with the mammoth and the cave-bear," is yet, according to Professor Huxley, "a fair average skull, which might have belonged to a philosopher, or might have contained the thoughtless brains of a savage." Of the cave-men of Les Eyzies, who were undoubtedly contemporary with the reindeer in the south of France, Professor Paul Broca says: "The great capacity of the brain, the development of the frontal region, the fine elliptical form of the anterior part of the profile of the skull, are incontestable characteristics of superiority, such as we are accustomed to meet with in civilised races."'—Wallace, *Contributions to the Theory of Natural Selection*, pp. 336 f.

Professor DU BOIS-REYMOND, Berlin:—'At a certain period of the development of life on the globe, an epoch of which we do not know the date, there arose a thing new and hitherto unheard of, a thing as incomprehensible as the essence of matter and force. The thread of our intelligence of nature, which mounts up to that infinitely distant time, is broken, and we find ourselves face to face with an impassable abyss. That new and incomprehensible phenomenon is thought.'—Du Bois-Reymond, *La Revue scientifique*, 10 Octobre 1874, p. 341.

(3) On the time requisite for the development hypothesis:—

'The subject [how long the earth has been habitable by plants and animals such as we see now] has been taken up very carefully within the last few years by Sir William Thomson, and the brief *résumé* I shall give of his results contains nearly all that is accurately and definitely acquired to science upon the subject. He divides his arguments upon it into three heads. The first is an argument from the internal heat of the earth; the second is from the tidal retardation of the earth's rotation; and the third is from the sun's temperature.

'Each of these arguments is quite independent of the other two, and is—for all tend to something about the same—to the effect that ten millions of years is about the utmost that can be allowed, from the physical point of view, for all the changes that have taken place on the earth's surface since vegetable life of the lowest known form was capable of existing there.

'But I daresay many of you are acquainted with the speculations of Lyell and others, especially of Darwin, who tell us that even for a comparatively brief portion of recent geological history three hundred millions of years will not suffice! We say so much the worse for geology as at present understood by its chief authorities; for physical considerations, from various independent points of view, render it utterly impossible that more than ten or fifteen millions of years can be granted.'—Professor Tait, *Recent Advances in Physical Science*, pp. 165 ff. Cf. Croll, *Climate and Time*, p. 355.

NOTE VII. p. 70.

HODGE AND BAXTER IN REGARD TO INSPIRATION.

The Church doctrine of plenary inspiration 'denies that the sacred writers were merely partially inspired; it asserts that they were fully inspired as to all that they teach, whether of doctrine or fact. This of course does not imply that the sacred writers were infallible except for the special purpose for which they were employed. They were not imbued with plenary knowledge. As to all matters of science, philosophy, and history, they stood on the same level with their contemporaries. They were infallible only as teachers, and when acting as the spokesmen of God. Their inspiration no more made them astronomers than it made them agriculturists. Isaiah was infallible in his predictions, although he shared with his countrymen the views then prevalent as to the mechanism of the universe. Paul could not err in anything he taught, although he could not recollect how many persons he had baptized in Corinth.'— Hodge, *Systematic Theology*, vol. i. p. 165.

'Those men who think that the human imperfections of the writers [of the Bible] do extend further, and may appear in some by-passages of chronology or history which are no proper part of the rule of faith and life, do not hereby destroy the Christian cause; for God might enable His apostles to an infallible recording and preaching of the gospel, even all things necessary to salvation, though He had not made them infallible in every by-passage and circumstance, any more than they were indefectible in life.

'As for them that say, "I can believe no man in anything who is mistaken in one thing, at least, as infallible," they speak against common sense and reason: for a man may be infallibly acquainted with some things who is not so with all. . . . A lawyer may infallibly tell you whether your cause be good or bad, in the main, who yet may misreport some circumstances in the opening of it. A physician, in his historical observations, may partly err as a historian in some circumstances, and yet be infallible as a physician in some plain cases, which belong directly to his art. I do not believe that any man can prove the least error in the Holy Scripture in any point according to its true intent and meaning; but, if he could, the gospel, as a rule of faith and life, in things necessary to salvation, might nevertheless be proved infallible by all the evidence before given.'—Baxter, *The Reasons of the Christian Religion*, Part II. c. x., Objection 17. Cf. also *The Catechising of Families*, c. vi., Q. and A. 11.

NOTE VIII. p. 83.

QUOTATIONS FROM THE NEW TESTAMENT FOUND IN THE FATHERS.

In looking into the early Christian writers for quotations from the New Testament, we must not expect them always to quote with perfect, or even modern exactness. They had no concordances, no convenient books such as we have, and no divisions into chapters and verses. As a rule we must expect them to quote from memory, and therefore with all the little inaccuracies of quotations of this kind.

It is in this very matter that the author of *Supernatural Religion* makes one of his grand mistakes as a practical critic. He seems almost to expect that the Fathers should have habitually quoted with all the accuracy of the modern recluse student, who has his concordance at hand, and turns up every verse before he writes it down; and because they do not so quote, he rashly infers that they must quote from Gospels different from those which we now possess. But nothing can be more unreal than such a view. He has only to attend a prayer-meeting or simple service conducted by any working minister, who prays without a prayer-book and speaks without a manuscript, in order to have an illustration of the true state of the case. He will find men in such circumstances habitually quoting Scripture inaccurately as to the words, and repeating the same inaccuracies from time to time. But this does not prove in the least that they draw their quotations from another source than the Authorized English Version.

On one occasion, after the publication of the work just mentioned, a company of ten city ministers happened to be present in my house, and in the course of conversation we fell upon the discussion of this author's mode of treating quotations. Attention was especially drawn to the use which he made of small inaccuracies, and the conclusions which he drew from them. One of the company was strongly impressed with the fact that similar phenomena might be met with over and over again in every Presbyterian service in the city every Lord's day, and suggested a very simple test. It was agreed that every one of the company should write down the apostolic benediction in the very form in which he was accustomed to give it in the Church services. We did so, and the result was found to be, that not two of the ten gave it in exactly the same words, and not one of the ten gave it in the exact words of the apostle (2 Cor. xiii. 14). Here there was not only variation, but the same variation repeated from service to service. But this did not prove that there were ten different sources whence the benediction was drawn. The man who has not shut himself up in his study all his life, but has had a little experience of practical Christian work, and has at the same time a little healthy common sense, will be prepared to expect such inaccuracy of quotation, more or less. He will have no difficulty in discounting it at its proper value; it will cause him no perplexity, and assuredly he will never think of requiring a new Gospel to account for every new inaccuracy. Indeed, we meet with similar inexactness in the quotations which the writers of the New Testament make from the Old Testament, and we can scarcely expect to find a different state of things in the early Christian authors.

I may add the following statement from a very high authority: 'The Fathers were better theologians than critics; they frequently quoted loosely or from memory, often no more of a passage than their immediate purpose required; and what they actually wrote has been found peculiarly liable to change on the part of copyists and unskilful editors. . . . In [many] cases, the same author perpetually cites the selfsame text under two or more various forms; and in the Gospels it is often impossible to determine to which of the three earlier ones reference is made.'—Scrivener, *Plain Introduction to the Criticism of the New Testament*, 3rd edition, pp. 416 f. Cf. Sanday, *The Gospels in the Second Century*, c. ii.

NOTE IX. p. 178.

J. S. MILL ON MIRACLES AS A 'VIOLATION OF LAW.'

'It will be said, however, that if these [miracles] be violations of law, then law is violated every time that any outward effect is produced by a voluntary act of a human being. Human volition is constantly modifying natural phenomena, not by violating their laws, but by using their laws. Why may not divine volition do the same? The power of volitions over phenomena is itself a law, and one of the earliest known and acknowledged laws of nature. It is true, the human will exercises power over objects in general indirectly, through the direct power which it possesses only over the human muscles. God, however, has direct power not merely over one thing, but over all the objects which He has made. There is, therefore, no more a supposition of violation of law in supposing that events are produced, prevented, or modified by God's action, than in the supposition of their being produced, prevented, or modified by man's action. Both are equally in the course of nature, both equally consistent with what we know of the government of all things by law.

'Those who thus argue are mostly believers in free-will, and maintain that every human volition originates a new chain of causation, of which it is itself the commencing link, not connected by invariable sequence with any anterior fact. Even, therefore, if divine interposition did constitute a breaking in upon the connected chain of events, by the introduction of a new originating cause without root in the past, this would be no reason for discrediting it, since every human act of volition does precisely the same. If the one is a breach of law, so are the others. In fact, the reign of law does not extend to the origination of volition. . . . The alleged [above] analogy holds good: but what it proves is only what I have from the first maintained — that divine interference with nature could be proved if we had the same sort of evidence for it which we have for human interference.'— Mill, *Three Essays*, pp. 226 ff.

NOTE X. p. 179.

THE MODE OF DIVINE INTERVENTION IN MIRACLES.

'The continuance of the creation is not conceivable without the action of the WILL which created its actual elements, and which alone can furnish the ground of their reciprocal action.

'We must affirm that every process of reciprocal action in nature, however insignificant, is possible only through the continual co-operation of the one true Reality, which in religion we call "God." Accordingly we cannot reject the continual active influence (*Einwirkung*) of God upon the course of nature, because of the theoretical objection that the order of nature cannot be interfered with.

'It is not correct to say that a miracle involves "the suspension of the laws of nature." Its peculiarity consists in this, that it really subjects itself to these, but with other proportions, magnitudes, and values in the co-operating elements than belonged to them by mere previous nature.

'When a miracle takes place, the divine influence does not aim at producing a change in the general laws of nature. We have much rather reason to hold that these laws must maintain their validity unchanged during the whole period of the world's existence. But an actual *course of nature* does not consist merely of *general laws*, which do not exist for themselves at all. On the contrary, it rather consists of innumerable elements, endowed with power of different kinds and measures, elements which are subordinate to the laws of nature. What these elements are and what their special condition at any time may be,—that is determined not by the *laws of nature*, but by the *plan of that world* which God, out of numerous possible world, has called into realization. Consequently, if this special plan [or idea] of the world demands a change in the *nature of the elements*, there is nothing whatever to hinder such an interference.

'Accordingly [in a miracle] God works by an immediate influence which changes the *inner nature of things*, so that while they work according to the *same* general laws, they nevertheless bring about the miraculous event, which they would *not* have produced *without* His influence.'—Lotze, *Grundzüge der Religionsphilosophie*, pp. 59, 60, 61.

That is, the continuance of nature and its operations depends directly and continually on the will of God. Miracles are therefore possible. But they are not a violation of the laws of nature. On the contrary, these laws remain the same. But God has direct access to the original elements which obey these laws, to change their inner nature and condition, and the force or power inherent in them. These elements so changed or modified continue to work according to the laws of nature, but in virtue of the change or modification they produce the miracle. In other words, the point where the divine will directly intervenes is not at the laws, but at the elements or forces which obey these laws while they bring about the miracle. Cf. also Lotze, *Mikrokosmus*, vol. ii. pp. 52 and 54; Dorner, *Christliche Glaubenslehre*, vol. i. pp. 603 ff.

'We are thus led to believe that there exists now an invisible order of things intimately connected with the present, and capable of acting energetically upon it; for, in truth, the energy of the present system is to be looked upon as originally derived from the invisible universe, while the forces which give rise to transmutations of energy probably take their origin in the same region.

'We have now reached a stage from which we can very easily dispose of any scientific difficulty regarding miracles. For if the invisible was able to produce the present visible universe with all its energy, it could, of course, *à fortiori*, very easily produce such transmutations of energy from the one universe into the other as would account for the events which took place in Judæa [at the advent of our Lord]. Those events are therefore no longer to be regarded as absolute breaks of continuity, a thing which we have agreed to consider impossible, but only as the result of a peculiar action of the invisible upon the visible universe.

'It appears to us as almost self-evident, that Christ, if He came to us from the invisible world, could hardly (with reverence be it spoken) have done so without some peculiar sort of communication being established between the two worlds.'—Professors B. Stewart and P. G. Tait, *The Unseen Universe*, pp. 199, 247, 248 (10th edition).

NOTE XI. p. 195.

ISAAC TAYLOR ON THE ARGUMENT FROM CONGRUITY.

'But is it not "reasoning in a circle" thus to believe the miracles because the religion is felt to be from heaven, and to believe the religion because it has been attested by miracles? Grant it that this *is* reasoning in a circle, when thus formally stated; but it does not follow that therefore the reasoning is not valid. A misapprehension on this ground has too easily been admitted, as well on the side of those who have conducted the Christian argument as with those who have impugned it. A sophism, boldly obtruded on the one side, has been timidly dealt with on the other.

'The very firmest of our convictions come to us in this same mode,—that is, not in the way of a sequence of evidences, following each other as links in a chain, and carrying with them the conclusion; but in the way of the CONGRUITY of co-ordinate evidences, meeting or collapsing in the conclusion. This is not the same thing as what is called "cumulative proof," nor is it proof derived from the coincidence of facts. Those impressions which command the reason and the feelings in the most imperative manner, and which in fact we find it impossible to resist, are the result of the meeting of congruous elements; they are the product of causes which, *though independent, are felt so to fit the one to the other, that each as soon as it is seen in combination authenticates the other;* and, in allowing the two to carry our convictions, we are not yielding to the sophism which consists in alternately putting the premise [and conclusion] in the place of each other, but are recognising a principle which is always true in the very structure of the human mind.

'Let the case be this—that you have to do with one who offers to your eye his credentials—his diploma, duly signed and sealed, and which declare him to be a Personage of the highest rank. All seems genuine in these evidences. At the same time, the style and tone, the air and behaviour, of this Personage, and all that he says, and what he informs you of, and the instructions he gives you, are in every respect consistent with his pretensions, as set forth in the instrument which he brings with him. It is not in such a case that you alternately believe his credentials to be genuine, *because* his deportment and his language are becoming to his alleged rank; and then, that you yield to the impression which has been made upon your feelings by his deportment, *because* you have already admitted the credentials to be true. Your belief is the product of a simultaneous accordance of the two species of proof: it is a combined force that carries conviction; it is not a succession of proofs in line.

'The same force of congruity, not a catena of proofs, gives us the most trustworthy of those impressions upon the strength of which we act in the daily occasions of life; and it is the same Law of Belief which rules us also in the highest of all arguments—that which issues in a devout regard to Him, by and through whom all things are. On this same ground, where logic halts, an instinctive reasoning prevails, which takes its force from the confluence of lines of reasoning.'—Isaac Taylor, *The Restoration of Belief*, pp. 94 f.

NOTE XII. p. 196.

MIRACLES NATURALLY TO BE EXPECTED OF CHRIST.

'We could not conceive of [Christ] as not doing such works; and those to whom we presented Him as Lord and Saviour might very well answer, Strange that one should come to deliver men from the bondage of nature which was crushing them, and yet Himself have been subject to its heaviest laws,—Himself "Wonderful" (Isa. ix. 6), and yet His appearance accompanied by no analogous wonders in nature,—claiming to be the Life, and yet Himself helpless in the encounter with death; however much He may have promised in word, never realizing any part of His promises in deed; giving nothing in hand, no first-fruits of power, no pledges of greater things to come. They would have a right to ask, "Why did He give no signs that He came to connect the visible with the invisible world?"'—Trench, *The Miracles of our Lord*, pp. 102 f.

NOTE XIII. p. 224.

ALLEGED EVIDENTIAL UNIMPORTANCE OF THE RESURRECTION OF CHRIST.

'M. Prudot, in his work *La Résurrection de Jésus Christ*, p. 299, gives a declaration signed at a general conference of pastors and elders of the French Protestant Church, held in Paris A.D. 1865, which contains the following statement:—

'"The undersigned pastors and laymen, considering that the modern religious conscience, instructed in the school of Jesus Christ Himself, and slowly developed by eighteen centuries of Christian education, has learned, on the one side, not to make the divinity of the Master's teaching depend upon His bodily reappearances; on the other, to consider as independent of this fact the certainty of eternal life, in such a manner that faith henceforth rests, not upon the perilous arguments of critical erudition unapproachable to simple believers, but upon the evidence of the truth itself:

'"Declare that, divided as they are among themselves upon the historical question, they frankly acknowledge the right of distinguishing between this question and Christianity itself, and of founding the living and simple demonstration of faith upon the agreement of the holy word of Jesus Christ with the principles and needs of the human soul."'—Professor Milligan, *The Resurrection of our Lord*, p. 259.

'It is difficult now, whether we look at the first rise of Christianity or at its later history, to admit that it hangs by a thread, as St. Paul declares, logically attached to the testimony of Cephas, and the Twelve, and the Five Hundred.'—*Natural Religion*, p. 253.

NOTE XIV. p. 245.

THE THEORY OF PROBABILITIES APPLIED TO THE EVIDENCE FOR CHRIST'S RESURRECTION.

It may be of importance to some minds that we should attempt to represent by the mathematical 'Theory of Probabilities' what are the chances that the witnesses to the risen Saviour were deceived by their senses. Of course, any attempt of the kind can only be an *approximation, an illustration and aid to thought* rather than a result mathematically exact.

The Law of Probabilities bearing on the case is thus laid down by Todhunter in his *Algebra:* (722) 'If there be any number of *independent* events, the probability that they will all happen is the product of their respective probabilities of happening.' To make this clear by a simple illustration, let us suppose that we have a bag with a hundred balls in it, of which one is white and ninety-nine are black. The chance that we draw the white ball at the first trial is only 1 to 100, or as it is represented arithmetically, $\frac{1}{100}$. The chance that we draw the white ball twice in succession is found by multiplying together the chance of drawing it the first time, which is $\frac{1}{100}$, by the chance of drawing it the second time, which is, of course, also $\frac{1}{100}$. In other words, the chance of drawing the white ball the first and second times in succession is $\frac{1}{100} \times \frac{1}{100}$ or $\frac{1}{10,000}$, *i.e.* 1 to 10,000. The chance of drawing it three times in succession is only 1 to 1,000,000, *i.e.* $\frac{1}{100} \times \frac{1}{100} \times \frac{1}{100}$, or $\frac{1}{1,000,000}$. In short, we get the ultimate chance by multiplying the original chance into itself the same number of times as the white ball is supposed to be drawn in succession. More briefly, the chance of drawing it n times in succession will be $(\frac{1}{100})^n$.

Now it is extremely easy to apply this principle to

the case of the witnesses of the risen Saviour. The only difficulty here is to be found in the calculation of the original chance that any one witness could be deceived. We may safely say that our eyesight in ordinarily favourable circumstances does not deceive us once in a million times. Let us say, however, that it does so once in a thousand times. That is, the chance that we may be deceived by our eyesight in fully favourable circumstances is 1 to 1000, or $\frac{1}{1000}$. We may with equal safety make the same assumption in regard to our sense of hearing. It does not in fully favourable circumstances deceive us once in a million times; but let us say once in a thousand times. That is, the chance that we are deceived by our hearing in the circumstances described is as 1 to 1000, or $\frac{1}{1000}$. Now, if we take a case in which we have the concurrent testimony of both our eyes and ears, the chance that they are both deceived is the product of the two chances, or $\frac{1}{1000} \times \frac{1}{1000}$, which is $\frac{1}{1,000,000}$. In other words, the chance that both eyes and ears should be deceived is only 1 to 1,000,000, and this is vastly more than the truth.[1]

Let us now apply this to the witnesses to our Lord's resurrection mentioned in 1 Cor. xv. 4–7. These witnesses saw and heard Christ, had the testimony of both their eyes and ears. The probability, therefore, that any one of these witnesses was deceived is only 1 to 1,000,000, *i.e.* $\frac{1}{1,000,000}$. The probability that two were deceived is of course $\frac{1}{1,000,000} \times \frac{1}{1,000,000}$, or $\frac{1}{1,000,000,000,000}$. That is, the chance that two of them were deceived is only 1 to 1,000,000,000,000, etc. But there are really twelve apostolic witnesses distinctly mentioned, most of whom saw the Lord at least twice. What then is the chance that all the twelve were deceived? To find the answer we must multiply $\frac{1}{1,000,000}$ into itself 12 times, *i.e.* $(\frac{1}{1,000,000})^{12}$. This, of course, gives a fraction whose numerator is 1 and whose

[1] Cf. Helmholtz, *Popular Lectures on Scientific Subjects*, p. 341.

denominator is 1 followed by 72 ciphers. That is, the chance that the twelve apostolic witnesses were deceived is only as 1 to the number which consists of 1 with 72 ciphers attached. If we take in the testimony of the 'more than five hundred brethren' on the same terms, the result is vastly more overwhelming. We have now 512 witnesses at the least who saw and heard the risen Lord. The chance that any one of them could be deceived is, as we have seen, only $\frac{1}{1,000,000}$; consequently the chance that all of them could be deceived is $(\frac{1}{1,000,000})^{512}$, *i.e.* the product of $\frac{1}{1,000,000}$ multiplied into itself 512 times, which gives a fraction whose numerator is 1 and its denominator 1 with 3072 ciphers attached. In other words, the chance that all of them could be deceived is only as 1 to the number which consists of 1 followed by 3072 ciphers, a number which it would take more than two pages of this appendix to express.

That is to say, the chance that the disciples and the five hundred were deceived as to the appearance of Christ is practically nothing; the probability that they were right and actually saw the Lord is practically the highest certainty. And Strauss says: 'There is no occasion to doubt that the Apostle Paul had heard this [about the appearances] from Peter, James, and perhaps from others concerned (comp. Gal. i. 18 ff., ii. 9), and that all of these, and even the five hundred, were firmly convinced that they had seen Jesus who had been dead, and alive again.'—*New Life of Jesus*, vol. i. p. 400. Surely all this points most clearly to the utter improbability of the hypothesis of visions which were the outcome of mere hallucination.

NOTE XV. p. 254.

HASE ON THE SOCRATES OF XENOPHON AND PLATO.

'The Socrates of Xenophon is different from the Socrates of Plato. Each has grasped that side which was to him the nearest and most congenial. Only from both representations conjoined can we recognise the true Socrates. The graphic simplicity of Xenophon carries with it the full impress of the truth of that which he relates. Nevertheless, this Socrates who moves about in the narrow circle of moral and political representations is not the complete Socrates, the wisest man of Greece, who called forth the great revolution in the minds of his people. On the other hand, the Platonic Socrates is much better fitted to be the creator of the new period of Greek philosophy, and accordingly appears as the Attic Logos, as having brought down the wisdom of heaven to the earth.'—Hase, *Geschichte Jesu*, p. 61; from the German, quoted in Schaff's *History of Apostolic Christianity*, vol. ii. p. 695. Cf. Stanley, *History of the Jewish Church*, Lecture xlvi.

NOTE XVI. p. 258.

THE TRULY JUST MAN AS DESCRIBED IN PLATO'S 'REPUBLIC.'

It may not be out of place here to remind the reader of Plato's well-known description of the truly just or righteous man, as given in his *Republic*. After having finished the picture of the unjust man, he continues :—

'Such being our unjust man, let us, in pursuance of the argument, place the just man by his side—a man of true simplicity and nobleness, resolved, as Æschylus says, not to seem, but to be good. We must certainly take away the seeming; for if he be thought to be a just man, he will have honours and gifts on the strength of this reputation, so that it will be uncertain whether it is for justice' sake, or for the sake of the gifts and honours, that he is what he is. Yes, we must strip him bare of everything but justice, and make his whole case the reverse of the former. Without being guilty of one unjust act, let him have the worst reputation for injustice, so that his virtue may be thoroughly tested, and shown to be proof against infamy and all its consequences; and let him go on till the day of his death, stedfast in his justice, but with a lifelong reputation for injustice.

'After describing the men [just and unjust] as we have done, there will be no further difficulty, I imagine, in proceeding to sketch the kind of life which awaits them respectively. They will say that in such a situation the just man will be scourged, racked, fettered, will have his eyes burnt out, and at last, after suffering every kind of torture, will be crucified.' — *Republic*, Book ii.; Davies and Vaughan.

If ever this test of the truly righteous man was fulfilled to the letter, it was fulfilled in Jesus of Nazareth, 'that Just One.'

NOTE XVII. p. 259.

TESTIMONIES TO THE CHARACTER OF JESUS.

In the following pages I venture to gather together a few of the testimonies of eminent negative or anti-supernaturalist writers to the moral character of Jesus. Of course these writers do not all occupy exactly the same position, some of them like Keim and Ewald, taking up a more favourable and friendly position ; and others, like Strauss in the last stage of his religious aberration, a position of extreme negation. It is instructive to contemplate the impression made by Christ upon the minds of upright and honourable men, who feel themselves unhappily constrained to take up a position outside of catholic Christianity, or even distinctly antagonistic to it.

I may state that the reader will find in Professor Schaff's book, *The Person of Christ*, a few of the testimonies given below, and a number of others in addition. I had all but finished this collection before I came across Dr. Schaff's interesting work.

(1) *Strauss.*

'If we ask how this harmonious mental constitution had come to exist in Jesus, there is nowhere in the accounts of His life that lie before us any intimation of severe mental struggles from which it proceeded. . . . In all those natures which were not purified until they had gone through struggles and violent disruption (think only of a Paul, an Augustine, and a Luther), the shadowy colours of this exist for ever; and something harsh, severe, and gloomy clings to them all their lives; but of this in Jesus no trace is found. Jesus appears as a beautiful nature from the first, which had only to develop itself out of itself, to become more clearly conscious of itself, ever firmer in itself, but not to change and begin a new life.'—*New Life of Jesus*, vol. i. pp. 282 f.

'Among these improvers of the ideal of humanity, Jesus stands, at all events, in the first class. He introduced features into it which were wanting to it before, or had continued undeveloped; reduced the dimensions of others which prevented its universal application; imported into it by the religious aspect which He gave it a more lofty consecration, and bestowed upon it, by embodying it in His own person, the most vital warmth; while the Religious Society which took its rise from Him provided for this ideal the widest acceptance among mankind.'—*New Life of Jesus*, vol. ii. p. 437.

It is right to state that Strauss held that there were 'defects' in Jesus, in regard, for example, to His teaching concerning man's relationship to the state, trade and art, citizenship, and 'the elegancies of life'! Cf. *New Life of Jesus*, vol. ii. p. 438.

(2) *Keim.*

'The question concerning the religious personality of Jesus leads us into the mysterious. Is it reality or is it a mere expression, if we call this virtuous, God-connected life the noblest blossom of a noble tree, the crown of the cedar of Israel? In a dry and barren age, a full and abundant life; among falling ruins, a construction; among broken natures, one upright and strong; among souls empty of God and God-abandoned, a son of God; among the sad and despairing, a joyous, hopeful, generous personality; among slaves, a freeman; among sinners, a Holy One; in this contradiction to the facts of the age, in this gigantic elevation over the depressed, flat, low level of the century; in this transmutation of stagnation, retrogression, and fatal sickliness into progress, health, the power and colour of eternal youth; finally, in this eminent distinction of His activity, His purity, His nearness to God, He makes, for new and endless centuries, which *through Him* have conquered stagnation and retrogression, the impression of mysterious loneliness, superhuman miracle, divine creation.'—*Geschichte Jesu von Nazara*, vol. iii. p. 662.

'There has been in the midst of us a true man, in whom the divine seed which is deposited in the bosom of human nature, by a miracle of divine power, has expanded to perfection. The innate communion of man with God has reached its consummation in Him, in a manner unique and valid for evermore. He is the ideal man, foreseen and loved of God from all eternity as the crown of the creation; in the contemplation of whom all the desires of the love of God the Creator are satisfied, because in the heart and face of that human Person He sees Himself.'—*Der geschichtliche Christus*, p. 198; quoted by Godet, *Conférences Apologétiques*, vi. p. 6.

(3) *Ewald.*

Of many passages which might be quoted from his *Life and Times of Christ*, the following may suffice. He speaks of Christ as one to whom 'not the smallest actual sin attached,' and says:—

'He brought the invincible gladness, strength, and activity of the purest divine love, pervading all perception no less than all action, fulfilling all the good laws already in existence, and not less alive to every new fact of knowledge and every new divine duty, authenticating itself to the world most distinctly in government, work, assistance, and guidance, but also in all obedience, self-limitation, and all self-sacrifice. Thus, He became the Son of God as no one had hitherto been, in a mortal body and in a fleeting space of time, the purest reflection and the most perfect image of the Eternal Himself. Thus He became the Word of God, speaking from God by His human word no less than by His whole appearing and work; and thus declaring to the world by an overwhelming force, an eternal, indelible clearness such as no one before had equalled and no one after surpassed, God's most hidden mind, and indeed the very spirit of His activity itself. . . . Is perfection in what is humanly imperfect, undying immortality in what is perishably mortal, possible? He shows that it is, and proves it as nothing else has done; and will eternally show and prove it to all those who do not flee from His light. . . . How far does Christ stand even above these greatest ones out of Israel [Socrates, Buddha, Confucius]! And if the kingdom of the two latter nevertheless still endures so wonderfully long, what is to be expected from the duration and stability of *His* kingdom!'

'O Christ, what after all these centuries, with all its ignoring and misdeeming of Thee, is the world of to-day seeking after and affecting? They who are Thine know Thee, as they always in the past perceived, and also in all the future will always perceive, that Thou art the sole unfailing instrument of the salvation of this world which history has brought to it.'—*History of Israel*, vol. vi. pp. 453 f., English translation (Longmans, Green, & Co.).

(4) *Rousseau.*

'Can it be that He whose history the gospel relates is but a man? Is that the tone of an enthusiast or an ambitious sectary? What sweetness, what purity in His manners! What touching grace in His instructions! What elevation in His maxims! What profound wisdom in His discourses! What presence of mind, what acuteness, what justness in His replies! What command over His passions! Where is the man, where is the sage, who can act, suffer, and die without weakness and without ostentation? When Plato paints his imaginary righteous man, covered with all the opprobrium of crime, and worthy of all the rewards of virtue, he paints feature for feature Jesus Christ. The resemblance is so striking that all the Fathers felt it, and it is impossible to mistake it. What prejudice, what blindness must we have, to dare to compare the son of Sophroniscus to the Son of Mary? What a distance the one is from the other! Socrates, dying without pain, without ignominy, easily sustained his character to the close; and if that easy death had not honoured his life, one might have doubted whether Socrates with all his genius was anything more than a sophist. They tell us he invented morality: others had put it into practice before he lived. He had but to say what they had done: he had but to reduce their example into the form of precepts. Aristides had been just before Socrates declared what justice was; Leonidas had died for his country before Socrates made patriotism a duty; Sparta was temperate before Socrates praised sobriety; before he had defined virtue, Greece abounded in virtuous men. But where did Jesus learn among His people that pure and elevated morality of which He alone has given us the precepts and the example? From the bosom of the most bigoted fanaticism, the highest wisdom makes itself heard, and the simplicity of the most heroic virtues honoured the vilest of all nations. The death of Socrates, philosophizing tranquilly with his friends, is the gentlest one could wish: that of Jesus expiring in anguish, reviled, mocked, cursed of a whole people, is the most horrible that one can fear. Socrates in taking the cup of poison blesses him who presents it weeping; Jesus in the midst of terrible agony, prays for His infuriated executioners. Yes, if the life and death of Socrates are those of a sage, the life and death of Jesus are those of a God. Shall we say that the gospel history is a mere invention? My friend, it is not so that men invent; and the facts concerning Socrates, of which no one entertains a doubt, are less attested than those concerning Jesus Christ. In reality this supposition is only to shift the difficulty a step farther back, not to banish it. It would be more inconceivable that several men should have united to fabricate that book, than that a single person should have furnished the subject of it. Jewish authors would never have invented either that style or that morality; and the gospel has marks of truth so great, so striking, so utterly inimitable, that the inventor of it would be more astonishing than the hero.'—*Émile*, Book iv. pp. 369 f. (Firmin-Didot).

(5) *Renan.*

'They—Sakya-Mouni, Plato, St. Paul, St. Francis of Assisi, St. Augustine—felt the divine in themselves. In the front rank of this great family of the true sons of God we must place Jesus. Jesus has no visions: God does not speak to Him from without: God is in Him: He feels Himself with God, and He draws from His own heart what He says about His Father. He lives in the bosom of God by a direct communication at every moment: He does not see Him, but He hears Him without the need of thunder and the burning bush like Moses, of a revealing tempest like Job, of an oracle like the ancient Greek sages, of a familiar genius like Socrates, or of the angel Gabriel like Mahomet. . . . He believes Himself in direct relation with God, He believes Himself the Son of God. The highest consciousness of God which has existed in the bosom of humanity was that of Jesus.'—*Vie de Jésus*, p. 75, 12th edition.

'Whatever may be the transformations of dogma, Jesus will remain the Creator of pure sentiment: the Sermon on the Mount will never be surpassed. Any revolution will only connect us in religion more closely with that grand intellectual and moral line at the head of which shines the name of Jesus.'—*Ibid.* p. 447.

'Jesus is the highest of those pillars which show to man whence he comes and whither he ought to tend. In Him is concentrated all that is good and elevated in our nature. . . . He found His very life in His Father, and in the divine mission which He believed it to be His duty to fulfil. . . . Whatever may be the unexpected phenomena of the future, Jesus will never be surpassed. His worship will renew its youth for ever; His story will call forth tears without end; His sufferings will melt the noblest hearts; all ages will proclaim that among the sons of men there is none greater than Jesus.'—*Vie de Jésus*, pp. 457 ff.

(6) *Keshub Chunder Sen.*

This eloquent Hindu, who died in 1884, was the well-known leader of the Brahmo-Somaj, or Indian theistic movement. Speaking of Christ, he says:—

'He was the son of a humble carpenter, and He laboured in connection with His ministry only three short years,—do not these simple facts conclusively prove, when viewed in reference to the vast amount of influence He has exercised on the world, that greatness dwelt in Jesus? Poor and illiterate, brought up in Nazareth—a village notorious for its corruption—under demoralizing influences, His associates the lowest mechanics and fishermen, from whom He could receive not a single ray of enlightenment, He rose superior to all outward circumstances by the force of His innate greatness, and grew in wisdom, faith, and piety by meditation and prayer, and with the inspiration of the Divine Spirit working within Him. Though all the external conditions of His life were against Him, He rose above them with the strength of the Lord, and with almost superhuman wisdom and energy, taught those sublime truths, and performed those moral wonders, for which succeeding ages have paid Him the tribute of gratitude and admiration. Verily He was above ordinary humanity. Sent by Providence in order to reform and regenerate mankind, He received from Providence the wisdom and the power for that great work.'—Keshub Chunder Sen, *Lectures and Tracts*, pp. 9 f. (Strahan).

'The two fundamental doctrines of gospel ethics which stand out prominently above all others, and give it its peculiar grandeur and its pre-eminent excellence, are, in my opinion, the doctrines of forgiveness and self-sacrifice; and it is in these we perceive the moral greatness of Christ. These golden maxims how beautifully He preached, how nobly He lived! What moral serenity and sweetness pervade His life! What extraordinary tenderness and humility—what lamblike meekness and simplicity! His heart was full of mercy and forgiving kindness; friends and foes shared His charity and love. And yet, on the other hand, how resolute, firm, and unyielding in His adherence to truth! He feared no mortal man, and braved even death itself for the sake of truth and God. Verily, when we read His life, His meekness, like the soft moon, ravishes the heart, and bathes it in a flood of serene light; but when we come to the grand consummation of His career, His death on the cross, behold how He shines as the sun in its meridian splendour!'—*Ibid.* pp. 37 f.

(7) *Theodore Parker.*

'Now here we see a young man, but little more than thirty years old, with no advantage of position; the son and companion of rude people; born in a town whose inhabitants were wicked to a proverb; of a nation above all others distinguished for their superstition, for national pride, exaltation of themselves and contempt for all others; in an age of singular corruption, when the substance of religion had faded out from the mind of its anointed ministers, and sin had spread wide among a people turbulent, oppressed, and downtrodden; a man ridiculed for His lack of knowledge, in this nation of forms, of hypocritical priests and corrupt people, falls back on simple morality, simple religion, unites in Himself the sublimest precepts and divinest practices, thus more than realizing the dream of prophets and sages; rises free from so many prejudices of His age, nation, or sect; gives free range to the Spirit of God in His breast;

sets aside the law, sacred and time-honoured as it was, its forms, its sacrifices, its temple, and its priests; puts away the doctors of the law, subtle, learned, irrefragable, and pours out doctrines, beautiful as light, sublime as heaven, and true as God.'—*Discourse of Matters pertaining to Religion*, p. 195 (Trübner & Co.).

'That mightiest heart that ever beat, stirred by the Spirit of God, how it wrought in His bosom! What words of rebuke, of counsel, comfort, admonition, promise, hope, did He pour out; words that stir the soul as summer dews call up the faint and sickly grass! What profound instruction in His proverbs and discourses; what wisdom in His homely sayings, so rich with Jewish life; what deep divinity of soul in His prayers, His action, sympathy, resignation! Persecution comes, He bears it: contempt; it is nothing to Him.'—*Ibid.* p. 197.

'He stands alone, serene in awful loveliness, not fearing the roar of the street, the hiss of the temple, the contempt of His townsmen, the coldness of this disciple, the treachery of that; who still bore up, had freest communion when all alone; was deserted, never forsaken; betrayed, but still safe; crucified, but all the more triumphant. This was the victory of the Soul; a Man of the highest type. Blessed be God that so much manliness has been lived out, and stands there yet, a lasting monument to mark how high the tides of divine life have risen in the human world. . . . Here was the greatest soul of the sons of men; a man of genius for religion; one before whom the majestic mind of Grecian sages and of Hebrew seers must vail its face. What man, what sect, what church has mastered His noblest thought!'—*Ibid.* p. 200.

(8) *J. S. Mill.*

'Above all, the most valuable part of the effect on the character, which Christianity has produced by holding up in a Divine Person a standard of excellence, and a model for imitation, is available even to the absolute unbeliever, and can nevermore be lost to humanity. For it is Christ, rather than God, whom Christianity has held up to believers as the pattern of perfection for humanity. It is the God incarnate, more than the God of the Jews or of Nature, who being idealized has taken so great and salutary a hold on the modern mind. And whatever else may be taken away from us by rational criticism, Christ is still left; a unique figure, not more unlike all His precursors than all His followers, even those who had the direct benefit of His personal teaching. It is of no use to say that Christ as exhibited in the Gospels is not historical, and that we know not how much of what is admirable has been superadded by the tradition of His followers. The tradition of followers suffices to insert any number of marvels, and may have inserted all the miracles which He is reputed to have wrought. But who among His disciples or among their proselytes was capable of inventing the sayings ascribed to Jesus or of imagining the life and character revealed in the Gospels? Certainly not the fishermen of Galilee; as certainly not St. Paul, whose character and idiosyncrasies were of a totally different sort; still less the early Christian writers, in whom nothing is more evident than that the good which was in them was all derived, as they always professed it was derived, from the higher source. . . . . About the life and sayings of Jesus there is a stamp of personal originality combined with profundity of insight, which, if we abandon the idle expectation of finding scientific precision where something very different was aimed at, must place the Prophet of Nazareth, even in the estimation of those who have no belief in His inspiration, in the very first rank of men of sublime genius of whom our species can boast. When this preeminent genius is combined with the qualities of probably the greatest moral reformer and martyr to that mission who ever existed upon earth, religion cannot be said to have made a bad choice in pitching upon this man as the ideal representative and guide of humanity; nor even now would it be easy, even for an unbeliever, to find a better translation of the rule of virtue from the abstract into the concrete than to endeavour to live so that Christ would approve our life.'—*Three Essays on Religion*, pp. 253 ff.

(9) *W. R. Greg.*

'It is difficult, without exhausting superlatives even to unexpressive and wearisome satiety, to do justice to our intense love, reverence, and admiration for the character and teaching of Jesus. We regard Him not as the perfection of the intellectual or philosophical mind, but as the perfection of the spiritual character, as surpassing all men of all times in the closeness and depth of His communion with the Father. In reading His sayings, we feel that we are holding converse with the wisest, purest, noblest being that ever clothed thought in the poor language of humanity. In studying His life, we feel that we are following the footsteps of the highest ideal yet presented to us on the earth.'—*Creed of Christendom*, vol. ii. p. 168.

'Such a one we believe Jesus to be, the most exalted religious genius whom God ever sent upon the earth; in Himself an embodied revelation; humanity in its divinest phase, "God manifest in the flesh," according to Eastern hyperbole; an exemplar vouchsafed, in an early age of the world, of what man may and should become, in the course of ages, in his progress towards the realization of his destiny; an individual gifted with a grand, clear intellect, a noble soul, a fine organization, marvellous moral intuitions, and a perfectly-balanced moral being; and who by virtue of those endowments saw further than all other men—

"Beyond the verge of that blue sky
Where God's sublimest secrets lie;"

an earnest not only of what humanity may be, but of what it will be, when the most perfected races shall bear the same relations to the finest minds of existing times, as these now bear to the Bushmen or Esquimaux. He was, as Parker beautifully expresses it, "The possibility of the race made real."'—*Ibid.* vol. ii. p. 177.

'I believe that [Jesus] was the greatest and purest of those great and pure souls to whom glorious intuitions are granted, or in whom they rise, or on whom they flow. I believe that these intuitions were to Him *convictions*, *certainties*, and that His belief in His mission to teach them was *a part of Him.*'—*Nineteenth Century*, Feb. 1883, p. 202; quotation from a letter.

(10) *W. E. H. Lecky.*

'The later Stoics had often united their notions of excellence in an ideal sage, and Epictetus had even urged his disciples to set before them some man of surpassing excellence, and to imagine him continually near them; but the utmost the Stoic ideal could become was a model for imitation, and the admiration it inspired could never deepen into affection. It was reserved for Christianity to present to the world an ideal character, which through all the changes of eighteen centuries has filled the hearts of men with an impassioned love; has shown itself capable of acting on all ages, nations, temperaments, and conditions; has been not only the highest pattern of virtue, but the strongest incentive to its practice; and has exerted so deep an influence that it may be truly said, that the simple record of three short years of active life has done more to regenerate and to soften mankind than all the disquisitions of philosophers and all the exhortations of moralists. This has indeed been the well-spring of whatever has been best and purest in the Christian life. Amid all the sins and failings, amid all the priestcraft and persecution and fanaticism, that have defaced the Church, it has preserved, in the character and example of its Founder, an enduring principle of regeneration.'—*History of European Morals*, vol. ii. pp. 8, 9 (5th edition).

(11) *Author of 'Supernatural Religion.'*

'The teaching of Jesus carried morality to the sublimest point attained or even attainable by humanity. The influence of His spiritual religion has been rendered doubly great by the unparalleled purity and elevation of His own character. Surpassing in His sublime symplicity and earnestness the moral grandeur of Sâkya Muni, and putting to the blush the sometimes sullied, though generally admirable teaching of Socrates and Plato and the whole round of Greek philosophers, He presented the rare spectacle of a life, so far as we can estimate it, uniformly noble and consistent with His own lofty principles, so that the "Imitation of Christ" has become almost the final word in the preaching of His religion, and must continue to be one of the most powerful elements of its permanence. . . . Whilst all previous systems had sought to purify the stream, [His system] demanded the purification of the fountain. It placed the evil thought on a par with the evil action. Such morality based upon the earnest and intelligent acceptance of divine law, and perfect recognition of the brotherhood of man, is the highest conceivable by humanity; and although its power and influence must augment with the increase of enlightenment, it is itself beyond development, consisting as it does of principles unlimited in their range and inexhaustible in their application.'—*Supernatural Religion*, vol. ii. pp. 487 f. (4th edition).

(12) *Napoleon Bonaparte.*

In the following we have the testimony of a genius of a totally different kind :—

'One of Napoleon's Generals was one day discussing in his presence the divinity of our Lord. Napoleon remarked : "I know men, General, and I can tell you that Jesus Christ is not a man. Superficial minds see a resemblance between Christ and the founders of empires, the conquerors, and gods of other religions. The resemblance does not exist.

'"Any one who has a true knowledge of things and experience of men will cut short the question as I do. Who amongst us, General, looking at the worship of different nations, is not able to say to the different authors of those religions,—No, you are neither gods nor the agents of the Deity ; you have no mission from heaven ; you are formed of the same slime as other mortals?

'"In Lycurgus, Numa, Confucius, Mahomet, I see lawgivers, but nothing which reveals the Deity. It is not so with Christ. Everything in Him amazes me : His mind is beyond me, and His will confounds me. There is no possible term of comparison between Him and anything of this world. He is a Being apart. His birth, His life, His death, the profundity of His doctrine, which reaches the height of difficulty and which is yet its most admirable solution, the singularity of this mysterious Being, His empire, His course across ages and kingdoms,—all is prodigy, a mystery too deep, too sacred, and which plunges me into reveries from which I can find no escape ; a mystery which is here under my eyes, which I cannot deny, and neither can I explain. Here I see nothing of man. Christ speaks, and from that time generations are His by ties more strict, more intimate than those of blood : by a union more sacred, more imperative than any other could be.

. . . What a gulf between my misery and the eternal reign of Christ, preached, praised, loved, adored, living in the whole universe! Is this to die? Is it not rather to live? Such is the death of Christ—the death of God."'—O'Meara, *Napoleon at St. Helena*, vol. ii. pp. 353 ff. (1888).

The above quotation is taken from a *brochure* which I have not been able to procure or consult, entitled *Sentiment de Napoléon sur la Divinité de Jésus Christ. Pensées recueillies à Ste. Hélène par M. le Comte de Montholon et publiées par M. le Chevalier de Beauterne.* This *brochure*, however, I find must simply be the Fifth Chapter of Beauterne's book, *Sentiment de Napoléon Ier sur le Christianisme* (new edition, Paris, 1868), which I therefore give as the original authority; the above extracts being found on pp. 87, 88, 93, 94, 118. As bearing on the trustworthiness of Beauterne's work, I may add that General Montholon, who was present at the conversations therein recorded, writes from Ham, on May 30, 1841, to that author: "I have read with lively interest your *brochure*, entitled *The Sentiments of Napoleon on the Divinity of Jesus Christ,* and I do not think it would be possible to express more accurately the religious belief of the Emperor."—*Sent. sur le Christianisme*, pp. viii., 156 f.

(13) *Jean Paul Richter.*

Perhaps I cannot do better than close this series of testimonies with the following extracts from that 'strange and tumultuous' genius, Jean Paul Richter:—

'Jesus, the purest among the mighty, the mightiest among the pure, with His pierced hand raised empires off their hinges, turned the stream of the centuries out of its channel, and still commands the ages. . . . Only one spirit of surpassing power of heart stands alone, like the universe, by the side of God. For there stepped once upon the earth a unique being, who merely by the omnipotence of holiness subdued strange ages, and founded an eternity peculiarly His own. Blooming softly, obedient as the sunflower, yet burning and all-attracting as the sun, with His own gentle might He moved and directed Himself and peoples and centuries at the same time towards Him who is the original and universal Sun. That is the gentle spirit whom we call Jesus Christ. If He really existed, then there is a Providence, or He Himself were Providence. Tranquil teaching and tranquil dying was the only music by which this higher Orpheus tamed wild men and charmed rocks harmoniously into cities.'—Jean Paul Richter, *Ueber den Gott in der Geschichte und im Leben;* Sämmtliche Werke, vol. xxv. pp. 53, 60 (Berlin, 1862).

Surely in view of such testimonies, all of them from men of the highest ability or literary repute, and most of them from men decidedly antagonistic to catholic Christianity, we may safely say without offence, in the words of Holy Scripture, 'Their rock is not as our Rock, even our enemies themselves being judges.'

NOTE XVIII. p. 277.

A PERFECT MORAL CHARACTER CONTRARY TO EXPERIENCE.

'Should a traveller, returning from a far country, bring us an account of men wholly different from any with whom we were ever acquainted,—men who were entirely divested of avarice, ambition, or revenge; who knew no pleasure but friendship, generosity, and public spirit,—we should immediately from these circumstances detect the falsehood, and prove him a liar, with the same certainty as if he had stuffed his narration with stories of centaurs and dragons, miracles and prodigies.'—Hume, *Inquiry concerning Human Understanding*, section viii.

That is, according to Hume, such perfect holiness as that of Christ is not to be found in mere human nature, is in short contrary to 'ordinary experience.' Since, however, in His case, it is a fact, it must therefore be supernatural in the emphatic sense.

NOTE XIX. p. 280.

THE INDEPENDENCE AND CONVERGENCE OF THE CHRISTIAN EVIDENCES.

'There is one quality or condition comprehended in these mixed and varied evidences of our religion which deserves to be further considered by itself; a condition highly characteristic of its truth, and, indeed, replete with the strongest confirmation of it. The condition is this, that the evidences are so exceedingly dissimilar in their several descriptions. They are not necessarily connected in their origin; they do not infer each the other; they are connected only in the subject which they conspire to attest. This independence of the component members of the argument is a material consideration. Perhaps it has not been urged in the defences of Christianity with the force it is entitled to. It affords, however, a very decisive criterion of truth, as the following remarks may serve to show.

'If man's contrivance, or if the favour of accident could have given to Christianity any of its apparent testimonies—either its miracles or its prophecies, its morals, or its propagation, or, if I may so speak, its Founder—there could be no room to believe, nor even to imagine, that all these appearances of great credibility could be united together by any such causes. If a successful craft could have contrived its public miracles, or so much as the pretence of them, it required another kind of craft and new resources to provide and adapt its prophecies to the same object. Further, it demanded not only a different art, but a totally opposite character, to conceive and promulgate its admirable morals. Again, the achievement of its propagation, in defiance of the powers and terrors of the world, implied a new energy of personal genius and other qualities of action, than any concurring in the work before. Lastly, the model of the life of its Founder, in the very description of it, is a work of so much originality and wisdom as could be the offspring only of consummate powers of invention; though, to speak more fairly to the case, it seems, by an intuitive evidence, as if it could never have been even devised, but must have come from the life and reality of some perfect excellence of virtue, impossible to be taken from, or confounded with, the fictions of ingenuity. But the hypothesis sinks under its incredibility. For each of these suppositions of contrivance being arbitrary, as it certainly is, and unsupported, the climax of them is an extravagance. And if the imbecility of art is foiled in the hypothesis, the combinations of accident are too vain to be thought of.'—Davison, *Discourses on Prophecy*, pp. 29 f. (4th edition).

'We have a system of proof; an evidence drawn from testimonies differing in kind but conspiring in effect, and combining together to an accumulated demonstration; in which neither the conclusiveness of any of the branches of the argument taken alone, is charged with the whole weight of the question; nor the imputed insufficiency of any of them, when so taken, can touch the validity of the collective inference.'—*Ibid.* pp. 34, 35.

NOTE XX. p. 323.

STATISTICS BEARING ON THE ALLEGED DECLINE OF MORALITY IN GERMANY.

'It is statistically demonstrated that immorality (*Unzucht*) has increased in a terrible degree of late years. During the last six years, in the eight older provinces of *Prussia*, crimes against morality have risen from 1072 to 2378—that is, an increase of 121 per cent. In the jury courts, before which only the more aggravated cases of criminality are brought up for decision, the following are the numbers of sentences passed for crimes against morality: 1871, 501; 1872, 614; 1873, 752; 1874, 982; 1875, 1013; 1876, 1382; 1877, 1975; in other words, an increase of 294 per cent. in six years. In *Bavaria* the same class of offences rose in the same years from 165 to 556—that is to say, 237 per cent. In *Baden*, during the period extending from 1872 to 1877, this class of crimes rosc from 144 to 321, or 122 per cent. In *Saxony*, in the six years from 1871 to 1877, from 345 (489, 519, 579, 607, 800) to 972, or 181 per cent. These numbers reveal a truly shocking state of things.

'In *Prussia*, in the eight older provinces, the number of investigations on account of crimes and misdemeanours rose, in the years 1877–1879, from 88,233 to 145,587, or 65 per cent. Amongst these, the cases of perjury rose from 491 to 1017, or 107 per cent.; assaults, from 7883 to 18,361, or 133 per cent.; cases of robbery and extortion, from 168 to 504, or 200 per cent. In *Saxony*, in the years 1860–1877, the civil processes that actually came before the courts rose from 78,539 to 138,817; the number of those condemned on account of crimes and misdemeanours rose from 9363 to 19,354, or more than the double. In *Bavaria* the sentences passed on account of perjury mounted, in the years 1872–1877, from 166 to 431, or 159 per cent. In *Württemberg*, during the same years, the sentences of the different courts rose from 7987 to 14,655, or about 83 per cent. These numbers require no comment.'—Luthardt, *Die modernen Weltanschauungen und ihre praktischen Konsequenzen*, pp. 100 f.

'In Berlin there stood under *police control* of women who notoriously lived by prostitution in 1852, 695; 1853, 980; 1854, 1156; 1855, 1338; 1856, 1338; 1866, 1360; 1867, 1447; 1868, 1625; 1869, 1776. The number of those *suspected* of prostitution increased in the following manner:—In 1853, 4500; 1855, 6000; 1863, 8000; 1864, 10,000; 1865, 12,006; 1867, 12,491; 1868, 13,610; 1869, 14,362; 1870, 11,382 (?); 1871, 15,064. The increase of prostitution amounted to double the increase in the population.'—*Ibid.*, p. 235.

'While the population of Berlin between 1858 and 1863 increased 20 per cent., public prostitution increased during the same time more than 66 per cent.'—Oettingen, *Moralstatistik*, p. 456. 1868.

The above, according to Luthardt, are some of the consequences of the prevailing atheistic materialism of Germany. It is said that Frederick the Great of Prussia, a most competent and impartial judge in such a matter, towards the close of his life expressed himself as follows: 'I would give my most glorious battle, if only I could again have religion and morality where I found them when I ascended the throne. I see well that I ought to have done more for this purpose.' What would he say if he were living now?

NOTE XXI. p. 333.

THE SADNESS OF ATHEISM.

'Forasmuch as I am far from being able to agree with those who affirm that the twilight doctrine of the "new faith" is a desirable substitute for the waning splendour of "the old," I am not ashamed to confess that, with this virtual negation of God, the universe to me has lost its soul of loveliness; and although from henceforth the precept "to work while it is day" will doubtless but gain an intensified force from the terribly intensified meaning of the words, "the night cometh when no man can work," yet when at times I think, as think at times I must, of the appalling contrast between the hallowed glory of that creed which once was mine, and the lonely mystery of existence as now I find it, at such times I shall ever feel it impossible to avoid the sharpest pang of which my nature is susceptible. For whether it be due to my intelligence not being sufficiently advanced to meet the requirements of the age, or whether it be due to the memory of those sacred associations which to me at least were the sweetest that life has given, I cannot but feel that for me, and for others who think as I do, there is a dreadful truth in these words of Hamilton,—philosophy having become a meditation, not merely of death but annihilation, the precept *know thyself* has become transformed into the terrible oracle to Œdipus—"Mayest thou ne'er know the truth of what thou art."'—Physicus, *A Candid Examination of Theism*, p. 114.

'Those who flatter themselves that they have shaken off the horror [of religion as a superstition], find a colder, more petrifying incubus, that of annihilation, settling down upon them in its place, so that one of them cries out, "Oh! take away annihilation, that abyss, and give us back Satan."'—*Natural Religion*, p. 239. See also the

DATE			
REFERENCE			

The Future of Teacher Power in America

By Marshall O. Donley, Jr.

Library of Congress Catalog Card Number: 77-089838
ISBN 0-87367-098-1

Bloomington, Indiana

TABLE OF CONTENTS

Introduction

The winter of 1976-77 was one of the coldest in years. Yet in the midst of the snow and wind, teachers were on picket lines in several states.

In Racine, Wisconsin, wrapped in ski parkas and heavily booted, nearly 1,000 teachers tramped the sidewalks outside school buildings and school board offices. The Racine teachers had been without a contract for more than two years; they decided finally that, cold winter or no, they would stay out of their classrooms until the school board agreed to put their rights in writing.

The impasse lasted a month and a half. The school board had hundreds of teachers arrested; the teachers association went to court to charge the board with unfair labor practices; the community refused to permit the nonworking teachers to get food stamps, so some teachers lived on contributions from other Wisconsin teachers. The Wisconsin Education Association Council and the National Education Association sent staff to help, provided interest-free loans for the strikers, and organized fund drives for the Racine teachers.

In mid-March the teachers won their contract and went back to work.

It was just one more instance of teacher militancy in the 1970s, but the Racine action would have shocked teachers and their communities at an earlier time in America's history. From the beginnings of the Republic, teachers were quiescent, modest, and meek. They were expected to act like servants. Their behavior in school and out was both prescribed and proscribed by the community. At different times and places, special rules regarding smoking, drinking, courting, and church-going were strictly enforced, even to the point of limiting teachers' rights to leave town without permission. Classrooms were entered regularly by the town fathers, who themselves tested pupils to see if they were learning. In the South, teachers were sometimes actually slaves—literate blacks assigned the task of imparting the ABCs to the children of the plantation.

Teachers who could not endure the restraints generally moved on to other jobs; teaching was, for many, a starting point for other professions, a way to earn a few dollars until other and better prospects were found. The dollars were indeed few. Throughout most of American history, teachers were earning just about enough to get by on. Between 1841 and the Civil War, for example, the wages of male teachers ranged from $4.15 to $6.30 weekly in rural areas, from $11.93 to $18.07 in the cities. Female teachers got less.

Teachers were not thought to deserve more money; some of them didn't even hope for more. In the words of a normal school teacher in 1839, "It is not to be expected that teaching will ever become a *lucrative* position."

This servant status began to change only when teachers began to organize. They learned the lesson that there is strength in unity. As one early Illinois teachers society noted, "Group petitions got a readier response from school boards than did the individual requests from the teachers." What the lone schoolmaster could not do, a union of educators could attempt.

The Earliest Teachers Organizations

The nation's first teachers association, the Society of Associated Teachers of New York City, was established in 1794. Five years later the School Association of the County of Middlesex, Connecticut, was founded. The Associated Instructors of Youth in the Town of Boston and Its Vicinity survived a few years following 1812. Countywide and citywide groups were set up in many states, and 30 state teachers associations were formed between 1840 and 1861.

When a national teachers group was formed in 1857, the invitation called on all "practical teachers" to assemble in Philadelphia for "the purpose of organizing a National Teachers Association." The invitations were mailed not to teachers, however, but to the presidents of the state education associations, 10 of whom accepted. Forty-three educators attended the organizing meeting, but few of them were classroom teachers. Total membership in the national group never topped 300 until the 1870s. At that time the organization merged with the National Association of School Superintendents and the American Normal School Association, both of which became departments of what was then called the National Educational Association.

The birth of these groups was attended by a kind of schizophrenia that has continued into the present. From the first, educators were torn between their desires to promote and improve public education and their determination to better their own conditions. In view of their genteel respectability, they could not very well strive only for the latter. Thus, teachers groups have been strained and occasionally torn apart by members' conflicting needs to serve society and to serve themselves.

"Associated effort" to some teachers meant labor unions. In 1897 the Chicago Teachers Federation was formed. It did not affiliate with the American Federation of Labor, however, so the honor of becoming the first bona fide teacher labor union went to teachers in San Antonio, Texas. They joined the AFL on September 29, 1902. Although the Chicago teachers "went labor" later the same year, they did not join the AFL, but did affiliate with the city labor council.

A national union of teachers, affiliated with the AFL, was set up on May 9, 1916, when several Chicago teachers unions and one in Gary, Indiana, formed the American Federation of Teachers.

Structure but Not Much Function

By the time of the First World War teachers had a mechanism for action, a structure upon which they could build their militancy. That mechanism—a national association of teachers, a national teachers union, state and local teachers associations, and local teachers unions—remained ineffective, however. For one thing, most teachers were not members. The National Education Association enrolled 2,332 educators in 1900. The number had grown to 6,909 by 1910, but even this represented but 1.3% of the nation's teaching force. State associations did better. They drew 14% of employed teachers in their states in 1907, 34% by 1916. Teachers union membership was smaller.

Further, these nascent groups did little *for* teachers. In many cases, they were dominated by superintendents and college professors; they blocked membership for women; they tiptoed around important issues such as salaries and spent much of their time on "professional" matters. In the words of one early member, "There was, at the start, too much *why,* not enough *what,* and hardly any *how* at all. Even the most practical schoolmen, when asked to prepare addresses, suffered an attack of pedantry and soared to cloudland."

Slowly, teachers organizations began to face some of the problems of teachers. In 1905 the NEA published its first salary study; by 1915 the association was passing resolutions calling for higher teacher salaries and greater financial security for teachers. State education associations claimed lobbying victories for minimum salary laws, tenure provisions, and pension plans. Codes of ethics for educators were promulgated, and a few associations explored the possibility of legal action on behalf of members who were fired without due process or cause.

Following World War I teachers began to join their associations in great numbers. In 1917 NEA membership was 8,466; by 1927 it had grown to 141,212; by World War II it topped 200,000. State teachers associations flourished in nearly every state. American Federation of Teachers membership rose to 32,000 by 1939.

Teachers Begin To Use Their Muscle

Hard hit by inflation following World War II, American teachers began flexing their organized muscles. "Teachers all over the United States are thinking about striking," progressive education leader George S. Counts told a Phi Delta Kappa seminar in 1947. He was not exaggerating. More than 100 strike threats were carried out from 1942 through 1959. These strikes involved more than 20,000 teachers. Further, the strikes were carried out by teachers groups affiliated with labor, those affiliated with the NEA and the state associations, and those independent of both. The strikes occurred across the nation in both large and small districts, but they were mainly for one purose: to obtain more money.

However, some of the strikes had other goals that, while secondary to salary gains, were becoming important. These included recognition of teachers groups as bargaining agents, stronger school personnel policies, and bigger school budgets.

The Norwalk, Connecticut, strike in 1946 is the first example in the nation's history of a teachers group walking out to achieve bargaining recognition. The teachers stayed out until the school board recognized the Norwalk Teachers Association as the sole bargaining agent for its members.

The Battle for Control of Teachers

By the late 1950s the potential in organizing teachers was clear to any who would see it. A variety of teachers, teacher-leaders, and unionists began to grasp the idea. Walter Reuther, leader of the Auto Workers, recognized this potential and began to finance teachers union organizing. Albert Shanker, an up-and-coming New York City teacher-leader, saw the opportunity for organizing as he moved toward the presidency of his union. A growing number of NEA leaders also recognized the direction teachers were going.

The New York City bargaining election of 1961 once and for all awoke teachers associations to the fact that militancy was in the cards for the American teacher—if the associations would not move into that future, teachers unions would.

In 1958, five New York City teachers groups had come together as the NEA Council. Two years later council leaders, along with representatives from four other teachers groups, asked NEA officials in Washington for help in developing collective bargaining. The NEA agreed to establish a regional office there, and on September 1, 1960, sent an assistant director of its membership division to the city with instructions to concentrate on service to city teachers.

Before the NEA had time to reorganize the city's teachers, however, the United Federation of Teachers played its first ace. The UFT called a strike on November 7. The strike, the union said, would win for teachers the right to bargain collectively. About 5,000 teachers stayed off the job for one day, and the union claimed it had won agreement from the Board of Education that an election would be held to choose a bargaining agent.

First, though, the board appointed a committee to study this question: "If collective bargaining is to be instituted for professional persons in the school system, what would be its most appropriate form?" At public hearings held by the committee, NEA-affiliated groups opposed the idea of collective bargaining; the UFT spoke out strongly for it. In May, 1961, the committee issued a report calling for a referendum by city teachers to see if they wanted collective bargaining. In a June referendum the vote was 26,983 for bargaining and 8,871 against.

When teachers returned to school in the fall of 1961, both groups began to gird for the inevitable battle. The UFT had the advantage and never lost it. It maintained unity throughout the campaign; it received at least $100,000 in direct aid and loans from other unions, especially (thanks to Reuther) from the Industrial Union Department of the AFL-CIO.

The NEA had no base to build on. To establish one, it combined the groups that had come to it a year earlier into a coalition of forces for collective bargaining. Called the Teachers Bargaining Organization (TBO) of New York City, it announced a few weeks later that it had established a bargaining committee in anticipation of winning the election.

Three organizations qualified for the ballot in December: the United Federation of Teachers, the NEA's Teachers Bargaining Organization, and the independent Teachers Union. The UFT received twice as many votes as did the TBO—20,045 to the NEA group's 9,770 (the Teachers Union got 2,575 votes). The UFT had won decisively and would from that time represent all of the city's teachers.

The union victory in New York City was probably the biggest single success in the history of teacher organizing in the United States. A lifesaver for the national union, the victory brought a huge increase in AFT membership, which stood at just 60,715 in the entire nation in 1961. It also spurred teachers unions in California, Colorado, Minneapolis, Chicago, and Detroit to new efforts. And the victory guaranteed continued financial support for the union from the AFL-CIO. It seemed to demonstrate to the nation that teachers were ready to "go union."

The greatest significance of the New York union victory probably was that it pushed the NEA and its state and local affiliates farther along a road they were already traveling. Even before it lost New York City, the NEA was developing guidelines for collective bargaining by teachers. Though it labeled the process "professional negotiation" to avoid labor terminology, the association was moving inexorably toward full recognition of the need to bargain for teachers. Ten years after the New York City election the NEA and its affiliates were bargaining, union style, for many more teachers than was the American Federation of Teachers and its local unions.

Contract Bargaining Becomes the Rule

Throughout the 1960s and 1970s teachers strikes seemed the major indicator of teacher militancy. And there were many strikes. Thousands of teachers "hit the bricks" during this period. But more important, *hundreds of thousands* of teachers were being covered by bargained contracts that gave them, usually for the first time, written, detailed provisions for salary, fringe benefits, and instructional standards. As early as 1964 the NEA estimated that 100,000 teachers in 346 school districts were serving under written contracts. By 1967 nearly 400,000 school personnel were under bargained contracts in 1,179 districts where teachers were represented by NEA affiliates. An additional 35 school districts had AFT contracts.

Teachers were bargaining in a number of states under new laws lobbied through the legislatures by teachers associations. By 1965 laws mandating school board-teacher bargaining were in effect in Connecticut and Washington; in Michigan teachers were choosing bargaining agents under the state's labor laws. Alaska passed a teacher negotiation law in 1959, New Hampshire in 1955, and Wisconsin in 1962. By 1966 California, Florida, Massachusetts, New Jersey, and Oregon had passed laws allowing teacher bargaining. The tide was irreversible.

By 1972 a total of 1,445,329 instructional personnel throughout the nation were covered by negotiated agreements.

Causes of Teacher Militancy

What brought about this huge rush to teacher bargaining, this massive increase in teacher militancy? I believe there were six major factors: a long history of economic injustice to teachers; growing professionalism as the teacher's role became more important in an increasingly complex society; growth in size and bureaucratization of the schools; changes in and among teachers organizations; growing availability of the mechanisms for militancy; and the changing social climate of the 1960s and 1970s. In 1975 a newspaper reporter asked the NEA's executive director, Terry Herndon, why the NEA had "suddenly" become so militant. Herndon's answer was that the NEA is a very democratic organization. It elects new officers each year or so, its policies are set by an annual assembly of thousands of teacher representatives. Many teachers, Herndon said, were militant in the 1950s and perhaps even earlier. But the majority of NEA members remained unwilling to accept strikes, collective bargaining, political action, etc., so the association's posture remained a conservative one. Sometime around 1970, Herndon concluded, 51% of the association's members moved into the militant camp; in a democratic organization, this reflected a change in the image of the NEA.

However it is analyzed, teacher militancy had become a reality by the time of the nation's Bicentennial. Most teachers were now working in districts where they had the right to negotiate with their employers. Most teachers were members of the NEA or of the AFT; 1974 figures showed that 72.4% of all teachers were organized; by 1976 this percentage probably exceeded 80, because the NEA and four state-level affiliates completed "unification" agreements in that period, thus mandating a larger NEA membership.

Further, teachers were expressing their militancy in other, newer ways. The most visible of these were 1) lawsuits brought by teachers organizations on behalf of their members' rights and 2) political action of organized teachers. The NEA, through its DuShane Fund, was spending hundreds of thousands of dollars yearly to guarantee that teacher contracts would be honored, to insure that black and other minority members would be dealt with fairly, to protect women's rights, and to assure teachers the right to free speech, freedom of dress, even freedom of sexual preference. The AFT had a similar, though smaller, fund for such actions. On the political front, teachers organizations were contributing thousands of dollars to campaigns of congressmen and senators who were considered pro-education. Thousands of teachers were volunteering to work on behalf of these candidates, proving themselves to be a valuable asset to politicians. Through its monthly newspaper sent to 1.7 million members, the NEA was publishing voting records of every member of Congress on issues relating to education. And in 1976, for the first time, the NEA endorsed a candidate for President of the United States.

One further aspect of teacher militancy appeared in the 1970s—the willingness of the education associations to work directly with other groups, including labor unions. The chief example of this cooperation was the Coalition of American Public Employees, founded jointly by the NEA and the American Federation of State, County, and Municipal Employees. The latter group, an AFL-CIO union led by Jerry Wurf, was a maverick in the house of labor and a long-time foe of AFT President Albert Shanker. Other public employee groups (nurses, doctors, IRS workers) also joined the coalition; statewide coalitions were formed by teachers and other unionists in a dozen or more states.

All of this militant action meant that most American teachers in the mid-1970s were organized, politically aware, and active.

Some observers have suggested that teacher militancy peaked at this point, and that teacher strikes, teacher bargaining, and teacher cooperation with other public employees could not go much further. There is evidence for such an argument. The downturns in the national economy in the 1970s moderated the money demands of many unions. Some state court decisions placed additional limits on the extent of teacher bargaining. A U.S. Supreme Court decision in 1976 seemed to cut off the possibility of a nationwide bargaining law for teachers and other public employees. Bankrupt city governments were blocking gains by municipal unions. Declining school enrollment raised fears of massive losses of teacher jobs. It was a time to ask, Had the steam gone out of the drive for teacher militancy?

To consider this question, let us look briefly at 10 other questions reflecting issues that will determine the future of teacher militancy in the nation. These questions are:

1. What is the outlook for legislation that will impede or promote teacher militancy?

2. What impact are court decisions having on the drive of teachers to organize and bargain?

3. Will the public attitude toward the militant teacher hinder that militancy?

4. Will increasing conservatism of teachers themselves slow their militancy?

5. Will the American economy support continued teacher militancy?

6. How will changes in the way schools are financed affect teacher militancy?

7. Is the supply of teachers exceeding the demand, and if so, how will this affect teacher activism?

8. Will conflicts between teachers organizations limit their thrust toward greater power for their members?

9. Will educators who are now unorganized join teachers associations or unions?

10. Will teachers continue their efforts to influence society through political action?

Laws and Court Decisions

What is the outlook for legislation that will impede or promote teacher militancy?

What impact are court decisions having on the drive of teachers to organize and bargain?

These two questions are closely related and need to be dealt with together, because the essential mechanism of teacher activism—collective bargaining—is affected both by legislation and by court decisions.

In 1977 teachers had the right to bargain, and *were* bargaining in most states of the Union. But the extent and effectiveness of that bargaining varied from negotiations conducted completely in the absence of a law allowing or forbidding bargaining, to full-scale contract bargaining with the right to strike as the ultimate weapon in the hands of the teachers (or other public employees). Thirty states allowed teachers to bargain by law. Seven states—Alaska, Hawaii, Minnesota, Montana, Oregon, Pennsylvania, and Vermont—stood at the most permissive end of the 30, allowing their teachers to bargain and to strike either by statute or by court rulings that specified that school boards could not automatically get injunctions blocking teachers from striking. In three additional states—Michigan, New Hampshire, and Rhode Island—court decisions limited injunctions against striking teachers to such an extent that, in practice, strikes went unimpeded in most cases.

At the other end of the spectrum were the so-called right-to-work states, in which union organizing was discouraged by laws requiring open shops, i.e., laws forbidding exclusive representation of worker groups. Unions consider a closed shop essential to negotiating employee-employer contracts. In 1977 the Virginia courts, in an action sought by Governor Mills E. Godwin, ruled that public employers in that state could not negotiate with their employees. This ruling for all practical purposes ended teacher-school board bargaining in the state.

Thus teachers and other public employees in the 50 states faced, in the 1970s, a variety of bargaining situations. NEA's chief counsel, Robert Chanin, called the situation "a patchwork quilt of state collective bargaining statutes ranging from fair to terrible." He added that "hundreds of thousands of teachers do not even have minimal collective bargaining rights."

Further, the U.S. Supreme Court itself had ruled in two cases that adversely affected teacher bargaining rights.

In a 6-3 decision in mid-1976, the Court ruled against teachers from Hortonville, Wisconsin, who argued that their school board, as a party to a contract dispute with them, could not then be an impartial determining agent in an action against them following the contract bargaining (the board had fired the teachers). A lower court agreed with the teachers ("It would seem essential, even in cases of undisputed or stipulated facts, that an impartial decision maker be charged with the responsibility of determining what action shall be taken"), but on appeal the Supreme Court disagreed, saying, "The sole issue in this case is whether the due process of the Fourteenth Amendment prohibits this school board from making the decision to dismiss teachers admittedly engaged in a strike and persistently refusing to return to their duties."

The second U.S. Supreme Court ruling, also in 1976, indirectly but crucially affected teachers' bargaining rights. In *National League of Cities v. Usery* the Court held that the U.S. Congress had exceeded its authority under the commerce clause of the Constitution when it extended the wage and hours provision of a federal law to most employees of state and local governments. The Court opinion did not deal directly with collective bargaining, but the implication of the decision to many observers was that Congress would be unable to pass any constitutional legislation requiring states and communities to bargain with its teachers and other public employees. If this implication held, the "patchwork quilt" of state statutes would be the best teachers could hope for.

Neither of these Supreme Court decisions, however, may block teacher bargaining as much as at first appeared to be the case.

In its Hortonville decision, the Court did not speak to the essential issues raised by the teachers. Ruling on the narrow question of the school board's right under the Fourteenth Amendment (regarding due process), the Court left unsettled such issues as the right of teachers to binding arbitration, the constitutional differences between public employee-employer relationships and those of workers in private industry, or even the due-process rights of teachers a school board intends to fire. Thus, as one Court expert noted, the Hortonville decision "doesn't mean it's 'open season' on striking teachers."

The *National League of Cities* decision could be the more important of the two for teachers. The reason is that in the early 1970s the National Education Association decided that the most effective way to guarantee the bargaining rights of its members (and of all teachers and public employees) would be the passage of a federal collective bargaining statute. Such a law, if Congress passed it, would end the "patchwork quilt" of state statutes and strengthen teacher bargaining in states which had no bargaining law at all.

The NEA began pursuing several versions of a federal collective bargaining law in the years prior to the *National League of Cities* decision. The association proposed and offered its support both for separate legislation to set up a national public employee law and for changes in the National Labor Relations Act that would include public employees under its rules. Either approach would give teachers the same rights to bargain (and strike) that other workers already have. Neither approach succeeded in Congress before 1976, partly because Congress itself was awaiting the *National League of Cities* decision. And when that decision came, many in Congress and in education circles assumed that the decision killed chances for federal legislation in the area of public employee bargaining.

In 1977, though, the NEA revised its position. Further analysis of the Court decision convinced NEA lawyers that a federal collective bargaining law could survive constitutional challenge if the law were written in a way to avoid the limitations set by the Supreme Court in *National League of Cities.* The thinking went this way: The Court decision did *not* say that *every* intrusion of the Congress into state sovereignty was unconstitutional; it said only that such intrusion is invalid if it "impairs the state's ability to function effectively within the federal system." In effect, the Court said that the amount of intrusion of federal law into state and local dealings that could be allowed must be balanced against the federal interest that brought about the particular federal law that intrudes.

NEA lawyers believed that several changes in the association's proposed bargaining bill would tip the balance to constitutional acceptance. The most important of these changes dealt with the right to strike and the use of binding arbitration. The NEA proposal now did not call for an unlimited right of teachers to strike, on the theory that such an unrestricted right would, in effect, allow employees to bring a state or local operation to a complete halt and thus intrude into the state's or community's rights. Instead, the new NEA proposal suggested that the right-to-strike language of the federal legislation include a proviso expressly authorizing a state to prohibit or limit the right to strike by passing appropriate laws. In other words, teachers would have the right to strike, but if a state legislature considered this right unacceptable, it could pass a law "opting out" of this part of the federal collective bargaining law. Teachers and other public employees would still have the protection and rights under the federal law, but they could not strike in that state.

The use of binding arbitration, too, would be an option under the new NEA proposal. The difference was that it would become not an "opt out" condition, as with the strike, but an "opt in" choice for the state. That is, the NEA-proposed legislation would make fact-finding with nonbinding recommendations the final step in bargaining; each state would have the option, though, of enacting legislation making the recommendations binding if it wanted to.

The NEA-proposed legislation would, the association said, leave teachers with several possible bargaining structures. In Chanin's words: "At best, they could have the structure set forth in the current [old] NEA proposal—that is, nonbinding recommendations with the right to strike unless the teacher organization waives that right in order to secure a binding decision. At worst, they could have what is available under most of the current state public sector collective bargaining statutes—that is, nonbinding recommendations with a strike prohibition."

To some, the new NEA proposal seemed too weak. AFT President Albert Shanker attacked it as "harmful to all employees, public and private, since it could set precedents for similar states' rights proposals for the private sector." The AFT said it would continue to demand a law giving teachers full bargaining rights, including the complete right to strike. The NEA counterattacked, pointing out that such a position was "self-defeating," since it would lead to the constitutional problems made clear in *National League of Cities.* NEA officials also said they doubted the AFT's sincerity; they suggested that the AFT would be the loser if *any* federal collective bargaining law passed Congress, because guarantees of bargaining rights for teachers would mean an end to AFT locals in communities where they had the minority of membership (a frequent condition). When California's strong bargaining law passed in 1976, for example, NEA-California Teachers Association locals won the vast majority of bargaining elections and, under the exclusive representation rules of the law, cut heavily into AFT strength. A federal law, NEA officials believed, would bring about a national situation of the same order.

So the answer to our two-pronged question—How will legislation and court decisions affect teacher militancy?—may lie in the answer to a single question: Will the Congress pass a constitutionally acceptable collective bargaining law for teachers and other public employees?

If such a law passes, the course of teacher (and public employee) bargaining will change greatly. If such a law is not passed, however, teachers groups will have to fall back on state legislation—not a happy prospect for them perhaps, but not a hopeless one either. As we have noted, 30 states have bargaining laws of some sort already. Ten states allow strikes by teachers. In several other states, teachers' proposals for bargaining laws are under consideration; the Kentucky Educational Association, for example, has as a major ingredient of its legislative package for the 1978 state assembly "a law to guarantee local education associations a formal procedure for negotiating with local boards of education."

In sum, a federal law that meets the Supreme Court's tests would greatly enhance teachers' opportunities for militancy, but failure to obtain that law is not likely to halt teachers' drives for bargaining rights.

Teachers and the Public

Will the public attitude toward the militant teacher hinder that militancy?

"Public Workers and Public on a Collision Course," *U.S. News & World Report* headlined in 1977. The article under the headline predicted that school would become a "major battleground as teachers unions grow stronger and try to protect their members' jobs in the face of dwindling classroom enrollments."

U.S. News identified the major conflict as that between hard-pressed local taxpayers and the financial demands of teachers. But the issue is more subtle. What is involved is not just money—money that admittedly must come from the taxpayer—but power. Perhaps the major cause of teacher strikes, for example, has been the desire of teachers to be recognized—to gain a place at society's bargaining table. Not that teachers will not use that position to press for higher salaries; certainly they have sought and likely will continue to seek a piece of the economic pie they have long been denied. But for teachers the point of organizing—forming unions—has been to force society to recognize them as first-class citizens. In the words of one teacher who struck in 1977, "We strikers are much more hungry for rights than we are for food. You can fill your stomach, but if in your soul, heart, and mind you're not at peace with what you believe, it's a much worse kind of hunger."

To feed this hunger, communities have to recognize teachers and their organizations as co-equal members of the local power circle. And it is at this point that resistance can build. Sometimes this resistance is expressed in rejected school levies, at other times in refusals to bargain with teachers.

The question is, Will this resistance increase?

Officials of teachers organizations in the late 1970s seemed convinced that the long-term battle for teacher acceptance was being won. AFT President Shanker, for instance, said in early 1977 that reports of school levy rejections should not be taken as dire omens. He suggested that these "no" votes were not necessarily aimed at teachers (and other public employees) but at "government in general"—as the only way citizens had to vent their anger at "the system." Shanker also suggested that teachers and other public employees would win public acceptance by effective political action and by involving themselves in "broad economic issues."

NEA leaders, by their actions in the 1970s, seemed to agree with the idea that broader involvement of teachers and their organizations in societal issues was both a need felt by teachers and an important way to help teachers express their concerns. The NEA greatly expanded its role in political action, its involvement in "noneducational" social issues, and its relationship with other public employees of the nation.

It is important to note that this rapid expansion of political action by teachers—endorsement of candidates, contributions to campaign funds, direct work on behalf of candidates—apparently did not affect the way the American public viewed the teacher. Gallup polls continued to show that the public rated teachers (and schools in general) high on their approval list. Lawyers, politicians, big businessmen, and big labor leaders dropped in public favor according to such polls, but professors and teachers remained near the top of "approved" groups. Few in the public were quoted as objecting to teacher involvement in broader, noneducational issues, either. Though many a city power broker may have wished that "teacher do-gooders" would stay out of things, few of these opinion leaders expressed this view publicly, and there was evidence that some of them even welcomed teacher involvement.

But what of a reported growing conservatism among the American people? By the late 1970s, observers were noting that the U.S. population's median age was rising and would be in the high twenties by the end of the century. Wouldn't this older population object to the demands of a militant teaching group? Several critical responses need be made to this question. One is to point out that, even assuming a correlation between age and conservatism, the American population had not been "young" and was not suddenly turning "old." Despite the cover stories in *Time,* the American median age had not fallen below 25 in the post-World War II years; the median age of the nation's population was much lower at the turn of the century, or in Thomas Jefferson's day, than in the middle of the twentieth century. Second, one needs to look at what is meant by conservatism. Even if the American population is becoming older and more conservative, we need to recall that "conservative" in 1990 might not be "conservative" by earlier standards. A conservative American in the 1920s might well have, and probably did, oppose Social Security, unions, and the expression of rights by minorities. What teachers groups were aiming for in the 1970s and will likely be working for during the rest of the century are such things as the right to bargain, the freedom to participate in politics, a voice in determining the working conditions and programs of their work situation. These are hardly ultraliberal goals; they are in fact the same goals already won by many other segments of society. It is by no means a certainty that even a more conservative population would object to them.

But the more basic answer to the question of whether the public's attitude will block teacher militancy may be that the public will have no choice.

In the 1970s teachers and other public employees began to work together. The NEA joined with the American Federation of State, County, and Municipal Employees (AFL-CIO) to form the Coalition of American Public Employees. The AFL-CIO itself established a Public Employee Department in 1974. By throwing their lot in with other public employees, teachers joined (some said *led*) a movement with considerable power. It is likely that the public has yet to feel the full force of that combined power. Labor columnist Victor Riesel expressed this idea in a 1975 article when he pointed out that "until garbage rots for two weeks on some city's streets, or the police pull some job action, or firefighters strike again as they have not too long ago, or teachers walk out again and again, the pubic won't realize the significance of the new era." In another article Riesel was more blunt: ". . . the public's seen nothing yet."

So the public may have no choice. Public employee groups are organizing and expanding far more rapidly than private sector labor. In Massachusetts and the District of Columbia, for instance, more than half of all state and local employees were organized by 1975.

The Coalition of American Public Employees, joined by nurses, some doctors, and others after its founding, was a potential spokesperson for nearly 14 million workers. An organized force of this size might not win enthusiastic support from the public, but it certainly would be able to demand respect.

Teacher Conservatism

Will increasing conservatism of teachers themselves slow their militancy?

If a conservative public-at-large does not slow teachers' militant actions, might the educators themselves edge toward conservatism and moderate their activism?

In the late 1970s the signs were mixed. Some trends seemed to indicate growing teacher conservatism; others tended toward a firm militancy.

At least four situations suggested growing teacher conservatism:

1. Starting early in the 1970s some teachers began joining the National Association of Professional Educators (NAPE) and its state and local affiliates. Led by Los Angeles educator Richard Mason, NAPE held annual meetings, collected dues, and generally ran a road show proclaiming the dangers of the teacher unionism displayed by the NEA and the AFT. NAPE leaders railed against collective bargaining, exclusive-agent contracts, big organizations, big government, etc. NAPE claimed adherents in dozens of states, but they could be found in significant numbers mostly in California, Texas, and parts of the South.

How many NAPE members were there? Despite claims by Mason that 40,000 educators "support NAPE," probably fewer than 10,000 teachers in the entire nation paid dues to NAPE or NAPE-like groups. Even in Los Angeles, birthplace of NAPE, its weakness was demonstrated in early 1977. Under the new California bargaining law, an exclusive agent was selected in Los Angeles by vote of the teachers. NAPE's loosely connected affiliate, the Professional Educators of Los Angeles (PELA), ran a far second to the merged NEA-AFT local, UTLA, which received 12,882 to PELA's 3,755, a number approximately matching its membership figure. In one California election (a 39-member unit in Imperial County), a NAPE group won a bargaining election. It was the only NAPE victory in the state.

To some observers it seemed ironic that a NAPE group would even be on the ballot in a bargaining election, because of NAPE's philosophy. PELA Business Manager John Harris explained, however, that had his group won the election, PELA would not have bargained as the exclusive agent for Los Angeles teachers but would have formed a joint bargaining front with UTLA and any other groups that got votes. "We're in favor of a collective bargaining contract," he said, "but we do oppose exclusivity and the agency shop."

2. After the NEA and its affiliates became politically active in the 1970s, some members objected to this political action. Under federal law the association had to reimburse thousands of members for the portion of their dues used for political action.

This membership protest apparently reflected two things. First, there was a philosophical difference between association-elected leaders and convention delegates (who tended to be politically liberal) and the NEA members at large (more than half of whom considered themselves politically moderate). Thus many members were objecting to what they saw as a difference in philosophy between their leaders and themselves. Second, given the closeness of the 1976 Presidential election, it is logical to assume that many association members voted for Gerald Ford. The NEA, through its Political Action Committee, had endorsed Jimmy Carter and Walter Mondale, and the pro-Ford members were expressing their objection to this choice.

To analyze properly the meaning of this membership objection to the movement toward teacher militancy, it would be necessary to know how many members were objecting to *the process* and how many to *the choice of a candidate they did not approve*. If members were objecting to the idea of teachers being involved in politics at all, this would be a sign of conservatism moderating teacher militancy. If, however, the objections reflected approval of the process but objection to the choice that was made, then one could argue that teachers were solidly behind the idea of involvement in political life and were merely arguing over how to carry out this involvement.

3. In the 1970s the NEA completed the process it calls "unified

California Teachers Association, a new and effective teacher bargaining act became law. Teachers now were able to seek exclusive representation either through demonstration of overwhelming numbers and automatic designation as the bargaining agent or through bargaining elections. As a result of the new law, teachers in California were soon bargaining through single agents in nearly every district in the state. The CTA, which won well over 90% of the designations and elections, was developing a coordinated bargaining program, with the goal of strong contracts for every teacher in the state.

Effective bargaining of the California type obviously leads to solidarity among teachers and strengthens their opportunities for activism.

3. By the 1970s many of the new teachers coming into America's school systems were young people who assumed routinely that associations or unions would bargain for them. These young people had never known a time when bargaining did not exist, and they took for granted their right to be represented by an organization.

A student NEA officer in the late 1970s reported that she was surprised at the militant positions of her colleagues in graduate school. This 22-year-old teacher-to-be thought that her ideas favoring teacher bargaining, political action, etc., would be minority views in her graduate seminars. But after one discussion session, her class voted on such questions as, Should teachers strike? Should teachers take part in politics? To her surprise the majority of students voted with her in favor of these militant positions. Her story is the stronger because she is a Texan and the class vote was taken in Austin. Texas is not known for its teacher militancy.

If today's student teachers are militant, can tomorrow's teachers be any different?

4. Teachers were not alone in their organizational drives in the 1960s and 1970s. "White-collar" union membership grew steadily from 1960. According to the Bureau of Labor Statistics, there was a growth from slightly more than two million to nearly six million in professionals joining unions between 1960 and 1974. These professionals included nurses, teachers, doctors, scientists, and engineers.

As recently as the 1950s teachers resisted joining organizations that looked like labor groups because, they maintained, it was "unprofessional" or "blue collar." Teaching had been a great avenue of escape from the blue-collar world for several generations of Americans, and many teachers did not want to "regress." But when airplane pilots earning $50,000 a year have a union, when young doctors are joining unions, when the American Medical Association favors collective bargaining for its members, and when thousands of professionals are recognizing that group action is needed in today's complex society, how can teachers feel second-class by joining too?

So teachers joined in huge numbers. NEA membership (1.8 million in 1976) doubled between the 1960s and 1970s; AFT membership climbed to a peak near 475,000 in 1976. These large numbers of organized teachers, a large percentage of them working under bargained contracts, suggest that unionism in its broadest sense was not a debatable topic as it had been 10 or 20 years earlier.

Teachers and the Economy

Will the American economy support continued teacher militancy?

Some observers have suggested that teachers will not be able to continue their push for higher salaries, smaller class sizes, and added benefits because the 1970s economy just will not bear it. They pointed to school levy losses, bankrupt school systems, and taxpayer resistance.

Several factors moderate this judgment, however. First, despite the funding problems of the schools, very few actually closed down. During the money-tight school year of 1976-77, for example, only a handful of school systems closed their doors because of money problems (several in Oregon, others in Connecticut and Ohio). The vast majority of the more than 16,000 school districts in the nation continued to operate. Second, there was no clear evidence that school closings (or other problems such as layoffs of teachers) diminished the efforts of teachers organizations. If anything, these problems may have reinforced organized efforts to increase school funding and to change structures rather than eliminate teacher jobs.

Further, any argument that recent economic slowdowns have tended to discourage teacher militancy would have to acknowledge the probability of a renewal of such militancy as the economy rebounds.

Cost problems of the schools, too, are affected by inflation, and this factor tends at times to distort the discussion. One observer, at Brandeis University, pointed out in 1977 that pundits who talk about school costs pricing people out of the market do not consider that school costs have not increased at a greater rate than other costs in our society. Although he was speaking of college costs, his argument could be extended to any school costs. He noted that in 1977 it cost $5,491 for a year of studies at Brandeis. The cost was $1,200 in 1949 and $1,735 in 1957. Now compare new family car prices over the same period, he suggested. A standard Ford automobile cost $1,346 in 1949, $2,433 in 1957, and $6,300 (with most of the options people want) in 1977. His conclusion was: "Can it be that [parents] would really rather have a Buick or a Ford than a quality education for their children?"

So perhaps the doomsday for educational costs did not arrive in 1977; perhaps the citizenry just hadn't adjusted to paying the "normal" inflationary increase for schooling.

It may be less realistic to ask, Can the economy afford schools? than to ask, How shall school funding change?

Federal School Financing

How will changes in the way schools are financed affect teacher militancy?

Two general trends in school finance were visible in the 1970s: a move, often inspired by court decisions, toward greater equalization of school costs within states; and a move toward more federal financial support of schools.

These trends have been heavily documented and extensively discussed, so we shall merely summarize them here. The movement toward equalization was brought about mainly by two circumstances. First, a number of states had budget surpluses in the early 1970s; they used these surpluses to improve their plans for providing additional school funds to less financially able communities. Second, court decisions typified by the *Serrano II* decision in California held that it was unfair for students in poorer communities to receive an inferior education just because the municipality in which they lived could not afford a good school program.

Federal support of public schools increased more than fivefold from 1961 to 1974 (from less than $760 million yearly to more than $4.2 billion). The preponderance of that federal aid went to educationally deprived children, to federally impacted school districts, and to vocational training.

It is important to note that these changes in school financing—both the state equalization and added federal aid—mainly benefited the poorer school districts.

It is likely that both trends will continue in the near future. Court decisions now on record should keep the pressure on for equalization. Certainly, the local property tax payer will be pushing for added state and federal aid. And the organized teachers of the nation have made it clear that their unions and associations will continue to push for more federal aid.

The question is, What effect are these trends having on the activism of teachers? The broad answer to this question seems to be that these trends are abetting teacher militancy. It seems, in general, that the farther from the locality the schools are financed, the better off teachers are.

The reasons for this are several. For one thing, the poorer the school district, the harder it is for teachers to negotiate salary gains and improved conditions. If the community is truly impoverished and aid is not forthcoming from the state or the federal government, the teachers are faced with a much more difficult task at the bargaining table. On the other hand, if state and federal monies are pouring into the district, teachers are bargaining from the start for a piece of a bigger pie. Further, when educational costs are relatively even throughout a state, teachers can organize and bargain for similar benefits throughout the state. In the 1970s such so-called coordinated bargaining became a reality in several Western states.

We could test our theory here by asking, If teachers gain more via school financing farther from the local community, how would teachers fare if *all* the school bills were paid by the farthest of sources—the federal government? An example of a modern industrialized nation where such a situation exists is France in the 1970s. There, teachers, well organized through the Federation de l'Education Nationale, have done very well. Because education is financed almost completely from a federal budget in France, the lack of city funds has not affected school budgets and the teachers have gained thereby. In contrast to other European countries (and the United States), teacher unemployment in France in 1976 was less than 1%, considerably lower than in neighboring countries where more traditional financing schemes were prevalent. Able to influence the national bodies that make educational decisions, French teachers negotiated reductions in class size each time the number of students in the school system declined.

This fact brings us to our next issue—the effect of a declining pupil population.

More Teachers, Fewer Students?

Is the supply of teachers exceeding the demand, and if so, how will this affect teacher activism?

The answer to the first part of this question is rather clearly yes. Enrollments in U.S. public elementary and secondary schools peaked in 1970-71 (at about 51 million pupils) and began to decline after that. The National Center for Education Statistics has predicted that the downward trend in enrollments will continue and level off at about 44.5 million pupils in the 1982-83 school year. During the same years, according to the U.S. Office of Education, the excess of teachers will range up to nearly 150,000 a year. (The figure will be lower if teacher turnover should be high.)

Instances of excess teachers were easy to find in the 1970s. New York City cut its teaching force by some 15,000; Chicago froze teacher hiring. The NEA estimated that, at the beginning of the 1975 school year, 200,000 qualified teachers were looking in vain for teaching jobs, although some 300,000 had left teaching for other work.

There were some countering trends. It was probable, for instance, that the greatest drop in teaching jobs had already occurred in the mid-1970s and that future declines would be less extensive. Further, the situation could turn around by the early or mid-1980s. Projections of school populations are based in large part on the declining birth rate—in 1976 American women were having an average of only 1.8 children each, a substantial drop from the 3.5 just after World War II. Some demographers have predicted a reversal in this trend, with a baby boom coming in the 1980s when women who have delayed bearing children begin to catch up. (Bureau of the Census officials have pointed out, however, that women in their thirties do not have large numbers of babies, for a variety of reasons, regardless of their desire to do so.)

A change in the ratio of teachers to pupils would of course vastly change the oversupply picture. NEA researchers pointed out in the mid-1970s that if class size were reduced to the levels of the NEA's recommendations there would be an instant shortage of some 500,000 teachers in the nation's schools. Another factor that could help teacher employment is the requirement, encouraged by court suits and federal laws, that handicapped children be educated in public schools. And finally, Census Bureau officials have stated that the tight teacher-employment situation does encourage earlier teacher retirement and job changes.

Despite these countering trends, it was the consensus of observers that the combination of fewer pupils and plenty of teachers meant a continuing oversupply of teachers, at least until 1982-83.

The question is, How will this oversupply affect the militancy of teachers?

At first blush, it might seem that an oversupply of teachers would curtail militancy. Fewer teachers in total number, for instance, means fewer members for teachers associations, and thus a smaller budget for these unions and associations. Further, with teacher demand low, it is logical to assume that teachers will be more timid about risking their jobs in militant actions. But these first assumptions do not seem to hold up. The smaller number of teachers, with their jobs threatened, apparently tend to join unions and associations to help guarantee job security. This is the "adversity brings cohesion" factor we have mentioned before. (One example of this cohesion is the effect the shortage of jobs for Ph.D.s has had: In 1977 Ph.D. holders were considering forming a union to lobby for themselves.) As to timidity, there were more than 50 teacher strikes in the opening days of the 1975-76 school year—a year of severe teacher oversupply. Although this number was down from some earlier years, apparently the threat to teacher jobs had not reached a level sufficient to wipe out the drive of teachers for rights and benefits.

In sum, the softening of the job market for teachers probably has not significantly affected the militancy of teachers. If teachers remained well organized, they were likely to remain activists.

Teachers Organizations

Will conflicts between teachers organizations limit their thrust toward greater power for their members?

First of all, we should lay to rest the hope of some conservatives that the NEA and the AFT will fade away. This was very unlikely in the 1970s. NEA membership grew from about 714,000 in 1960 to 1.8 million in 1976; AFT membership went from some 60,000 in 1960 to 475,000 in 1976. Although about 200,000 of these were joint members of the NEA and the AFT in 1976, the total number of organized teachers that year exceeded two million. There were few indications of any diminution in those numbers. The NEA's unification program (requiring local, state, and national membership) had locked in most organized teachers outside of some major cities; and in those cities (e.g., New York, Chicago, Detroit, and Philadelphia) the AFT held its members.

During the 1976-77 school year, NEA-AFT conflicts in New York, Florida, and California changed the complexion of organized teacher membership to some degree. The NEA, having disaffiliated the New York State United Teachers, lost most of its members in New York state, though it retained some 30,000. The AFT lost at least 40,000 members through New York City layoffs and the decision of thousands of teachers to join the new NEA affiliate, the New York Educators Association. In Florida, the NEA and the AFT had split the state, but between them continued to enroll most Florida teachers. In California, because of the success of the NEA-California Teachers Association in winning representation rights under a new state bargaining law, AFT membership was down. But these changes in the complexion of teacher membership did not substantially change the *numbers* of teachers who were organized.

The NEA-AFT conflict continued into 1977, and there were few if any indications that it would die down later in the decade. In addition to the New York, Florida, and California disputes, the two organizations were head to head on such issues as a federal collective bargaining law especially designed for teachers (the NEA for it, the AFT against it); affiliation of teachers with the AFL-CIO (the NEA against, the AFT maintaining that it helps teachers to be part of a labor organization); and cooperation with other public employees (the AFT charging that the NEA's relationships with public employee unions was divisive because the NEA was "not in the mainstream" of American labor).

Merger between the two organizations was not under active consideration in 1977; both groups seemed content to go their separate ways. NEA officials were confident that their much larger numbers, combined with their working relationships with other public employees, would ultimately yield the greater benefits for teachers. AFT officials remained adamant about labor affiliation; AFT President Shanker was a member of the AFL-CIO Executive Council. Further, the AFT had other matters on its hands, the financial crisis in New York City being one of the most urgent.

Anti-teacher organization people could hope for, at the most, a weakening of the AFT. But even this was a two-edged sword. The *American School Board Journal* noted this fact in a 1977 article warning its members not to celebrate the declining fortunes of the United Federation of Teachers (the AFT's New York City flagship affiliate). Said the *Journal:* "The UFT's parent union, the AFT, is locked in mortal combat with the far more lethal NEA. If the UFT crisis cripples its parent union severely enough, the NEA could gain an irreparable advantage. So, before giving ourselves up to indecent pleasure, we might consider this: The more the AFT withers, the more the NEA flourishes, and nonaligned teachers will find it harder than ever to remain independent."

It seemed likely as of 1977, then, that teachers organizations would grow stronger and continue to press their members' demands in the face of the dwindling classroom enrollments.

Organizing the Unorganized

Will educators who are now unorganized join teachers associations or unions?

Not only were teachers organizations likely to continue to wield their strength, they were, in the 1970s, looking to the unorganized members of the education world in the search for even more members. Among the groups wooed were professors, teacher aides and paraprofessionals, parochial school teachers, and retired teachers.

Of the efforts to organize the unorganized, the greatest push in the 1970s was toward recruiting college faculty. By the end of 1976 more than 100,000 of the nation's 600,000 professors were members of bargaining groups. NEA affiliates alone had contracts covering some 80,000 faculty. The AFT, too, was coming on strong on campuses. And the American Association of University Professors finally, in the 1970s, gave in to the pressure to establish bargaining units; it represented some 20,000 faculty members under contract by 1977. (The NEA attempted to co-opt the AAUP contracts by offering a merger plan that would provide NEA expertise in bargaining to AAUP members, with dues going to both organizations, but as of mid-1977 the AAUP had not taken the bait.)

Faculty organizing proceeded at a sluggish pace during the early 1970s, but economic pressures on colleges (where the loss of students was soon to hit), combined with NEA and AFT needs for more members, might bring a speeding of campus recruitment by the 1980s. Several observers believed that college faculties were ripe for organizing; Ford Foundation official Fred Crossland predicted in 1976 that "in the not too distant future, faculty unionization and collective bargaining will be the national norm."

Paraprofessionals—teacher aides, school secretaries, and others—were being pursued by the AFT and the NEA (and also by the AFL-CIO American Federation of State, County, and Municipal Employees) in the 1970s. The AFT has several strong paraprofessional union affiliates. In 1977 the NEA made proposals to bring these aides into full association membership. The NEA also negotiated jurisdictional agreements with AFSCME to avoid conflict with a union that was a founding member, along with the NEA, of the Coalition of American Public Employees.

The AFT was working throughout the 1970s to organize teachers in Catholic schools, mainly in the large cities. Organizing these teachers was a slow process, however, hampered by court actions at times, for the courts ruled that separation of church and state meant that these teachers could not choose a union to represent them. The AFT pressed on, however, and in 1977 called a walkout by lay teachers in the Catholic secondary schools in the Los Angeles area as part of its efforts to get church officials to accept an AFT local as a bargaining agent.

Organizing retired teachers was under consideration by the NEA in the late 1970s. The association had once retained a percentage of its teachers who retired through life membership and through a relationship with the National Retired Teachers Association; but in recent years that effort lagged as life memberships were discontinued and NRTA became independent. Whether large numbers of retired teachers could be lured back into the NEA fold was an unsettled question.

If any of these groups—professors, paraprofessionals, parochial school teachers, or retired teachers—could be added to NEA or AFT rolls, however, they could bring added growth to organizations that had already recruited nearly all of the nation's regular public elementary and secondary school teachers.

Political Action by Teachers

Will teachers continue their efforts to influence society through political action?

Of all the questions we have raised, this one has perhaps the clearest answer, for teachers groups seem fully committed to continued political action.

Organized teachers jumped deeply into the political pond in the 1970s, and they loved it. During the 1974 congressional campaign, the NEA and its affiliates contributed an estimated $2.5 million toward electing "friends of education"; the AFT added another $1 million. Teachers groups found that politicians were as eager for teacher volunteer workers as for their dollars, so when federal election laws began limiting the amounts of contributions they could make, the NEA and the AFT were not discomfited—they found just as much success through the use of smaller, carefully placed contributions combined with volunteer efforts and well-publicized endorsements as was gained through larger donations.

In the 1976 campaign, the NEA endorsed a Presidential candidate (Jimmy Carter) for the first time in its history. It supported candidates, too, in hundreds of Congressional races, and scored a high percentage of wins for those it backed.

NEA state affiliates, too, were turning to political action in the 1970s. The California Teachers Association waded into political action so extensively that one state assemblyman, speaking of the CTA's political clout, told the *Sacramento Bee* that "There are only three things I fear—God, my redheaded wife, and the CTA."

Led by UFT President Shanker, a man who made New York City politics his union's agenda, the AFT, too, continued its political action programs. Thus there seemed in the 1970s little reason to expect a lessening of teachers groups' political efforts. NEA Executive Director Terry Herndon made this position clear in a Washington Press Club statement in 1975. In careful phrases he said, "We perceive an absolute need and responsibility to exert maximum influence on the political system."

The Future of Teacher Power

Looking back over the 10 questions we have raised about teacher power, we can see that some questions are more important than others—more crucial to our understanding of teacher militancy.

For example, the first question—about the potency of laws allowing teachers to bargain—offers an excellent index to the movement of teacher activism in the future. For should a federal collective bargaining law for teachers be enacted, this factor alone could expand teacher militancy more than any other we have reviewed. Collective bargaining, the mechanism for teacher militancy, is the key to that militancy. Wishes without implementation are sterile; give more teachers the tools for bargaining and you provide the weapons they need for militancy.

Looking at the other side of the coin, however, it is not equally true that failure of teachers to get a federal bargaining law will greatly limit their militancy. After all, teachers have conducted strikes, statewide walkouts, political campaigns, court suits, and all the other manifestations of their militancy without a federal bargaining law. So, although the passage of such a law would greatly stimulate teacher militancy, its absence would merely divert that militancy to a state-by-state effort for bargaining rights.

Another measure of teacher militancy lies in the combined answers to the last three of our questions: How effectively will teachers groups continue their drives, organize the unorganized, and press their political efforts? Regardless of the unpredictable economy, the directions taken by the courts, and the ravages imposed by teacher oversupply, if teachers organizations remain effective, militancy is likely to continue. As we have seen, teachers began the march to militancy more than 100 years ago when they realized that they had to organize—that there was a greater readiness by school boards to deal with *group* petitions.

American teachers to a large extent shed their modesty between 1945 and 1975. Many—perhaps most—have been willing to stand up and say, "As a professional in our society, I have a right to make reasonable demands on behalf of my economic status; further, as a professional I want the right to have a say in how the schools of our nation are run. I don't think this is wrong; I think it is right and will help our schools do their job better."

The answers to the 10 questions we have examined can help tell us what forces, if any, in our society would deny teachers these rights.

Some Books Dealing with the History and Directions of Teacher Militancy

Bendiner, Robert. *The Politics of Schools: A Crisis in Self-Government.* New York: Harper & Row, 1969.

Blum, Albert A., ed. *Teacher Unions and Associations: A Comparative Study.* Urbana, Illinois: University of Illinois, 1969.

Clark, James M. *Teachers and Politics in France: A Pressure Group Study of Federation de l'Education Nationale.* Syracuse, New York: Syracuse University, 1967.

Curti, Merle. *The Social Ideas of American Educators* (revised). Paterson, New Jersey: Littlefield, Adams and Co., 1963.

Donley, Marshall O., Jr. *Power to the Teacher: How America's Educators Became Militant.* Bloomington, Indiana: Indiana University and Phi Delta Kappa, 1976.

Kahn, Herman, and Wiener, Anthony J. *The Year 2000: A Framework for Speculation on the Next Thirty-Three Years.* New York: Macmillan, 1967.

Lynd, Robert S., and Merrell, Helen. *Middletown: A Study in Contemporary American Culture.* New York: Harcourt, Brace and Co., 1929.

Mayer, Martin. *The Teachers Strike, New York, 1968.* New York: Harper & Row, 1969.

National Education Association, Research Division. *Achievements and Services of the State Education Associations.* Washington, D.C.: The Association, October, 1964.

Schnaufer, Pete. *The Uses of Teacher Power.* Chicago: The American Federation of Teachers, 1966.

Wesley, Edgar B. *NEA: The First Hundred Years.* New York: Harper and Brothers, 1957.

Zitron, Celia Lewis. *The New York City Teachers Union 1916-1964.* New York: Humanities Press, 1968.